by David E. Scott

Whitecap Books
Vancouver/Toronto

Edited by Tim Dunn
Cover and interior design by Warren Clark
Cover illustration by Warren Clark
Typeset by Warren Clark

Printed and bound in Canada

Canadian Cataloguing in Publication Data

Scott, David, 1939-
    Ontario place names

    ISBN 1-55110-093-2

    1. Names, Geographical—Ontario. 2. Ontario
—History, Local. I. Title
FC3056.S36 1993   917.13'0014   C93-091532-1
F1056.4S36 1993

Contents

Introduction

This book explains the origin of the name of every community in Ontario with a population greater than 200, and succinctly chronicles the history of each of those places, with an emphasis on events that were historically significant, offbeat, or humourous.

Humour is spread thinly through the book because Ontario's settlers had a tough row to hoe and survival had to come well ahead of humour on their priority lists. Nevertheless, there are nuggets scattered through the book—usually where you'd least expect to find them!

The origin of the names is a fascinating historical anecdote, in many cases, and the explanations range from vanity to chance, from prejudice to clerical error, from favouritism to egotism, from nepotism to homesickness, from legend to political legerdemain, from whimsy to rancour.

And bureaucracy then, as now, sometimes dealt with the wishes of the people with a heavy hand—to wit the Irish settlers who petitioned the government of the day for a post office named Emmett, after the Irish patriot hanged for rebellion in 1803. The government provided a post office, but named it Chepstow. Chepstow was the residence of Earl Strongbow, the first English invader of Ireland.

Dealtown is so named because the post office just couldn't get the right name right. The name was supposed to be Erieus but a clerical error turned it into Ericus. That was corrected and then the post office closed for a time. When it reopened it was given the name Ouvry. Residents petitioned to have the name Erieus restored, but postal officials responded by naming the post office Dealtown, after Deal in England.

And the bureaucrats picked on poor old Clarence Bissillon as well. Postmasters have traditionally had the right to name their offices after themselves, but when postmaster Bissillon requested his name be used, his request was turned down on the grounds that his name was too difficult to spell. The post office then named the office Val Caron after the first missionary in the district, Rev. Father Hormisdas Caron. Bissillon seems easier to spell than Wunnummin, Penetanguishene, or Dubreuilville, but post office decisions don't seem to have ever been open to discussion.

Despite extensive research in many quarters, including the files of the Ontario Geographic Names Board in Toronto, no historical detail or origin of the name was found for some entries in this book. In other cases, a number of possible origins have been offered; I found one set of options so hilarious that my uncontrolled outburst of laughter unfortunately startled some of the sequestered denizens of the Names Board office.

A portion of the file card for Calabogie follows so you can share the humour of the detailed research that has obviously been done on this unusual name: "(1) from *calladh bogaidh,* Gaelic for "marshy shore"; (2) in Spanish, *cala boga* refers to a body of water where rowing is necessary; (3) Indian word for "sturgeon"; (4) "callibogus" was an early Newfoundland beverage concocted from spruce beer and rum."

Henry Hudson is believed to have been the first white man to see Ontario, in 1610. The first community in Ontario was settled in 1673 and real immigration started a decade later when United Empire Loyalists began moving north from the United States to hack new homes and new futures from the wilderness of what was then Upper Canada.

The process of carving homes and communities from the wilderness is still going on in Ontario. There are still tens of thousands of square miles of wilderness, even though Southern Ontario is criss-crossed by multi-lane paved highways and liberally sprinkled with glass-sheathed highrise buildings and acres of asphalt-paved shopping mall parking lots.

In researching *Ontario Place Names,* every effort was made to achieve historical accuracy and to explain the origin of every place listed. Sadly, very little information is on file about a number of Ontario communities. Even though there must be people still living in some of the younger places who can recall the early days and such details as the origin of the place name, the information hasn't found its way to the authorities who gather and store this material for future generations.

Many communities and regions have active historical societies whose members have over the years gathered a wealth of information about their communities. Much of that information, I suspect, hasn't been shared with provincial record keepers, simply because the record keepers and the historical societies may be unaware of each other's existence.

Any historian or historical society in possession of information that could fill any of the many gaps in this book is urged to share it with me; I'll include it in an updated edition of *Ontario Place Names,* and also pass it along to Michael B. Smart, executive secretary of the Ontario Geographic Names Board.

Mr. Smart and his staff have the expertise and facilities to store new information so that it will be available for the enrichment of this and future generations. And by acting as a "go-between," I'll be repaying in some measure their kind assistance in compiling the facts, figures, and anecdotes that have gone into this book

David E. Scott
P.O. Box 131
Ailsa Craig, Ontario
N0M 1A0

Acknowledgements

A number of writers "broke trail" for my effort to provide an inexpensive thumbnail history of Ontario places and the origin of their names. For their enormous help, I thank them; without it I would likely have fallen by the wayside, probably very early in the alphabet.

Nick and Helma Mika of Mika Publishing Company, Belleville, spent at least a decade compiling material and writing their three-volume set, titled *Places in Ontario*. That work, published 1977 through 1983, attempts to explain the origins of more than 5,000 place names and covers more than 2,100 pages.

Floreen Ellen Carter of Oakville produced a similar work in 1984, on which she had spent at least a decade attempting to track down the origins of all geographic names in Ontario. Her two-volume, 1,492-page *Place Names of Ontario* was published by Edward Phelps of Phelps Publishing Company, London, Ontario.

This book lists all places in Ontario that have a population of 200 or more and are listed on the 1993 *Official Road Map of Ontario*. For their help with various explanations, my thanks to Bryan Porter, information processing officer, topographical map unit, Ministry of Transportation of Ontario and his supervisor, John Fernandes.

Because I used so many sources for historical background, there were frequently different versions of events or different origins for the same name. Every discrepancy was checked against the files of the Ontario Geographic Names Board in Toronto, which were my ultimate authority.

For access to those files (and in some cases the files behind the files), I am deeply indebted to Michael B. Smart, executive secretary of the Ontario Geographic Names Board and coordinator of geographic names for the Land and Resource Information Branch of the Ministry of Natural Resources of Ontario. And for the infinite patience and cheerful assistance of Carol Haire, toponymist with the same department, I am also most grateful.

For his guidance and encouragement and prolonged loan of valuable research material, I am also indebted to Edward Phelps, Collections librarian, D. B. Weldon Library, University of Western Ontario, London.

Finally, for his his patient and skilled nitpicking in the interests of accuracy and easy reading, my warmest thanks to editor Tim Dunn.

AAA

ACTON

Pop. 6,975. In Reg. Mun. of Halton on Acton Creek at Hwys. 25 & 7, 56 km W of Toronto. Settled in 1820 as Danville. The name was changed to Adamsville in 1852 to honour the first settlers—Zenas, Rufus and Ezra Adams. In 1844 postmaster Robert Swan renamed the place after his hometown in Northumberland, England. Acton has long been known for its tanning industry. In the mid-1870s the Nelles tannery was producing up to 20,000 sides of leather annually.

AILSA CRAIG

Pop. 814. In McGillivray T., Middlesex C., on the Ausable River and Hwy. 7, 40 km NW of London. Settled in 1835 by David Craig, who donated land for the first railway station on condition it be named Craig's Station. Another place of that name existed, so the settlement was named Ailsa Craig after the witches' rock in the mouth of Scotland's Clyde River.

AJAX

Pop. 45,046. In Reg. Mun. of Durham on Hwy. 401, 37 km E of Toronto. Began as a shell-filling factory in 1941 when 3,000 acres (1,215 ha) of farmland were turned into a munitions plant to supply the Canadian Armed Forces. The community was named after one of three British cruisers that scuttled the German battleship *Graf Spee*. After the Second World War, Ajax became a temporary campus of the University of Toronto. At its peak, more than 3,300 students were enrolled in the Faculty of Applied Science and Engineering. In 1949 the university withdrew, and the Central Mortgage and Housing Corporation established Canada's first fully planned community.

ALBAN

Pop. 340. In Bigwood and Delamere ts., Sudbury Dist., on Hwy. 64, 4 km E of Hwy. 69, 69 km SE of Sudbury. The first known settler was Edouard Daoust, who arrived in 1910. Alban was established as a farming community, but its proximity to Eighteen Mile Bay, part of the French River system, has made it a popular fishing and tourist area whose summer population swells to over 3,000. A Roman Catholic parish was organized in the community in 1934 under Father Alban Filiatrault, after whom the village was named. A church, which replaced the first house of worship, was destroyed by fire and with it were lost all records of the early residents. The post office was established in 1937.

1

ALDERSHOT

Pop. 16,500. Part of the City of Burlington, Reg. Mun. of Halton, on Hwy. 403 just N of Hamilton. First settled in 1783 by David Fonger and known as Brown's Wharf after a landing built by a Colonel Brown in the 1840s. The Post office opened in 1856 under the name Aldershott, which through usage became Aldershot. The origin of the name is unknown.

ALEXANDRIA

Pop. 3,229. In Lochiel T., Stormont, Dundas, and Glengarry C., on the Garry River and Hwys. 34 & 43, 110 km E of Ottawa. In 1794, 40 families from various Highland clans emigrated from Scotland under the leadership of Alexander MacLeod and settled near the site of present-day Alexandria. The community, first known as Priest's Mills, was founded in 1819 when Rev. Alexander Macdonnell built a grist mill. Macdonnell was later the first Roman Catholic to be appointed Bishop of Upper Canada. The post office opened in 1825 as Alexandria, honouring the pioneer, Alexander MacLeod.

ALFRED

Pop. 1,095. In Alfred T., Prescott and Russell C., on Hwy. 17, 63 km E of Ottawa. Settled in the early 1800s and first known as Bradyville after Thomas Brady the first hotelier. When the post office was established in 1842, the community was named Alfred after the township, which honours Prince Alfred, son of George III of Great Britain.

ALLANBURG

Pop. 475. Part of the City of Thorold, Reg. Mun. of Niagara, on the Welland Canal and Hwy. 20, 10 km W of Niagara Falls. The community came into existence in 1824 when the sod was turned for the first Welland Canal, an historic site now marked by a cairn. The place was first called New Holland because of the many Dutch and German United Empire Loyalist settlers. A village was laid out in 1832 by Samuel Keefer. It was named Allanburg to honour two men: William Allan, a Toronto banker who was vice-president of the Canal Company, and John Vanderburgh, the first settler.

ALLENFORD

Pop. 270. In Amabel T., Bruce C., on the Sauble River and Hwy. 21, 21 km W of Owen Sound. The Indians knew the place as Driftwood Crossing. The post office, established in 1868, was named after James Allen, who had settled in 1857.

ALLISTON

Pop. 4,885. In Tecumseth T., Simcoe C., on the Boyne River (a tributary of the Nottawasaga) and Hwy. 89, 35 km SW of Barrie. In 1847 settler

William Fletcher and his son, John, built a log shanty. The following year they built a sawmill and a frame house. Fletcher named the place Alliston after his native town in Yorkshire, England. In 1891 a fire destroyed most of the town's business establishments. Alliston has two famous sons. Sir Frederick Grant Banting was born just north of town. In 1923 Banting shared a Nobel Prize with his University of Toronto department head, Dr. J.J.R. MacLeod, for isolating insulin, which is used in the treatment of diabetes. His family's former homestead, still a private residence, is identified by a plaque. Theodore Pringle Loblaw was born in the nearby hamlet of Elm Grove in 1872. An orphan, he went to work in a Toronto grocery store. By the age of 28 he owned his own shop, and in 1919, in partnership with J. Milton Cork, he founded Loblaws Groceterias Ltd. They built a grocery chain that at one time owned 158 stores in the United States and more than 100 in Ontario.

ALMA
Pop. 322. In Peel T., Wellington C., on C. Rds. 7 & 17, 30 km N of Kitchener. Alexander MacCrea and his wife came from Port Hope in 1848 and settled where the townships of Peel, Nichol, and Pilkington now meet. When the post office was established in 1854, the place was called MacCrae's Corners. In 1870 when the Wellington, Grey and Bruce Railway arrived, the name was changed to Alma. The origin of the name is unknown.

ALMONTE
Pop. 4,026. In Ramsay T., Lanark C., on Hwys. 15 & 44 and the Mississippi River, 56 km SW of Ottawa. Settled in 1819 by David Shepherd and first known as Shepherd's Falls. In 1821 Daniel Shipman built a sawmill and the following year a grist mill. For a time, the place was called Shipman's Mills. Later, it was variously called Shipman's Falls, Ramsay, Ramsay Village, Victoria, Victoriaville, Watford, and Waterford. In 1852 the post office was named Almonte to honour Juan N. Almonte, Mexican ambassador to the United States.

In 1930 Robert Tait McKenzie (1867-1938) (a surgeon, physical educator, and noted sculptor who designed many war memorials in Canada, the United States, and Great Britain) opened a studio here in an old mill that he renovated and renamed after his ancestral home. The Mill of Kintail is now a museum. An historic plaque marks the childhood home (4.5 km NW of Almonte) of Dr. James Naismith, the inventor of basketball. Dr. Naismith (1861-1939) creatively combined the professions of physical educator and medical doctor. In 1891, responding to the demand for an indoor team sport to occupy students during winter months, he devised the game of basketball, using a soccer ball and two half-bushel peach baskets.

ALTON

Pop. 475. Part of the Town of Caledon, Reg. Mun. of Peel, on the West Branch of the Credit River and Hwy. 136, 82 km NW of Toronto. The place was settled in the 1830s by members of the Thomas Russell family, who for three years were the only inhabitants. As others took up land in the area, the name Williamstown was used. When the post office was being established in 1854, postmaster John S. Meek suggested the community be called Alton after a town in Illinois.

ALVINSTON

Pop. 793. In Brooke T., Lambton C., on the Sydenham River and Hwy. 79, 1.6 km N of Hwy. 80, and 60 km SE of Sarnia. The place was settled in 1837 by Archibald Gardiner, who built a grist mill. It was first called Gardiner's Mill. A short time later, Gardiner became converted to the Reorganized Church of Jesus Christ of the Latter Day Saints and moved to Illinois. In 1846, Gardiner and his family and others abandoned their homes and businesses and joined the Mormons in Salt Lake City, Utah. The settlement got a new lease on life as Brennan's Mills when J. W. Brennan built a mill. Later, it was called Brooke's Mill. In 1854 the post office was named Alvinston after a village on the Isle of Wight.

AMHERSTBURG

Pop. 8,211. In Malden and Anderton ts., Essex C., on the Detroit River and Hwy. 18, 24 km S of Windsor. From about 1727 and for 20 years, the Bois Blanc mission occupied lands in this area, but the first permanent settlement was started in 1784 by a number of former Indian Department officers. In 1815 the place was named Amherstburg to honour Lord Jeffery Amherst, governor general of British North America from 1760 to 1763. In 1796 the British established Fort Malden just north of the town after evacuating Detroit. In 1838 Fort Malden's garrison and the local militia repelled four attempts by the "Patriot" filibusters to invade Canada. The fort was garrisoned by British regiments until 1851, occupied by military pensioners until 1859, and then abandoned. Today it is fully restored and operated by Parks Canada as a tourist attraction.

On Dalhousie Street South, at the southern approach to Amherstburg, is one of the finest remaining examples of Georgian architecture in Ontario. "Bellevue" was built in 1816 by Robert Reynolds as the commissary to the garrison at Fort Malden. Another historic attraction is the Park House, now a museum. The home was originally built in 1796 on the U.S. side of the Detroit River. When the United Empire Loyalist owner moved to Canada, he dismantled his house, floated the materials across the river and re-assembled it in what is now Amherstburg around 1799. The solid log structure with clapboard siding and cedar shake roof seems an unlikely "pre-fabricated" house. One of the oldest Anglican churches in the province is Christ Church, built in 1819 to serve the garrison at Fort Malden and a local civilian population.

AMHERSTVIEW

Pop. 6,110. In Ernestown T., Lennox and Addington C., on Hwy. 33, 11 km W of Kingston. The present day residential community was planned in the 1950s and named for the view of Amherst Island, which it overlooks. The site has a long history of settlement. In Fairfield Historical Park in Amherstview, the St. Lawrence Parks Commission maintains a public museum in an historic home. William Fairfield Sr., a United Empire Loyalist from Vermont, completed the clapboard house in 1793, and six generations of Fairfields lived there during the next 150 years. A plaque just west of Amherstview on Hwy. 33, honours Madeleine de Roybon d'Allonne, (1646-1718), the first known female landholder in present-day Ontario. She was the daughter of a French nobleman and came to Kingston (then Fort Frontenac) about 1679. On land granted to her by René Robert Cavelier, Sieur de LaSalle, she built a house and barns, grew crops and grazed cattle, and established a small trading post. Amherstview was also the home of Lt.-Col. Edwin Albert Baker (1893-1968). He was blinded while serving with the Canadian army in Belgium in 1914 and devoted the rest of his life to the rehabilitation and training of blind people. He helped found the Canadian National Institute for the Blind in 1918 and served as its managing director for more than 40 years.

ANCASTER

Pop. 19,728. In the Reg. Mun. of Hamilton-Wentworth on Hwy. 2, 8 km W of Hamilton. In the summer of 1790 Jean Baptiste Rousseaux and James Wilson settled the site, and Wilson built a mill. The place was called Wilson's Mills until 1794 when Rousseaux bought the mill. Around 1800 Rousseaux Mills, as it had come to be known, was named Ancaster after a village in Lincolnshire, England. In 1814, 19 men charged with treason during the War of 1812 stood trial in George Rousseaux's log hotel. Fifteen were convicted and eight were hanged, drawn, and quartered at nearby Burlington Heights. The remainder were exiled. The trial is known as "The Bloody Assize" of Ancaster.

ANGUS

Pop. 3,000. In Essa T., Simcoe C., 19 km SW of Barrie on Hwy. 90 and the Nottawasaga and Pine rivers. To encourage settlement in the area, the government ordered the survey of the Sunnidale Rd. west of Barrie in 1833, but settlement was slow. Jonas TarBush bought a farm site near the proposed village site, and when the Northern Railway line was being built nearby in 1857, TarBush and William Proudfont laid out a village site, which they named Angus in honour of Angus Morrison, a director of the railway and a member of the Parliament of Upper and Lower Canada.

APPLE HILL

Pop. 257. In Kenyon T., Stormont, Dundas, and Glengarry C., on C. Rd. 20, 25 km N of Cornwall. The area was settled primarily by Scots. When the Canadian Pacific Railway was built, the right-of-way ran through an apple orchard on high ground owned by Sandy Kennedy. When the post office opened in 1882 it was named Apple Hill.

APSLEY

Pop. 375. In Anstruther T., Peterborough C., on Eel's Creek and Hwys. 28, 504, 620, and A620, 60 km NE of Peterborough. The first settlers arrived in 1862. Charles J. Vizard built a sawmill on Eel's Creek and became the first postmaster when a post office was established in 1865. The origin of the name is unknown.

ARISS

Pop. 287. In Guelph T., Wellington C., on C. Rds. 51 & 86, 9 km NW of Guelph. The post office was established in 1908. The origin of the name is unknown.

ARKONA

Pop. 517. In Bosanquet and Warwick ts., Lambton C., on Hwys. 7 & 79 and C. Rd. 12, 56 km E of Sarnia. Asa Townsend settled in 1821. The community was first called Eastman's Corners because many families named Eastman had settled there. The post office opened in 1851 as Bosanquet, after the township. The village was known as Smithfield for a time, but in 1857 some settlers of German extraction had the name changed to Arkona after Cape Arkona on Germany's northern coast.

ARMSTRONG

Pop. 600. In Thunder Bay Dist. on Hwy. 527, 242 km N of Thunder Bay, 26 km NW of Lake Nipigon. The community started as a divisional point on the CNR in the early 1900s. It was named for either Hector Armstrong, an English railroad financier of the late 1800s, or William Armstrong, a Thunder Bay-area landowner of that era.

ARNPRIOR

Pop. 6,002. In McNab T., Renfrew C., on Chats Lake (a widening of the Ottawa River at the mouth of the Madawaska River) and Hwys. 17 & 29, 67 km W of Ottawa. In 1823, Archibald McNab, 13th chief of the Clan McNab, came to Upper Canada with 80 Scottish Highlanders and took control of an unsettled township, which he named after himself. He built a log house that he called Kennell Lodge and established the patriarchal rule of a Scottish chief, compelling settlers to pay illegal fees for their lands. In 1831, McNab met George and Andrew Buchanan in Montreal and persuaded them to settle in his township. The Buchanans named the place Arnprior after their native home in Scotland. In the 1830s the Toronto *Examiner* exposed McNab's illegal activities and, following a government investigation, he lost his settlement rights in 1840 and returned to Scotland.

AROLAND

Pop. 315. In Danford T., Thunder Bay Dist., on the Kawashkagama River 2 km NW of Kawashkagama Lake and Hwy. 643, 78 km N of Geraldton. The Aroland Logging Company built a sawmill here in the 1930s. A post office was in operation from 1936 to 1944, in 1953, and from 1972 to 1974. From Aroland a first-class gravel road maintained by Kimberly Clark Canada Inc. runs 80 km northwest to the Ogoki River. Between 1977 and 1980, the federal government built a steel and concrete bridge across the Ogoki River at a cost of $1 million. On the far side of the bridge there is only enough cleared ground in which to turn a vehicle around; hence its nickname: "The Bridge To Nowhere." The 64 km highway to the bridge may have cost the government another $3 million.

ARTHUR

Pop. 1,967. In Arthur and West Luther ts., Wellington C., on the Conestogo River and Hwys. 6 & 9, 40 km NW of Guelph. The site was surveyed in 1841, and the village, at the south end of the Garafraxa Colonization Road, was laid out by a Mr. Silverthorn in 1846, and named after Arthur Wellesley, duke of Wellington. The early settlers came mainly from England and Ireland.

ASHBURN

Pop. 200. Part of the Town of Whitby, Reg. Mun. of Durham, on C. Rd. 5, 17 km NW of Whitby. One of the early settlers, in 1832, was Richard Butler, sergeant of a troop in the Rebellion of 1837, who owned a large tract of land, and after whom the community was first named Butler's Corners. When a post office was approved in 1852, community resident David Bowler proposed the name Ashbourne after his hometown in England. The name was approved but the post office sent out a cancellation hammer with the name Ashburn on it. The error was never corrected.

ASTORVILLE

Pop. 250. In East Ferris T., Nipissing Dist., on the SW shore of Lake Nosbonsing, 21 km SE of North Bay. The first settlers, in 1886, were brothers Cleophas, Alexandre, Joseph-Alphonse, and Alvarez Roberts Levesque who paddled their canoe to the head of the lake and built themselves a house. The tiny settlement was first known as Levesque.

Rev. Moise Legault was the first priest to visit the pioneer settlers. In 1887 a chapel was built under the guidance of Rev. Georges-Thomas Gagnon. It was replaced in 1902 by a church built by residents under the direction of Father Joseph-Antonin Astor, who ran the mission, Tête du Lac (head of the lake). Two years later the church was destroyed by fire. In 1913 a hurricane heavily damaged the church erected on the same site. In 1965 an impressive new structure, the Church of St. Thomas Aquinas, was built. The post office, first named Nosbonsing after the lake, was renamed Astorville to honour Father Astor.

ATHENS

Pop. 882. In Yonge and Escott ts., Leeds and Grenville C., on Hwy. 42, 25 km W of Brockville. The first settler was John Dixon in 1784, and the settlement was called Dixon's Corner until the post office opened in 1836 as Farmersville. One of the first agricultural exhibitions in Ontario was held there, and it was the site of one of the first sanatoria in the province. In 1888 the prosperous merchant Arza Parish suggested the name Athens because, like its namesake in Greece, the town had become an educational centre. It had a grammar school in 1860, a model school in 1877, and a high school in 1888. Since 1986 the town has invited artists to create large murals on the outside walls of buildings as a tourist attraction.

ATHERLEY

Pop. 370. In Mara T., Simcoe C., on the Narrows between Lake Couchiching and Lake Simcoe and Hwy. 12 and C. Rd. 44, 5 km E of Orillia. The post office was established as Atherley in 1851. Shortly after the area was settled, land-hungry settlers forced the relocation of a band of Ojibway led by Chief William Yellowhead. The Indians were moved in 1838-39 to a new reserve in nearby Rama Township. Atherley was incorrectly named after the Township of Azerley in Ripon, Yorkshire, England.

ATIKOKAN

Pop. 4,389. In Freeborn & Schwenger ts., Rainy River Dist., on the Atikokan River and Hwy. 11, 208 km W of Thunder Bay. The first settlers were prospector Tom Rawn and his wife, who arrived by canoe in 1899 and the following year built the Pioneer Hotel on the site of the present Atikokan Hotel. As early as 1897 it was believed that a substantial body of iron ore lay beneath the waters of Steep Rock Lake, but it was not until 1938 that ore was actually discovered. Mining began six years later, and over the following 20 years more than 36 million tons (32.652 million tonnes) of ore were mined. The town's name is derived from the Indian word, believed to mean "bone of caribou," or from similar Indian words *Akkoka* or *Attikoka*, meaning "one who is skilful at doing anything."

ATTAWAPISKAT

Pop. 975. In Kenora Dist., 12 km W of the mouth of the Attawapiskat River and Akimiski Strait on the W side of James Bay, 210 km NW of Moosonee. This Cree Indian settlement is a trading post on the site of an old Hudson's Bay Post. It can only be reached by air or water. The meaning of the Cree name Attawapiskat is not known.

AUBURN

Pop. 217. In East and West Wawanosh and Hullett ts., Huron C., on the Maitland River and C. Rds. 8, 22, & 25, 17 km NE of Goderich. Although the place had come to be known as Manchester, the post office was established as Auburn in 1854 and the community was incorporated under that name in 1895. The origin of the name is not known.

AURORA

Pop. 24,545. In the Reg. Mun. of York on Hwy. 11, 29 km N of Toronto. Settled in 1804 by Richard Machell, and known as Machell's Corners because Machell acquired the corner of Yonge and Wellington streets. In 1853 the first train to run in Ontario arrived in Aurora from Toronto. In 1854 postmaster Charles Doan renamed the community Aurora for the Greek goddess of the dawn. A fire in 1886 destroyed much of the town on the west side of Yonge Street. Aurora is the home of St. Andrew's College, a well-known boys' school. The two-story white brick school, built in High Victorian style in 1886, now houses the Aurora Museum.

AVONMORE

Pop. 308. In Roxborough T., Stormont, Dundas, and Glengarry C., on the Payne River, Hwy. 43 and C. Rd. 15, 26 km NW of Cornwall. In 1842 the very versatile John Hough settled. Hough built the first sawmill, kept a store, built houses, acted as the local preacher, blacksmith, magistrate and doctor, and also manufactured coffins. The place was first known as Hough Mills. When the post office was established in 1864 the community was renamed Avonmore, a Gaelic word for "deep water."

AYLMER

Pop. 5,457. In Malahide T., Elgin C., on Catfish Creek and Hwys. 3 & 73, 18 km E of St. Thomas. The area was settled in the 1830s and first known as Troy. John Van Patten from New York State was the first settler. In 1835 a meeting was held to choose an official name to be submitted to postal authorities. Many favoured retaining Troy, but Aylmer won majority support. The name honours Lord Aylmer, governor-in-chief of Canada from 1831 to 1835. Aylmer is the home of the Ontario Police College.

AYR

Pop. 1,295. In the Reg. Mun. of Waterloo on the Nith River and C. Rds. 49 & 50, 16 km SW of Cambridge. Settled in 1824 when Abel Mudge built a saw and grist mill on Smith's Creek, now called the Nith River. First called Mudge Hollow, then Mudge's Mills, and later Nithvale. In 1840, store owner Robert Wyllie established a post office. The first postmaster, James Jackson, renamed the community Ayr after his native Ayrshire, Scotland.

AYTON

Pop. 425. In Normanby T., Grey C., on a branch of the Saugeen River and C. Rds. 3 & 9, 72 km S of Owen Sound. The government laid out a townsite in 1855, and the first to settle were William Butcher and Henry McMahon. Many of the early settlers were of German descent. It is said the place had no name until settler Charles Ayton suggested his family name. Many of the businesses in town were destroyed by fire in 1939.

AZILDA

Pop. 4,300. Part of the Town of Rayside-Balfour, Reg. Mun. of Sudbury on Hwy. 144, 9 km NW of Sudbury. CPR construction worker Joseph Belanger was the first settler in the area, around 1880. His bride, the former Azilda Brisbois, so impressed township residents that they asked authorities to name the post office St. Azilda in her honour. In 1891 the post office was established under that name. When it was found that there was no such saint, the post office changed the name to Rayside, in 1900, after the township. Residents succeeded in having the name St. Azilda reinstated the following year, but the St. was dropped a few months later.

BADEN

Pop. 1,058. In Wilmot T., Reg. Mun. of Waterloo, on Spring Creek, a tributary of the Nith River and C. Rd. 1, 16 km SW of Kitchener. Jacob Beck from the Grand Duchy of Baden in Germany laid out the village in 1855 and named it after his hometown. His son, later Sir Adam Beck, introduced a bill in the provincial legislature in 1906, creating the Ontario Hydro-Electric Power Commission. He became its first chair and is remembered by Adam Beck Memorial Park in Baden. In the 1820s, with the assistance of Mennonites already established in the area, Christian Nafziger arranged for a number of European Amish families to settle on a tract of land in what later became Wilmot Township. Baden is noted for its Limburger cheese.

BAILIEBORO

Pop. 283. In South Monaghan T., Peterborough C., on Hwy. 28 and C. Rd. 2, 22 km NW of Port Hope. By the 1860s, the community, founded by United Empire Loyalists, had been known for some time as Bloomfield. Because there was another community of the same name, a name change was required before a post office could be established. James Aiken suggested Bailieboro, for his hometown in Ireland, and the post office took that name in 1861. An historic plaque at the Pengelley Burying Ground, six km east of Bailieboro, recalls Joseph Medlicott Scriven (1819-1886). He was a native of County Down, Ireland, and a graduate of Trinity College, Dublin. After coming to Upper Canada in 1847, he was engaged by Robert Pengelley as tutor to his children and lived in the Rice Lake area. He was the author of the hymn, *What a Friend We Have in Jesus*.

BALA

Pop. 527. In Muskoka Lakes T., Dist. Mun. of Muskoka, on Bala Bay and Hwy. 169, Lake Muskoka, 25.5 km NW of Bracebridge. The first settler was Thomas Burgess, in 1868, who used the falls on the Musquosh River to operate a sawmill. The community was known as Musquosh Falls and then Muskoka, but was named Bala in 1871 after Bala Lake in Wales. In 1914 it was incorporated as a town without first becoming a village, and was believed to have been Canada's smallest incorporated town. In 1971 Bala amalgamated with the villages of Port Carling and Windermere and the townships of Cardwell and Watt to form the Township of Muskoka Lakes. A provincial plaque at Bala describes the Pre-Cambrian Shield, one of the oldest rock formations in the earth's crust, which covers about two-thirds of the surface of Ontario.

BALM BEACH

Pop. 412. In Tiny T., Simcoe C., on Nottawasaga Bay and C. Rd. 29, 15 km SW of Midland. A summer post office was established in 1931. The origin of the name is not known.

BALMERTOWN

Pop. 1,341. In Balmer T., Kenora Dist., Patricia Portion, on Red Lake and Hwy. 105, 169 km N of Hwy. 17 and 212 km NW of Dryden. The community started after rich deposits of gold were discovered on the shores of Red Lake in 1925. The post office was established in 1848 and named after Balmer Township.

BALMY BEACH

Pop. 446. In Sarawak T., Grey C., on Owen Sound and C. Rd. 1, 7 km N of Owen Sound. The origin of the name is not known, but the place was likely named in the summertime.

BANCROFT

Pop. 2,248. In Faraday T., Hastings C., on the York River and Hwys. 62 & 28, 104 km NE of Peterborough. First settled by the Clark family in 1853 and known as The Branch, then York Branch, then York Mills. When the post office was established in 1861 the community was called York River. In 1879, the community's leading businessman, Billa Flint, later a senator, renamed it Bancroft in honour of his wife, the former Phoebe Bancroft. In 1873 Bancroft was the eastern terminus of The Monck Road, built from Lake Couchiching to Bancroft as a settlement road and a military route between the Upper Great Lakes and the Ottawa Valley. Lumbering and a wool mill built Bancroft. In 1949, prospector Arthur Shore discovered uranium. Production started in 1957 and continued until the early 1960s. The Bancroft area contains many types of minerals. The annual Rockhound Gemboree draws gemologists from across North America.

BARRIE

Pop. 49,818. City in Simcoe C. at the head of Kempenfelt Bay off Lake Simcoe and Hwys. 11, 26, 27, 90, 93, and 400, 78 km N of Toronto. The first building was a Hudson's Bay Company storehouse in 1812 and the first dwelling was a log house built in 1815 for Sir George Head, who had come to supervise a proposed naval establishment at Penetanguishene, 49 km northwest of Severn Sound off Georgian Bay. The settlement was first called Nine Mile Portage. The portage was cleared during the War of 1812 as a supply route to military establishments at Penetanguishene. It ran from the site of present-day Barrie at the headwaters of Kempenfeldt Bay to Willow Creek.

In 1812 the site of Barrie was surveyed by Captain Oliver of the Royal

Navy, who bought land and called the place Barry for Capt. Robert Barry, commander of the 15th Regiment of York. When the post office opened in 1832, it was named Barrie after (British) Commodore Robert Barrie, who commanded the warships at Kingston at that time. In 1831, nine black veterans of the War of 1812 accepted land grants along what is now Wilberforce Street, forming the only government-sponsored black settlement in Upper Canada. A community of about 100 settlers flourished briefly, but the poor soil and harsh climate discouraged them and the settlement was gradually abandoned.

Barrie has been home to many prominent people over the years. Hewitt Bernard (1825-1893) was a native of Jamaica who settled in Barrie in 1851 and opened a law practice. He accompanied John A. Macdonald to the Charlottetown conference in 1864 and served as secretary of the Quebec and London Conferences, which laid the groundwork for Confederation. Andrew Frederick Hunter (1863-1940) was an active member of the Canadian Institute and the Ontario Historical Society. He undertook extensive research on the history and archaeology of Huronia, and his published writings encouraged the study of local history throughout the province. William Edward Gallie (1882-1959) was a distinguished surgeon and teacher. While practising at the Hospital for Sick Children in Toronto he devised revolutionary techniques in tissue transplant and bone repair that are now practised throughout the world. The city holds North America's largest annual dog show, Canada's largest flea market, and a winter carnival on the frozen waters of Kempenfelt Bay. Barrie's oldest public building is an octagonal jail completed in 1842 and still in use.

BARRIEFIELD
Pop. 1,250. In Pittsburgh T., Frontenac C., at the mouth of the Cataraqui River on Hwy. 2, 1.5 km E of Kingston. Immediately south is Point Frederick where the Royal Naval Dockyard was established in the early 1800s, many of whose employees settled at Barriefield. St. Mark's Church, an early Gothic Revival structure, was built in 1843 with funds subscribed by the British Admiralty and early settlers. The community is named after Robert Barrie, commander of the Kingston dockyard from 1818 to 1835.

BARRY'S BAY
Pop. 1,109. In Sherwood T., Renfrew C., on the bay of the same name, an inlet of Lake Kamaniskeg, and Hwys. 60 & 62, 83 km SW of Pembroke. The community originated as a stopover point on the Opeongo Colonization Rd., which was largely completed by 1854. The settlement, first named Barry's Camp on the Bay, after a pioneer family, was settled mainly by Polish immigrants who arrived in the 1870s, drawn by the

lumbering industry. The post office was named Barry's Bay when it opened in 1876. Today the pretty village is the main shopping and outfitting centre for the Madawaska Valley tourist region.

BATAWA

Pop. 261. In Sidney T., Hastings C., on the Trent River and Hwy. 33, 10 km N of Trenton. The community was created in 1939 by Czechoslovakian shoe manufacturer Thomas Bata and named after him. Bata established the Canadian branch of his worldwide chain of shoe factories there. While facilities were being built in Batawa, the company produced shoes in an old paper mill in nearby Frankford.

BATH

Pop. 1,059. In Ernestown T., Lennox & Addington C., on the North Channel of Lake Ontario opposite Amherst Island, on Hwy. 33, 24 km SW of Kingston. Land was first granted to the Loyal Rangers in 1777. (The Rangers was a Loyalist force raised in 1776 in the neighbourhood of Albany by Edward Jessup [1735-1816].) The land was surveyed in 1783 and named Ernest Town after the fifth child of King George III. It was settled in 1784 by about 400 United Empire Loyalists led by Col. Edward Jessup. The first Anglican services west of Kingston were held in the home of Capt. Jeptha Hawley, a United Empire Loyalist from Arlington, Vermont. Hawley's original cabin, at the west edge of the village on Hwy. 33, is the oldest structure in the area. The stone portion was likely added in the 1790s to serve as quarters for the Rev. John Langhorn, the area's first resident Anglican clergyman. The settlement's first criminal court was held in Finkle's Tavern, and the first hanging in Upper Canada was from a tree near the tavern about 1790. In 1811, Bath Academy was founded by local subscriptions and opened briefly as a public school before being requisitioned as a military barracks during the War of 1812. It later reopened, and, by offering an extensive curriculum, gained an excellent reputation for scholarship.

In 1812 the community was named after the famous English health resort. In the same year the first significant naval action of the War of 1812 took place about 8 km west of Bath, when the British warship *Royal George* escaped its American pursuers by adroitly navigating the gap between Prince Edward County and Amherst Island. After an exchange of fire in Kingston harbour the following day, the American fleet was forced to withdraw. The first Canadian steamship, the *Frontenac*, was launched here in 1816, and Bath was also site of the first brewery/ distillery in Upper Canada. The population of more than 2,000 began to decline in the 1850s, when the Grand Trunk Railway line between Toronto and Montreal turned inland at Collins Bay, just west of Kingston, and bypassed Bath.

BAYFIELD

Pop. 711. In Stanley and Goderich ts., Huron C., at the mouth of the Bayfield River and Lake Huron on Hwy. 21, 21 km S of Goderich. The townsite was surveyed in 1832 and the first home was built the following year. The town grew rapidly, and a post office was established in 1847. By 1870 the population exceeded 700, but in that decade the Grand Trunk Railway line to Goderich bypassed the village by several miles to the east, and the population began to decline. The community was named after the Admiralty Surveyor of the Great Lakes, Henry Wolsey Bayfield. Today it is a quiet summer resort with an excellent beach and marina, several historic inns, and a number of beautifully restored Victorian homes.

BAYFIELD INLET

Pop. 596. In Parry Sound Dist., on Georgian Bay and at the terminus of C. Rd. A529, 12 km W of Hwy. 69, 54 km NW of Parry Sound. Although this place was likely named after Henry Wolsey Bayfield, the official origin of the name is not known.

BAYSIDE

Pop. 500. In Sidney T., Hastings C., on the Bay of Quinte and Hwy. 2, 12 km SW Belleville. The place was first settled in the early 1800s and known as Rhinebeck. The post office opened in 1883 as Bayside because the village sits on the shore of the bay. An Anglican church built near Bayside in the 1820s is believed to have been the first church in Sidney Township.

BAYSVILLE

Pop. 205. In Lake of Bays T., Dist. Mun. of Muskoka, at the S end of Lake of Bays and on Hwy. 117 and C. Rd. 2, 20 km NE of Bracebridge. The land on which most of Baysville is located was granted in 1871 to William H. Brown from the Brantford area, who built the settlement's first sawmill. The post office was established in 1874. The community takes its name from the regional topography.

BEACHBURG

Pop. 681. In Westmeath T., Renfrew C., on C. Rds. 21 & 12, 25 km SE of Pembroke. David Beach, the first settler, was a United Empire Loyalist, who was granted 1,000 acres (405 ha) of land in 1835. With his five sons and four daughters he established a community, which was called South Westmeath when the first post office opened in 1848. The hamlet was damaged by a major fire in 1851. In 1858 the community was renamed Beachburg to honour the first settler.

BEACHVILLE

Pop. 919. In West Oxford and North Oxford ts., Oxford C., on the Thames River and Hwy. 2, 6 km SW of Woodstock. The first settler was John Carroll, who came from New Jersey in 1784. The village is in a dairy-farming region, and limestone is quarried. Beachville was named by its first postmaster, William Merigold, in 1832, to honour Andrew Beach, owner of the first grist mill.

BEAMSVILLE

Pop. 5,000. Part of the Town of Lincoln, Reg. Mun. of Niagara, about 3 km from Lake Ontario on Hwy. 8 and 16 km W of St. Catharines. The first settler, Jacob Beam, was a United Empire Loyalist, who arrived in 1788, and after whom the town was named when the post office opened in 1832. Beamsville held its first country fair in 1857 at which was exhibited a 24-inch (60 cm) carrot. Robert L. Gibson, a skilled stonecutter, established a quarry in 1875. It flourished and provided many jobs. In 1895 the quarry was permanently shut down during a strike for higher wages. In 1961, a harness-racing world record was established when Fred Hill won all eight races on the card. It was the first time in harness-racing history that one driver had won all the races in one day.

BEARDMORE

Pop. 523. In Summers T., Thunder Bay Dist., on the Blackwater River, 12 km E of Lake Nipigon and Hwy. 11, 80 km N of Nipigon. The community was settled in 1920 as a CNR flagstop and named Beardmore Station after the Beardmore family—early settlers. In the 1930s, when gold was discovered, the community was also known as West Beardmore Mines and Buffalo Beardmore Mines. The gold mines are no longer operating, and today the community is supported by pulpwood logging, hunters, and sport fishermen.

BEARSKIN LAKE

Pop. 336. In Kenora Dist., 610 km NW of Thunder Bay. The post office was established in 1961. The origin of the name is unknown.

BEAVERTON

Pop. 1,952. Part of Brock T., Reg. Mun. of Durham, on the E. shore of Lake Simcoe at the mouth of the Beaverton River and C. Rds. 23 & 15, 38 km SE of Orillia. Scottish settlers first arrived in 1822. The community was known as Milltown, Milton, and Beaver River until the Beaverton post office opened in 1836. The Indians originally referred to the place as Beaver because there were many in the river of the same name. St. Andrew's Presbyterian Church, known locally as the Old Stone Church, was built from fieldstone over 13 years by members of its congregation, starting in 1840. Services were conducted in English and Gaelic.

BEETON

Pop. 2,189. In Tecumseth T., Simcoe C., at C. Rds. 1 & 10, 38 km S of Barrie. The first settler, William Hammill, arrived in 1827, and a village named Clarksville was established after Robert Clark, a blacksmith, began selling lots in 1852. In 1860, the Tecumseth post office, which had been operating 5 km from the village, moved to Clarksville, but kept its name. (The original post office, opened in 1842, was named for one of the two ships—the *Nawash* and *Tecumseth*—sunk in Penetanguishene Harbour in 1819.) David Allanson Jones, who was to become the "Bee King" of the 19th century, moved to Clarksville in the 1860s. He purchased two swarms of bees from a neighbour in 1870 and became Canada's first commercial beekeeper and a pioneer in large-scale honey production. He developed beekeeping equipment, printed a bee journal, and founded the Ontario Beekeepers' Association. Since honey bees were not then indigenous to North America, Jones established an apiary in Cyprus where he raised queen bees to bring back to Canada. A fire in 1893 destroyed the plant where Jones printed a weekly journal, and the rising cost of importing bees finally bankrupted him. In 1876 a name change was needed at Clarksville since mail was being directed to a number of other "Clark" places. Beeton was chosen to honour Jones' contribution to the apiary industry.

BELFOUNTAIN

Pop. 300. Part of the Town of Caledon, Reg. Mun. of Peel, on the West Branch of the Credit River and C. Rds. 1, 11, & 52, 24 km NW of Brampton. The area was settled before 1850, and by 1852 the community was known as Tubtown. This name came about because a blacksmith by the name of Henderson used large octagonal iron tubs to cool hot metal. The tubs sat outside his shop and dominated the centre of the village. When a Mr. McCurdy built a mill, the name changed to McCurdy's Village, but the post office opened in 1853 as Belfountain, sometimes spelled Bellfountain. The origin of the name is unknown.

BELGRAVE

Pop. 276. In East Wawanosh and Morris ts., Huron C., on Hwy. 4, 35 km NE of Goderich. The first settlers came from County Fermanagh in Ireland in 1851. When a post office was established in 1865, postmaster Simon Armstrong submitted the names Bornholm, Rosehall, and Belgrave to the post office. Belgrave is the name of a town in Leicestershire, England.

BELLE RIVER

Pop. 3,764. In Rochester T., Essex C., on Lake St. Clair at the mouth of the Belle River and Hwy. 2 and C. Rd. 27, 31 km E of Windsor. Most of the settlers, in the early 1800s, were of French extraction and came from the Detroit River area. The post office was established in 1854 as Rochester, but in 1874 the name changed to Belle (French for "beautiful") River.

BELLEVILLE

Pop. 35,326. In Thurlow T., Hastings C., on the Bay of Quinte at the mouth of the Moira River on Hwys. 2, 14, and 37, 81 km W of Kingston. Founded in 1790 by United Empire Loyalist Capt. John Walter Meyers and first known as Meyer's Creek. Upper Canada's first brick house was built nearby in 1794. The first post office in 1816 was called Singleton's Corners after a Capt. George Singleton, who operated the store. In 1816 the name was changed to Belleville in honour of Arabella, wife of Lt.-Gov. Francis Gore of Upper Canada. Belleville's City Hall, built in the 1870s, is a fine example of High Victorian architecture and is well preserved. The official establishment of the Methodist Church resulted from a series of meetings held in Belleville in 1884, and was the culmination of years of debates and mergers between Methodist groups of British and American origin. In 1966 the Belleville Seminary, founded in 1857, was rechartered as Albert College, an affiliate of the University of Toronto. Five years later it became an independent, degree-granting institution. The Ontario School for the Deaf, the first provincial school for deaf children, opened here in 1870. The residential institution combines elementary school subjects with vocational training. Sir Mackenzie Bowell (1823-1917), long-time resident of Belleville, served as prime minister of Canada from 1894 to 1896.

BELL EWART

Pop. 400. In Innisfil T., Simcoe C., on Cook Bay of Lake Simcoe, 19 km SE of Barrie. The place was named after James Bell Ewart, who owned the site before it was surveyed in 1855. The community that started there soon developed into an important lumber manufacturing centre. Logs were brought to the mills from around the lake, and millions of feet of lumber were shipped to Toronto by the Northern Railway. The timber resources began diminishing and a disastrous fire destroyed the steam sawmills and most of the town. The railway branch line was torn up, and the once busy wharves gradually rotted away.

BELMONT

Pop. 1,090. In South Dorchester T., Elgin C., on Kettle Creek and Hwy. 74 and C. Rd. 35, 22 km SW of London. First settled in 1832 by Joshua S. Odell and known as Kettle Creek. In 1849 the name was changed to Plymouth. In 1853 a post office was established as Plymouth, one mile (1.6 km) north of the settlement known as Belmont. The people of

Belmont wanted the post office, so they requested that the name of the post office be changed to Belmont. When that was done, they petitioned that the Belmont post office be moved one mile south to Belmont, which was done in 1854.

BETHANY

Pop. 382. In Manvers T., Victoria C., on Hwy. 7A, 22 km SW of Peterborough. Bethany came into being when the Midland Railway line was being built from Port Hope to Lindsay in the 1850s. The place was named by a Mr. McAllister, a community leader and religious man, who took the name from the Bible. In 1911 a fire destroyed half the village, including the community hall. Devil's Elbow ski area is 1.5 km north of Bethany.

BEWDLEY

Pop. 598. In Hamilton T., Northumberland C., on the S shore of Rice Lake and Hwy. 28 and C. Rd. 9. The first settler, in 1800, was Nelly Grant, a United Empire Loyalist widow. The place was named by William Banks for his native town in England. A post office opened in 1857.

BIG TROUT LAKE I.R.

Pop. 600. Indian reserve in Kenora Dist., Patricia Portion, on the N shore of Big Trout Lake, 256 km N of Pickle Lake. The post office, named Big Trout Lake, was established in 1957.

BLACKBURN

Pop. 9,687. In Gloucester T., Reg. Mun. of Ottawa-Carleton, on C. Rds. 28 & 30, 4.8 km S of the Ottawa River and 11 km E of Ottawa. First known as Daggville, the community was renamed Blackburn when the post office was established in 1876. The place is believed to have been named after Robert Blackburn, a member of Parliament, early mill owner, and reeve.

BLAIR

Pop. 275. In the Reg. Mun. of Waterloo on the Grand River, 5 km NW of Cambridge. Pioneers of the area were predominantly Mennonites who came from Pennsylvania in the early 1800s. Blair Cemetery dates to 1804. The first mills in the village were built by Daniel and Jacob Erb. The community was first known as Shinglebridge because of a shingled covered bridge, then Durhamville, and New Carlisle after mills in the area. When the post office was established in 1858, the community was named Blair after Adam Blair, an early settler. The first school in Waterloo County was established at Blair, and the community was the first in Ontario to have a paved main street.

BLENHEIM

Pop. 4,336. In Harwich T., Kent C., on Hwys. 3 & 40 and C. Rds. 8 & 19, 19 km SE of Chatham. The first settlers built log homes in 1834, and the community was named Rondeau when the post office opened in 1849. In 1883 the post office name was changed to Blenheim, after the estate of the duke of Marlborough in Oxford, England. It is the centre of a rich agricultural area.

BLEZARD VALLEY

Pop. 1,090. Part of the Town of Valley East, Reg. Mun. of Sudbury on C. Rd. 15, 16 km NW of Sudbury. The township was surveyed in 1883 and named after Thomas Blezard, a Scot who was then the member of Parliament for East Peterborough. The township and the community of Blezard Valley developed as the Canadian National Railway was being pushed through the area. When the timber resources were depleted, settlers turned to farming. When the post office was established in 1899, the community took its name from the township and added "Valley" because of the valley in which it is located.

BLIND RIVER

Pop. 3,263. In Cobden T., Algoma Dist., near the mouth of the Mississagi River and the N Channel of Lake Michigan and Hwy. 17, 123 km SE of Sault Ste. Marie. Champlain noted the location on his map of 1632 as "the place where the savages gather yearly to dry blueberries and raspberries." It was known to the Indians as Penebawabikong, meaning a sloping rock, but the sheltered settlement site got its name in 1837 from voyageurs who were unable to see the mouth of the river until they were very close to it. The name Mississagi, or Mississauga, means "that which opens its mouth to strike," and was the name given by the Ojibway to the rattlesnake. Early settlers came to work for lumber companies, an industry that continues, along with uranium mining. The Pronto Mine, 19 km east, was Ontario's first producing uranium mine, opening in 1955. A post office was established in 1877, when mail was hauled by dog team across the ice from Parry Sound. Timber Village Museum just east of town contains relics of pioneer lumbering operations and a full-scale replica of a logging camp.

BLOOMFIELD

Pop. 677. In Hallowell T., Prince Edward C., on Bull Creek and Hwys. 14 & 33, 27 km S of Belleville. The first land grants were made in 1799 to the Hon. Richard Cartwright, one of Lord Dorchester's appointees, and the townsite was settled in the early 1800s. The community was first known as Bull's Mills, but the post office, opened in 1832, was called Bloomfield, for Capt. A. Bloomfield, skipper of several boats operating in the nearby Bay of Quinte.

BLOSSOM PARK
Pop. 6,792. In Gloucester T., Reg. Mun. of Ottawa-Carleton, on Hwy. 417, 10 km SE of Ottawa. The post office was established in 1956. The origin of the name is unknown.

BLUEVALE
Pop. 240. In Turnberry T., Huron C., on the Little Maitland River and Hwys. 86 & 87, 7 km SE of Wingham. The first settler, Alexander Duncan, arrived in 1853, and his wife, Margaret Hood, named the place Bluevale after a suburb of Glasgow, Scotland. In 1856 the Leech brothers purchased land from Jacob Cantelon and built the first grist mill in the township.

BLYTH
Pop. 899. In East Wawanosh T., Huron C., on Blyth Brook, Hwy. 4 and C. Rd. 25, 25 km E of Goderich. First settled in 1851 and known as Drummond, or Drummondville, after William Drummond, who surveyed the village in 1853. When the post office opened in 1853, the place was called Blythe after the Blyth Estate in England, which at the time owned a large percentage of the townsite. The "e" was later dropped. The village has an active summer theatre.

BLYTHESWOOD
Pop. 250. In Mersea T., Essex C., on Hwy. 77, 8 km N of Leamington. The community was settled in the late 1850s by pioneers from Scotland and Quebec. Donald Cameron opened the first store in the settlement. When a post office was established in his store in 1858, he named the village Blytheswood after a town in Scotland.

BOBCAYGEON
Pop. 1,944. In Verulam T., Victoria C., on three islands formed by the Little Bob and Big Bob rivers and the Trent Canal at the junction of Pigeon and Sturgeon lakes and Hwy. 36 and C. Rd. 8, 37 km NE of Lindsay. The community was founded as a mill centre in 1832 by Thomas Need, who had been given 400 acres (162 ha) of government land on which to build a saw and grist mill for the township. The name derives from the Indian name Bob-ca-je-won-unk, meaning "shallow rapids." A lock in the town centre was built in 1833 to connect Pigeon and Sturgeon lakes, in the Trent Canal system. The town now is the hub of the Kawartha Region, which thrives on summer tourism.

BOLSOVER
Pop. 348. In Eldon T., Victoria C., on the Talbot River and Hwy. 48 just W of Hwy. 46, 40 km NW of Lindsay. The settlement was founded in 1850 by Duncan McRae, a minister of the provincial parliament. McRae

built several mills and named the place Onnacome. When the post office was established in 1864 the community was renamed Bolsover. The origin of the name is not known.

BOLTON

Pop. 7,500. Part of the Town of Caledon, Reg. Mun. of Peel, on the Humber River, Hwy. 50 and C. Rds. 9 & 11, 35 km NE of Brampton. First settled in 1824 by James Bolton and his nephew George Bolton, who built the village's first mill, giving the place its first name of Bolton Mills. The first post office, in 1832, was named Albion for the township, but in 1892 the name was changed to Bolton.

BOND HEAD

Pop. 538. In West Gwillimbury T., Simcoe C., at Hwys. 27 & 88, 10 km SW of Bradford. The community was named in honour of Sir Francis Bond Head, lieutenant-governor of Canada, by postmaster Joel Flesher Robinson, in 1832. In 1851 a plank road was built to Bond Head from Bradford, and one of Ontario's first grammar schools opened there. The community was the birthplace of Sir William Osler (1849-1919), a famous physician and author, and Sir William Mulock (1843-1944). As postmaster general of Canada, Mulock introduced Imperial penny postage.

BONFIELD

Pop. 540. In Bonfield T., Nipissing Dist., on the NE tip of Nosbonsing Lake at the mouth of the Kaibuskong River at the end of Hwy. 531, 3 km S of Hwy. 17, 24 km E of North Bay. In the 1880s, Bonfield was a stop on the great lumber drive from Lake Nipissing to the Ottawa River, and most of its settlers were drivers from eastern Canada, who took up land grants in the township. When the CPR main line arrived in 1882, the station was named Callander, now the name of a community a few kilometres to the west. In 1896 the name Bonfield was adopted for both the station and the post office, honouring James Bonfield of Eganville, MPP for South Renfrew.

BONVILLE

Pop. 269. In Cornwall T., Stormont, Dundas, and Glengarry C., on Hwy. 138, 13 km NW of Cornwall. The post office was established as McPhail's Corners in 1889. In 1892 the name was changed to Bonville. The name translates from French as "good city," but its origin is not known.

BORDEN C.F.B.

Pop. 5,000. In Tosorontio T., Simcoe C., on C. Rd. 10 just south of Angus, 16 km SW of Barrie. Camp Borden was established in 1916 as a training centre for Canadian Expeditionary Force battalions and up to 32,000 troops were based there. The following year an air training program was instituted under the Royal Flying Corps, Canada. Camp Borden was known briefly as Anderson Park in 1967, but is now called C.F.B. Borden (Canadian Forces Base). It is named after Sir Frederick William Borden, a member of Parliament and minister of militia in the early 1900s.

BOTHWELL

Pop. 876. In Zone T., Kent C., near the Thames River on Hwy. 79 and C. Rds. 21 & 24, just N of Hwy. 2, 40 km NE of Chatham. Settlement started in 1852, when the Great Western Railway built a line through the township. In 1854 the Hon. George Brown purchased 4,000 acres (1,620 ha) in the area and laid out a townsite, which he called Bothwell after the Town of Bothwell in Scotland. Brown was owner of the Toronto *Globe*, in which he advertised the lots for sale. Speculators bought up the lots but were unable to profit from their investment because the "metropolis" advertised by Brown did not materialize. When John Lick discovered oil in 1863, the community became a boom town, rapidly growing to 7,000. The first well produced 30,000 barrels of oil before it was accidentally blown up. Many of those drawn by the oil boom were Americans, and as the Fenian raids accelerated in 1866, they returned to the U.S. In the same year the price of crude oil dropped, and in 1867 a major fire destroyed most of the community's business district. Today Bothwell has some small industries and is the centre for a region of mixed farming.

BOURGET

Pop. 1,150. In Clarence T., Prescott and Russell C., on Bear Brook, a tributary of the South Nation River at County Rds. 2 & 8, 41 km E of Ottawa. The post office, opened in 1880, was named The Brook. In 1910 the name was changed to Bourget to honour Bishop Ignace Bourget.

BOWMANVILLE

Pop. 12,979. Part of the Town of Newcastle, Reg. Mun. of Durham, on the N shore of Lake Ontario at the mouth of Bowmanville Creek and Hwys. 2 and 401 and C. Rds. 14 & 57, 67 km E of Toronto. The community has a fine (though undeveloped) harbour. The site was first settled in 1792 as Barber's Creek, named for early settler Augustus Barber. It was successively known as Port Darlington, Darlington Port, Darlington Mills, Darlington Village and, when the post office opened in 1826, as Darlington. The name was later changed to Bowmanville after Charles Bowman, who owned all the town lots. He was never a resident and died in Italy in 1848. Bowmanville native Lt.-Col. Charles McCullough is considered the founder of the Canadian Club movement. (Canadian Clubs are dedicated to fostering throughout Canada an interest in public affairs. The first club was inaugurated in 1893.)

BRACEBRIDGE

Pop. 9,968. In Dist. Mun. of Muskoka, on the Muskoka River and Hwys. 11 & 118 and C. Rd. 14, 55 km N of Orillia. The townsite was discovered by John Bell in 1861. He named it North Falls, and when a mill was built the name was changed to North Mills. In 1864 Bracebridge was named by the postmaster general of Canada after the book, *Bracebridge Hall*, by Washington Irving. Nearby Gravenhurst was named after a place mentioned in the same book. One of Ontario's few remaining three-story octagonal houses was built in 1882 for mill owner Henry James Bird. It is now the home of the Bracebridge Museum. Since 1956, Santa's Village, an amusement park 6 km south of town, has delighted youngsters of all ages. Bracebridge Fall Fair has been held since 1867.

BRADFORD

Pop. 16,679. In West Gwillimbury T., Simcoe C., on the Holland River and Hwys. 11 & 88, 35 km S of Barrie. The first settler, Letitia McGee, had a log cabin on the townsite in 1815. In that year a group of Scottish settlers, disheartened by crop failures and the antagonism of North West Company agents, left Lord Selkirk's Red River settlement and came to Upper Canada. Many of them settled in this area. When William Milloy built a tavern there in 1829, the place became known as Milloy's Tavern and later as Edmanson's Corners. Early storekeeper Joel Flescher Robinson named the settlement for his hometown in Yorkshire, England. The town is a centre for the major market-gardening industry in adjacent Holland Marsh.

BRAESIDE

Pop. 483. In McNab T., Renfrew C., on Lac des Chats, (a lake formed by the Ottawa River) and Hwy. 3, 6 km NW of Arnprior. The post office opened in 1872 as Braeside. The name, chosen by founder W. J. McDonald, is Scottish for "the side of a hill."

BRAMALEA

Pop. 45,000. Part of the City of Brampton, Reg. Mun. of Peel, on Hwy. 7, 3 km E of Brampton. This development started in 1958. The name is a composite of the BRA of Brampton, the MA of Malton, and LEA, as in "meadow." The post office was established as Bramalea in 1962.

BRAMPTON

Pop. 192,045. In the Reg. Mun. of Peel on the Etobicoke River and Hwys. 7 & 10, 32 km W of Toronto. The community was settled in the early 1820s and first known as Buffy's Corners. In 1832 the post office called the place Chinguacousy. The first settler, John Elliot, cleared land and laid out village lots. In 1851 he named the place after his former home in Cumberland, England. The town now is nicknamed "Flower Town" because of the world-famous roses and other flowers produced by the Harry Dale Estate Nurseries. Toronto architect William Kauffman designed the Peel County Court House in 1865 in a pleasing and eclectic style described as Venetian Gothic.

BRANCHTON

Pop. 278. In Reg. Mun. of Waterloo on C. Rd. 13, 9 km SE of Cambridge. Branchton had its beginnings, and derived its name, from the Great Western Railway, which in the early 1850s built a branch line through it from Harrisburg to Galt. The post office was established in 1852.

BRANTFORD

Pop. 75,465. City in Brant C. on the Grand River and Hwys. 2, 24, 53, 54, and 403, 38 km W of Hamilton. In 1626 an Indian village called Kandoucho existed at the site of what is now Brantford and was visited by Father Daillon. The village was in the middle of an area called Beavers Happy Hunting Ground because game was always plentiful. In 1784 Joseph Brant (Thayendandgea) settled with his Six Nations Indians, and the place was known as Brant's Ford. One of Brantford's most important tourist attractions is Her Majesty's Royal Chapel of the Mohawks. The beautifully wrought frame chapel of St. Paul's was built in 1785 with funds given to Joseph Brant by George III. It was the first Protestant chapel in present-day Ontario and was designated a royal chapel by Edward VII in 1904. The post office was established and named Brantford in 1825.

Brantford calls itself the "Telephone City" because the device was invented in 1874 at nearby Tutela Heights by Alexander Graham Bell, whose family home is preserved there as a museum. Also on the site is Canada's first telephone office building, which was set up in the home of Rev. Thomas Henderson in 1877. When Henderson realized the economic potential of the telephone, he resigned the Baptist ministry to administer the office. Another nickname for Brantford is "Combine Capital of the World," because, on a farm just outside the city, Alanson Harris produced the first Canadian-designed farm machine, a business that grew into the giant Massey-Ferguson Company. The first railway "sleeper" car was also produced at Brantford.

Brantford was the home of Hon. Arthur Sturgis Hardy (1837-1901). Hardy was elected to the Ontario legislature in 1873 as the member for South Brant and assumed the portfolios of attorney general and premier after the death of Sir Oliver Mowat in 1896, becoming Ontario's fourth premier. Brantford native Lawren Harris (1885-1970), was a member of the Group of Seven Canadian painters. Journalist and author Sara Jeannette Duncan (1861-1922) was also born in Brantford and earned international recognition for her writing. Of her many novels, only *The*

Imperialist is set in Canada. William Charles Good (1876-1967) was a leading spokesman for agrarian and cooperative movements. He helped found the United Farmers of Ontario in 1914 and from 1921 to 1945 served as president of the Co-operative Union of Canada. One of the oldest national organizations of musicians in Canada was established in Brantford in 1909. The Royal Canadian College of Organists is primarily an examining body dedicated to maintaining a high standard of excellence in organ playing, choral directing, and musical composition. In 1872 The Ontario School for the Blind opened in Brantford with 11 pupils. By 1881 more than 200 students were receiving academic instruction combined with manual and vocational training at what is now the W. Ross Macdonald School.

BRECHIN
Pop. 200. In Mara T., Simcoe C., on Hwy. 12, 26 km SE of Orillia. J. P. Foley came to the area around 1860 and laid out the village. He was appointed the first postmaster in 1863 and the post office was named by his wife for her hometown in Scotland.

BRIDGENORTH
Pop. 1,633. In Smith T., Peterborough C., on the E shore of Chemung Lake and C. Rd. 18, 9 km NW of Peterborough. The first house was erected by William Valley some time after 1818 and operated as a tavern. When Corneluis Herrington, a tailor, arrived in 1840, he and Asa Dunbar, then owner of the tavern, were the only two residents. In 1852 the Kelly family built a mill, and the community began to grow. The post office was established as Bridgenorth in 1854. The origin of the name is not known.

BRIGDEN
Pop. 603. In Moore T., Lambton C., on Hwy. 80, 25 km SE of Sarnia. Founded in 1873 and named after John Brigden, construction engineer of the Courtright branch of the Canada Southern Railway, later part of the New York Central Railway.

BRIGHT
Pop. 325. In Blandford-Blenheim T., Oxford C., on C. Rds. 8, 22, & 42, 21 km NE of Woodstock. George Baird was the first settler. He established a store and named the community after John Bright, an English statesman. The Grand Trunk Railway reached the village in 1857, and the post office was established in 1863.

BRIGHTON
Pop. 3,686. In Brighton T., Northumberland C., on the N shore of Lake Ontario and Hwys. 2 & 30, 32 km SW of Belleville. First settled in 1796 by United Empire Loyalist Obediah Simpson and known as Singleton's

Corners. The community was named Brighton in 1831, presumably after the city in England since there were many immigrants from the British Isles. A plaque just south of Brighton off Hwy. 2 recalls the loss of the schooner *Speedy* in 1804. The *Speedy* sailed from Toronto in October carrying members of the circuit court to attend a murder trial in the Newcastle District. All on board—including the lawyers, witnesses, and the accused—were drowned when the *Speedy* foundered off Presqu'ile Point and sank.

BRIGHTS GROVE

Pop. 2,500. In Sarnia T., Lambton C., at the S end of Lake Huron on C. Rd. 7, 16 km NE of Sarnia. In 1829 Henry Jones attempted to establish a socialist settlement or commune similar to those of the Hutterites and along lines advocated by social reformer Robert Owen. It failed by 1830, and a community called Maxwell grew in its place. By 1835 the place was known as Maxwell Settlement, and in 1863 a post office opened called Perch Station. John Bright owned a lakefront farm with a grove of trees near the beach, and the pretty resort community took the name Bright's Grove in 1935.

BRINSTON

Pop. 236. In Matilda T., Stormont, Dundas, and Glengarry C., on C. Rd. 2, 20 km NW of Morrisburg. When two men named McDonald and Brouse were awarded the contract to build the Matilda plank road, they built a sawmill on a site that developed into Brinston. George Barton opened the first store and a hotel and was then bought out by Thomas Brinston. When Charles Lock became postmaster in 1873 the place was known as Brinston's Corners. In 1909 the name was shortened to Brinston.

BROCKVILLE

Pop. 20,607. City in Leeds and Grenville C., on the St. Lawrence River and Hwys. 401, 2, & 29, 75 km NE of Kingston. Connecticut-born William Buell settled in 1784 and donated land for a village green, thus making Brockville the only municipality in Ontario with a New England-type town square—surrounded by a courthouse green with a church on each corner. The place was first known as Buell's Bay, and the first post office, in 1789, was known as Elizabethtown. The community was also known as Williamstown and Charlestown, and there was so much controversy over the names that the town was nicknamed Snarlington. During the War of 1812, the community was named Brockville to honour Gen. Sir Isaac Brock.

At one time Brockville was said to have more millionaires per capita than any other place in Canada. Hotel magnate George Boldt, who built a castle on one of the nearby Thousand Islands on the U.S. side, is credited—along with his chef—with having invented the Thousand Islands salad dressing at Brockville. The city also has the oldest railway tunnel in Canada, built between 1854 and 1860 to carry the Brockville and Ottawa Railroad under the town to the riverfront. It is no longer in use. In 1851, long-time Brockville resident James Morris became the first Canadian postmaster general. He introduced the first Canadian postage stamps, standardized postal rates, and reduced the letter rate from 16 cents to five cents—likely the first and last reduction ever made in Canadian postal rates. Ogle Robert Gowan (1803-1876) founded the Grand Orange Lodge of British North America in 1830, a year after settling in Brockville. He used his newspaper, the *Brockville Statesman*, to promote his political views.

BRONTE

Pop. 2,029. Part of the Town of Oakville in the Reg. Mun. of Halton, at the mouth of Twelve Mile Creek at Lake Ontario on Hwys. 2 & 25, 46 km SW of Toronto. Philip Sovereign settled in 1814. He was of German descent and a Royalist, fleeing from the United States. The community was named to honour Admiral Lord Nelson, one of whose titles was duke of Bronte.

BROOKLIN

Pop. 1,600. Part of the Town of Whitby in the Reg. Mun. of Durham on Lynde's Creek and Hwys. 7 & 12, 9 km north of Whitby. In 1840 John and Robert Campbell built a flour mill, and a settlement formed called Winchester. The post office, opened in 1847, changed the name to Brooklin. The origin of the name is unknown.

BROUGHAM

Pop. 300. Part of the Town of Pickering, Reg. Mun. of Durham, at the headwaters of Duffin's Creek on Hwy. 7 and C. Rd. 1, 10 km NW of Pickering. In 1807 Thomas Hubbard and John Major built log homes on what is now the townsite. The place was known as Howell's Hollow and Bentley's Corners before the post office was established as Brougham in 1836. The name was chosen by early pioneer Nicholas Howell to honour Lord Brougham, an eminent Scottish peer of that era.

BROWN HILL

Pop. 250. In Georgina T., Reg. Mun. of York, on C. Rd. 32, 1 km E of Hwy. 48, 48 km N of Toronto. The first settlers arrived in the 1860s, and Paul Chappelle opened a general store in 1875. In 1878 the Grand Trunk Railway built a line through the settlement and named its station Blake Station. The post office was established in 1886, and Brown Hill is believed to have been named by the first postmaster, John Brown.

BROWNSVILLE

Pop. 419. In Dereham T., Oxford C., on C. Rds. 10 & 20, 10 km W of Tillsonburg. The place was first known as the Dean Settlement after David Dean who had bought land in the area prior to 1840. In 1841 Brinton Paine Brown, a Methodist minister, arrived with his family from New York State. They were followed by the Loucks and Dennis families. By 1854 the community had been named Brownsville after one of the pioneer families.

BRUCEFIELD

Pop. 200. In Stanley and Tuckersmith ts., Huron C., on Hwy. 4, 29 km SE of Goderich. The first settler of what is now Brucefield was Peter McMullen who arrived about 1833. A Mr. McGowan established the first store and is said to have named the community in honour of Major Bruce, a brother-in-law of Lord Elgin and his aide-de-camp during his term as governor general of Canada.

BRUCE MINES

Pop. 565. In Plummer Additional T., Algoma Dist. on the N shore of Lake Huron's North Channel opposite St. Joseph Island, on Hwy. 17, 62 km SE of Sault Ste. Marie. In 1846 the first mining claim was filed by James Cuthbertson, and the following year the Montreal Mining Company commenced production, making Bruce Mines the first copper mining town in Canada. The mines were also the most productive on the continent until declining profits forced their closure in 1876. The town was named in honour of James Bruce, Lord Elgin. Cornishmen, brought from England to work the mines, were known as "Cousin Jacks," and their wives as "Cousin Jennies." The ore was shipped directly to Wales for smelting. The American demand for copper ceased during the Civil War and the mine closed in 1876.

BRUSSELS

Pop. 991. In Morris and Grey ts., Huron C., on the South Branch of the Maitland River and C. Rds. 12 & 16, 32 km E of Goderich. Settled in 1852 by William Ainley of Yorkshire, England as Ainleyville. The post office, opened in 1856 was called Dingle. In 1872 residents sought a more sophisticated name for their community and chose Brussels after the city in Belgium. Between 1860 and 1875 Brussels had three disastrous fires, but the arrival of the Wellington, Grey and Bruce Railway assured prosperity.

BUCKHORN

Pop. 243. In Harvey T., Peterborough C., on Hwys. 36 & 507 and C. Rd. 16 between Buckhorn Lake and Stony Lake, 30 km N of Peterborough. In 1828, Irish native John Hall, who was operating a successful business in the United States, bought land on both sides of the Buckhorn River. Within two years he built a dam, a saw- and grist mill, a wooden bridge, and homes for his workers. The place became known as Hall's Bridge. Hall pursued his business interests in the U.S. and did not move to Canada until the 1850s, when he settled permanently at Hall's Bridge. A post office was established in 1860 as Hall's Bridge, and John Hall became the first postmaster. Hall was an avid hunter and proud of his prowess at killing game. He mounted his trophies on the side of his mill for all to see. In 1941 the community's name was changed to Buckhorn because of the plentiful game in the area and Hall's collection of animal horns.

BURFORD
Pop. 1,461. In Burford T., Brant C., on Hwy. 53, 14 km west of Brantford. Benagah Mallory built the first home in Burford in 1794, the year after it was surveyed and named after an English town. Pipe organs made by the Burford Organ Builders are in many Canadian churches.

BURGESSVILLE
Pop. 358. In Norwich T., Oxford C., on Big Creek and Hwy. 59, 14 km SE of Woodstock. Elias Snyder settled in 1811, and for a time the community was named Snyder's Corners. E. W. Burgess was a later settler, but when the post office was established in 1853 the place was renamed Burgessville.

BURKETON
Pop. 215. In the Town of Newcastle, Reg. Mun. of Durham, 22 km NW of Bowmanville. The post office was established as Burketon in 1885. The origin of the name is not known.

BURK'S FALLS
Pop. 903. In Armour T., Parry Sound Dist., on the Magnetawan River and Hwy. 11, 40 km N of Huntsville. Named after the first settler, David Francis Burk, who arrived from Oshawa in 1876. The site of the present village was known to lumbermen before Burk settled. They camped there while guiding logs over the falls. In 1879 the steamship *Pioneer* was launched on the Magnetawan River, and for the next 50 years it provided the only efficient means of transportation between the railhead at Burks Falls and small settlements along the river.

BURLINGTON
Pop. 118,546. City in the Reg. Mun. of Halton at the W end of Lake Ontario on Hwys. 2, 5, 6, & 403, directly N across the bay from Hamilton. In 1669, explorer René Robert Cavelier, Sieur de LaSalle, set out from Montreal on the first of several voyages of exploration, seeking a passage to the Far East. On this trip he was accompanied by the Sulpician

missionaries François Dollier de Casson and René François de Bréhan de Galinée. They reached Burlington Bay, travelled inland for a time, and then returned to Montreal. The city grew from what started as Brant's Block, a tract of 3,450 acres (1,397 ha) of land given to Iroquois Chief Joseph Brant (Thayendanegea) by King George III for services during the American Revolutionary War. The first settler on the site was August Bates, who arrived in 1800. In 1807 James Gage purchased 338 acres (136.89 ha) from Brant's widow and laid out a village site, which he called Wellington Square. Wellington honoured the duke of Wellington and Square was the shape of the survey. In 1873 the hamlets of Wellington Square and Port Nelson amalgamated and became Burlington, believed to be a corruption of Bridlington, a resort town in Yorkshire, England. In 1954, William Breckon of Burlington became the first Ontario farmer to win the World Wheat Championship at the Royal Agricultural Winter Fair with his Genesee grain.

BUTTONVILLE

Pop. 200. Part of the Town of Markham, Reg. Mun. of York on C. Rd. 8, 2 km N of Hwy. 7, 18 km NE of Toronto. United Empire Loyalist Major John Button was the first settler and arrived at the close of the War of 1812. When the post office was established in 1851 it honoured Button by naming the community after him. There is a small airport nearby named Buttonville Airport.

CACHE BAY

Pop. 720. In Springer T., Nipissing Dist., on a bay on the NW shore of Lake Nipissing, 40 km W of North Bay. The community was settled in the 1880s by pioneers from Renfrew County. Cache comes from the French for "hide," and the "hidden" bay was likely a place where early voyageurs and fur traders cached their furs and supplies.

CAESAREA

Pop. 600. In Scugog T., Reg. Mun. of Durham, on the E shore of Lake Scugog 32 km N of Oshawa. Originally called Lasherville after the first innkeeper, John Lasher. In 1836 the Caesar family acquired 1,000 acres (405 ha) in the area. In 1853 the post office opened as Caesarea.

CALABOGIE

Pop. 500. In Bagot T., Renfrew C., at the head of the Madawaska River where it leaves Calabogie Lake and C. Rds. 511 & 508, 34 km SW of Arnprior. In the early 1800s the settlement was a supply centre for log drivers on the Madawaska River. In 1895 the largest black graphite deposit in the Americas was discovered at Calabogie. The Black Donald Graphite Mine remained in production until 1954, and during a period of peak production following the First World War it accounted for 90 percent of all graphite mined in Canada. The files of the Ontario Geographic Names Board list four possible origins for this unusual name: (1) from *calladh bogaidh*, Gaelic for "marshy shore"; (2) in Spanish, cala boga refers to a body of water where rowing is necessary; (3) Indian word for "sturgeon"; (4) "callibogus" was an early Newfoundland beverage concocted from spruce beer and rum. The name is sometimes misspelled as Calaboogie.

CALEDON

Pop. 33,538. On the Credit River and Hwy. 10, 24 km NW of Brampton. A town formed by regional government in 1974 by the incorporation of the communities of Alton, Belfountain, Caledon, Cataract, and Inglewood; the villages of Bolton and Caledon East, and the Township of Albion. The present town name, however, has a long history. Settlement in this hilly region started in 1819 when the government opened a rough sleigh track for surveyors. The first town meeting was held in 1824 near Belfountain when settlers appointed a clerk, tax collector, and constable. The community was first called Raeburn's Corners and then Charleston. The name was changed to Caledon in 1839.

Caledon was the political name for a part of Scotland, the name believed to have been derived from the Latin verb *celare* (to conceal.) Caledonians were people skilled at concealing themselves in woody shelters. There were a number of clashes and near riots during the 1830s because many of Caledon's Scottish settlers supported William Lyon Mackenzie and his Reformers, and just as many others were staunch Tories. On one occasion, the story goes, a group of Orangemen broke up a Reformers banquet (just as grace was being said) by storming the meeting place and eating all the food in sight. In 1864 James McLaren, son of one of the township's pioneers, built a castle with a Norman tower at Caledon. For a century the castle was a well-known landmark, and here the Grangers, Ontario's first farmers' cooperative, used to hold their meetings. The castle was destroyed by fire in 1964.

CALEDON EAST
Pop. 1,300. Part of the Town of Caledon, Reg. Mun. of Peel on C. Rds. 7 & 22, 24 km NW of Brampton. The place was first known as Tarbox Corners after the first settlers, United Empire Loyalists Elisha and Elizabeth Tarbox who settled on her 200-acre (81 ha) grant of land in 1821. The first postmaster was James McDougall, but James Munsie, a later postmaster was such a popular man that the place was called Munsie's Corners for a time before it came to be called Paisley. In 1857 the settlement was named Caledon East because of its location at the eastern border of Caledon Township.

CALEDONIA
Pop. 4,237. Part of the Town of Haldimand, Reg. Mun. of Haldimand-Norfolk, on the Grand River and Hwys. 6 & 54, 22 km SW of Hamilton. The first settler, Ronald McKinnon, arrived in 1835 and worked for the Grand River Navigation Company. The community was called Seneca until 1880, from the Indian word *Sinaka*, meaning "stone snakes." Caledonia is a poetic form of an early name for Scotland.

CALEDON VILLAGE
Pop. 301. Part of the Town of Caledon, Reg. Mun. of Peel on Hwys. 10 & 24, 24 km NW of Brampton. William Stubbs and George Bell settled in 1821, and the first store was opened by George Wright. The post office was established as Charleston in 1838, and the following year the name was changed to Caledon.

CALLANDER
Pop. 1,158. In North Himsworth T., Parry Sound Dist., on the E end of Lake Nipissing, 11 km SE of North Bay. The first settlers were lumbermen from nearby Wasi Falls just south of the village. A post office was opened in 1881, and George Morrison, the first settler and the postmaster, suggested the name of Callander, his hometown in Scotland. In 1934 the

Dionne quintuplets were born in a farmhouse near Callander, delivered by Dr. Allan Roy Dafoe, the district's general medical practitioner. News of the multiple birth reached the world when the father, Elzire Dionne, went to the North Bay *Daily Nugget* to place five birth notices.

A plaque at a lookout over Lake Nipissing, 1.5 km south of Callander, explains the creation of the lake. When glacial ice began to retreat, about 9000 BC, the Nipissing Basin formed an eastern extension of Georgian Bay and drained into the Ottawa and Mattawa Rivers. With the gradual tilting of the land, the lake began to drain westward about 7,000 years later, creating the French River.

CAMBORNE
Pop. 220. In Hamilton T., Northumberland C., on C. Rd. 18, 10 km NW of Cobourg. The community was first known as Spring Mills. In 1858 the post office was established as Camborne. The origin of the name is unknown.

CAMBRIDGE
Pop. 80,657. City in the Reg. Mun. of Waterloo on the Grand River and Hwys. 8 & 24, 14 km SE of Kitchener. Cambridge was formed in 1973 by the amalgamation of the city of Galt in North Dumfries Township and the towns of Hespeler and Preston in Waterloo Township. Cambridge is named after an earlier settlement, itself named after the duke of Cambridge, son of George III. (See entries under Galt, Hespeler, Preston.)

CAMDEN EAST
Pop. 205. In Camden T., Lennox and Addington C., on the Napanee River and C. Rds. 1 & 4, 8 km NE of Napanee. Albert Williams, son of a United Empire Loyalist family, was one of the first to settle, in 1800. In 1818, Abel Scott built the first sawmill and then sold the rights to Samuel Clark, who added a grist mill and a wool mill. The community then became known as Clark's Mills. The post office was established in 1832 as Camden; in 1835 the name was changed to Camden East, after the township, which was organized in 1787 and named to honour the earl of Cameron, Lord Chancellor of Great Britain in the late 1700s. Sir Gilbert Parker (1862-1932), a native of Camden East, was a journalist in Australia before moving to England in 1889. There he gained a considerable reputation as a writer of historical novels, many of which were set in French Canada. One of the best-known of his works is *The Seats of the Mighty*.

CAMERON
Pop. 221. In Asphodel T., Peterborough C., on Hwy. 35, W of Sturgeon Lake, 11 km NW of Lindsay. The place is believed to be the site where Samuel de Champlain fought a battle with Indians in 1613. It has been

known as Cameron Line and Cameron Settlement. The community is named after Chief Justice Sir Matthew Crooks Cameron, MPP and provincial secretary and commissioner of Crown lands, who died in 1887.

CAMLACHIE

Pop. 234. In Plympton T., Lambton C., on C. Rd. 7, 17 km E of Sarnia. The settlement came into being with the arrival, in 1859, of the Grand Trunk Railway line from Stratford to Sarnia. One of the first settlers was Duncan McDonald, who arrived in the early 1860s and became the first postmaster, in 1864. McDonald named the community Camlachie after a suburb of Glasgow, Scotland.

CAMPBELLFORD

Pop. 3,408. In Seymour T., Northumberland C., on the Trent River and Hwy. 30, 53 km E of Peterborough. The first settlers came to the area in 1806, but in the early 1830s there was an influx of military men who had received land grants for their services. Maj. David Campbell and his brother, Lt.-Col. Robert Campbell, were granted 1,800 acres (729 ha) in 1831. The Trent River was crossed by a ford a short distance from the present bridge in the centre of town, and since the Campbells owned the site, it became known as Campbell's Ford. The town is headquarters of Ontario's first Fish and Game Protective Association, founded in 1878.

CAMPBELLVILLE

Pop. 720. Part of the Town of Milton, Reg. Mun. of Halton, on Sixteen Mile Creek and C. Rds. 1 & 9, just S of Hwy. 401, 9 km SW of Milton. The place was settled in 1832 by Scottish immigrant John Campbell, who built a sawmill on the creek. The community is named after him.

CAMPDEN

Pop. 253. Part of the Town of Lincoln, Reg. Mun. of Niagara on C. Rds. 22 & 73, 14 km W of St. Catharines. There were a few log homes in the area as early as 1812, and by the 1850s Campden had a number of businesses. The place was first known as Moyer's Corners for Jacob Moyer and his seven sons, who owned most of the land in the area. When a post office was established in 1862 it was given the name of Camden, an English town.

CANFIELD

Pop. 250. Part of the Town of Haldimand, Reg. Mun. of Haldimand-Norfolk, on Hwy. 3, 17 km NW of Dunnville. When a branch of the Grand Trunk Railway crossed the Talbot Road on its route from Goderich to Buffalo in 1852, a settlement slowly developed there. The place was first called Azoff after a village in Russia, which had gained prominence during the Crimean War. When the railway was completed in 1859, the station was named Canfield to honour Albert Canfield, local builder and contractor. When the post office was established in 1854 it took the same name.

CANNIFTON

Pop. 356. In Thurlow T., Hastings C., on the Moira River, 5 km N of Belleville. The community was founded by John Canniff in 1806. The Canniff family built a flour mill in 1812. When the post office was established in 1853, the place was named Bridgewater, but the following year the name was changed to Cannifton. In the 1860s Cannifton was made a stage junction and became the gateway to the northern townships of Hastings County. The population reached 1,000, but as the lumber and flour trade began to decline by 1870, so did the population.

CANNINGTON

Pop. 1,623. In Brock T., Reg. Mun. of Durham, on the Beaverton River and C. Rd. 12 between Hwys. 12 & 46, 58 km NW of Oshawa. Joel Horner settled in 1827 and built the first saw- and grist mill. In 1833 the McCaskill brothers acquired the mill and the community became known as McCaskill's Mills. When the post office opened in 1849, the community was called Cannington to honour the British statesman, the Hon. George Canning. Artist Robert Holmes was born in Cannington in 1861. He was an expert watercolourist and specialized in painting Canadian wildflowers. His work hangs in the National Gallery and the Art Gallery of Ontario.

CAPE CROKER

Pop. 378. On an Indian reserve of the same name on a peninsula on the Georgian Bay shore of the Bruce Peninsula, 25 km NE of Wiarton. The 17,000 acre (6,885 ha) tract of land was one of five set aside in a treaty signed in 1854. The first fur traders called the place Pointe au Portage and the Indians called it Neiyosheonegaming. The peninsula was named after William Croker, an early secretary to the British Admiralty. Peter Kegedonce Jones, who came to the peninsula with his wife in 1852, was elected the first chief of the reserve. Before then the Indians had been ruled by hereditary chiefs.

CAPREOL

Pop. 3,531. In the Reg. Mun. of Sudbury, W of Wanapitei L., on C. Rd. 84, 24 km N of Sudbury. The community began as a divisional point on the Canadian Northern Railway, which was constructing a line from Port Arthur, via Capreol, to Ottawa in 1911. The community was named after Frederick Chase Capreol, a Toronto railway promoter who was the driving force behind the Ontario, Simcoe and Huron railways in the 1850s.

CARAMAT

Pop. 325. In Thunder Bay Dist. on Hwy. 625 and the Canadian National Railway, 78 km SE of Geraldton. Railway superintendent A. J. Hills named the place, somewhat whimsically, by spelling backwards the tree name *tamarack* in its French form in which the final K is dropped. The community got a post office in 1923.

CARDIFF

Pop. 575. In Cardiff T., Haliburton C., on Hwy. 121 & C. Rd. 9, 15 km SW of Bancroft. The area was opened for settlement in 1862, and the community was named after the township, which is itself named after Cardiff, a town on the Bristol Channel in Glamorganshire, Wales.

CARDINAL

Pop. 1,578. In Edwardsburgh T., Leeds and Grenville C., on the St. Lawrence River and Hwy. 2, 35 km NE of Brockville. The place was settled in 1784 by United Empire Loyalists and first known as Munro's Point after founder Capt. Hugh Munro. Because of strong currents, boats had to be poled around Munro's Point. When shipping increased, the Galops Canal and locks were built in 1846. The canal was filled in when the St. Lawrence Seaway replaced it. The community, also known as Point Cardinal, Port Elgin, and Edwardsburgh, was named Cardinal in 1880 in honour of Cardinal Richelieu.

CARGILL

Pop. 208. In Brant and Greenock ts., Bruce C., on the Teeswater River and C. Rd. 52, 11 km NW of Walkerton. Brothers William, James, Donald, Charles, and Malcolm McNeil were among the first settlers of this community. In the late 1850s they started building a mill dam and a mill, which they sold to George Elphick, who completed the construction and opened a grist mill. Charles Mickle Sr., the next owner of the property, built a sawmill and began shipping lumber from the nearby railway station, which became known as Mickles. The community was called Yokassippi, a corruption of the Indian name for the river they called "Drowned Lands River." James Cargill, later MP for South Bruce, had acquired most of the land in the Greenock Swamp and bought the sawmill in 1879. He cut canals to float timber out of the swamp to his sawmill. The canals also drained the swamp and turned Cargill's holdings into farmland. When the post office was established in 1880, Cargill became the first postmaster and named the community Cargill.

CARLETON PLACE

Pop. 6,634. In Beckwith & Ramsay ts., Lanark C., on the Mississippi River and Hwys. 7, 15, & 29, 45 km SW of Ottawa. Founded in 1818 by Edmond Morphy and his three sons from Tipperary, Ireland, the place was first known as Morphy's Falls. In 1824, established Protestant settlers, jealous of government assistance to new Irish Catholic immigrants, were involved in riots in which one immigrant was killed, several were injured, and a number of buildings were destroyed or damaged. The riots, known as The Ballygiblin Riots, were put down by Col. James Fitzgibbon. In 1830 the community was named Carleton Place after a square in Glasgow, Scotland. Capt. A. Roy Brown (1893-1944) of Carleton Place is credited with shooting down Germany's First World War ace Baron Manfred von Richthofen in 1918. Richthofen, nicknamed The Red Baron, had shot down 80 Allied planes.

CARLSBAD SPRINGS

Pop. 525. In Gloucester T., Reg. Mun. of Ottawa-Carleton, on Bear Brook, 16 km SE of Ottawa. Surveyors laying out the townsite in the early 1860s called the place Cathartic because of the six natural mineral springs they discovered. In 1867 Danny Eastman built a roadside inn to cater to guests seeking the supposedly curative powers of the mineral waters, and the place became known as Eastman's Springs. In 1906 the community was named after a famous health spa in Czechoslovakia.

CARTIER

Pop. 700. In Cartier T., Sudbury Dist., on Hwy. 144, 57 km NW of Sudbury. In 1885 the community was known as Archer. In 1888 it was officially named Cartier after the township, which was named to honour Sir George Etienne Cartier, a joint premier of United Canada from 1857 to 1862.

CASSELMAN

Pop. 2,021. In Cambridge T., Prescott and Russell C., on the South Nation River and C. Rds. 3 & 7, just north of Hwy. 417, 48 km E of Ottawa. First called High Falls, the community was named Casselman in 1898 after Martin Casselman, the first settler, who arrived in 1830.

CASTLETON

Pop. 298. In Cramahe T., Northumberland C., on C. Rds. 22 & 25, 30 km NE of Cobourg. Joseph A. Keeler, son of the township's first settler, built a grist mill at Castleton in 1795. The post office was established as Castleton in 1852. The origin of the name is unknown. In the community's heyday, the mid-1800s, there were four sawmills and a number of other industries, which sustained a population of 700 people. The surrounding forests were depleted by the 1880s; the sawmills began closing and the inhabitants moved away to seek new jobs.

CATARAQUI

Pop. 625. In Kingston T., Frontenac C., near Little Cataraqui Creek on Hwy. 2, 5 km NW of Kingston. The name, Indian for "rocks rising out of the river," originally was given to a fort built by Louis de Buade, Comte de Palluau et de Frontenac, governor of New France from 1672 to 1682 and from 1689 to 1698. The fort, also known as Fort Frontenac, was built in 1673 at the mouth of the Cataraqui River. The present community was first called Sandville and then Waterloo, to commemorate the British victory over Napoleon Bonaparte at the Battle of Waterloo in 1815. In 1868 the village was named Cataraqui to end confusion in mail delivery with the town of Waterloo. Sir John A. Macdonald, Canada's first prime minister, is buried here in Christ Church Cemetery.

CAT LAKE I.R.

Pop. 227. In Kenora Dist. on the N shore of Cat Lake, 250 km N of Ignace. The community was so named because in the 1940s a bobcat was shot on the shores of the lake.

CAVAN

Pop. 367. In Cavan T., Peterborough C., on a tributary to the Otonabee River and Hwy. 7A and C. Rd. 10, 16 km SW of Peterborough. A post office was established in the community in 1830. The place was named after the township, which early settlers had named after a county in Northern Ireland.

CAYUGA

Pop. 1,164. Part of the Town of Haldimand, Reg. Mun. of Haldimand-Norfolk, on the Grand River and Hwys. 3 & 54, 40 km S of Hamilton. The first settlers arrived in 1833 after an Indian Treaty gave the government permission to sell the lands for settlement. The community was named for the Cayugas of the Six Nations Indians, who were granted land in 1784 by Sir Frederick Haldimand, then governor of Upper Canada, as compensation for the loss of their lands in New York State. Cayuga became part of the Town of Haldimand in 1974 under regional government.

CEDAR SPRINGS

Pop. 432. In Raleigh T., Kent C., on Hwy. 3 and C. Rd. 10, 19 km SE of Chatham. Nelson Chapman is credited with founding the settlement in 1855, when he opened an inn on the Talbot Colonization Road. The signboard for the inn was made from a pair of buck's horns, and when the post office was established in 1859 the place was called Buckhorn. In 1885 the name was changed to Cedar Springs.

CENTRALIA

Pop. 200. In Stephen T., Huron C., on Hwy. 4, 42 km NW of London. Centralia was one of a number of settlements that sprang up in 1833 along the London Colonization Road. It was first known as Devon and took that name when the post office was established in 1852. In 1873 the name was changed to Centralia. The origin of the name is not known.

CHALK RIVER

Pop. 832. In Buchanan T, Renfrew C., on the Chalk River and Hwy. 17, 35 km NW of Pembroke. It is believed that the river's name originated from the practice of marking timber with chalk at Rafting Bay, where the river meets the Ottawa River. The community of Chalk River was settled in the mid-1800s by men who worked in lumber camps in the winter and farmed in summer. In 1945 the first nuclear reactor outside the United States started operating at a plant on the shore of the Ottawa River 8 km east of Chalk River. The ZEEP (Zero Energy Experimental Pile) was designed by Canadian, British, and French scientists and was the forerunner of more powerful reactors at Chalk River used to produce radioactive isotopes.

CHAPLEAU

Pop. 3,184. In Chapleau T., Sudbury Dist., at the headwaters of the Kapuskasing River and Hwy. 101, 272 km NW of Sudbury. A divisional point on the CPR, settled in the early 1800s and known by the Indians as Nemegosee. Mrs. Noel de Tilley, wife of the first CPR engineer to live there, named the settlement after Sir Joseph Adolphe Chapleau, premier of Quebec from 1879 to 1882 and lieutenant-governor of Quebec from 1892 to 1898. Louis Hémon, author of the novel *Maria Chapdelaine*, is buried in the Chapleau Roman Catholic Cemetery. He was killed by a transcontinental train while walking to Western Canada along the CPR tracks, gathering material for future writings.

CHAPUT HUGHES

Pop. 709. In Teck T., Timiskaming Dist., on Hwy. 66, 3 km SW of Kirkland Lake. The post office was established as Chaput Hughes in 1932. The origin of the name is not known.

CHARING CROSS

Pop. 321. In Raleigh T., Kent C., on C. Rds. 8 & 10, 12 km SE of Chatham. The first settlers were an Englishman named Cook and a man named Samuel Hall. The place was first known as Cook's Corners. When the post office was established in 1860 the community was named Charing Cross. The name likely came from the English hamlet of Charing Cross, now completely absorbed by London.

CHARLTON

Pop. 254. In Dack T., Timiskaming Dist., on the Blanche River and Hwys. 560 & 573, 42 km S of Kirkland Lake. Louis G. Hooey and Tom McLaughlin, who both arrived in 1902, were the first settlers. A townsite was laid out in 1904, and settlers came overland through the bush from New Liskeard or by water up the Blanche River from Tomstown, 16 km east. When the post office opened in 1904, residents requested the name Auralynn, meaning "golden falls," but the name was refused by the post office department. The origin of the name Charlton is unknown.

Sawmills were operating here by 1904, and a branch line of the Timiskaming and Northern Ontario Railway was built to Charlton in 1907. By 1913 the erection of a power dam and generating station made it one of the first rural communities in the north with electricity. The place was a bustling community of more than 500 residents when, in 1922, a bush fire destroyed 1,200 square miles (3,108 sq km) of timber and left only the powerhouse and two homes standing in Charlton. After the fire, the town council met for a time in a streetcar on the site of the former courthouse. The community has gradually rebuilt, but with the timber supplies destroyed and a drop in world silver demand, growth has been slow.

CHATHAM

Pop. 41,840. City in Kent C. at the head of navigation of the Thames River and Hwys. 2 & 40, 3 km N of Hwy. 401, 74 km NE of Windsor. First surveyed in 1790 by Patrick McNiff and named by Lt.-Gov. John Graves Simcoe after Chatham in England. The first post office, in 1816, was called McGregors Mills because a mill owned by John McGregor operated just outside the town limits. During the War of 1812, Shawnee Chief Tecumseh became one of the most heroic figures in Canadian history, fighting on the side of the British in many battles. He was allied with General Proctor, commander of the British forces, who ordered a retreat up the Thames River in the face of strong American forces. Tecumseh urged Proctor to stay and fight at the junction of the Thames and McGregors Creek, but Proctor withdrew, leaving Tecumseh and his warriors to fight at a nearby swamp called Moraviatown. Tecumseh was killed, and Proctor was court-martialled and publicly reprimanded. The town was also known as Chatham Mills, Chatham Village, and Chatham West before being named Chatham in 1850.

CHATSWORTH

Pop. 442. In Holland T., Grey C., on Hwys. 6 & 10, 13 km S of Owen Sound. The first settler, in 1842, was a Mr. Coyer, who built a log tavern at the site of the present community on the Garafraxa Colonization Road. The place was first called Johntown for early landowner John

Deavitt, and Holland for the township. When the post office opened in 1851, it was named Holland East. In 1857 the name was changed at the suggestion of postmaster Henry Cardwell to Chatsworth, after Chatsworth near London, England, his hometown and seat of the duke of Devonshire. Writer, temperance leader, and women's activist Nellie Letitia McClung was born in Chatsworth in 1873. She moved to Manitoba when still a child and lived in Western Canada until her death in 1951.

CHELMSFORD
Pop. 7,400. Part of the Town of Rayside-Balfour, Reg. Mun. of Sudbury, on the Whitson River and Hwy. 144, 19 km NW of Sudbury. Established when the CPR line passed through the area in 1886 and named after a town in England. There were silver, lead, copper, and zinc mining booms in the 1890s and 1920s. A fire in 1909 destroyed many businesses.

CHELTENHAM
Pop. 475. Part of the Town of Caledon, Reg. Mun. of Peel, on the Credit River 19 km NW of Brampton. The founder of the village was Charles Haines, who began clearing land on the Credit River in 1820. In 1827 he built a grist mill that became the nucleus of a small settlement. Haines, a native of Cheltenham in England, gave that name to his new home.

CHENEY
Pop. 450. In Clarence T., Prescott and Russell C., on C. Rd. 2, 37 km E of Ottawa. The first settler was A. Hagar, but the community is named for Samuel T. Cheney, who built a sawmill and a store and ran the post office, which was established in 1900.

CHEPSTOW
Pop. 210. In Greenock T., Bruce C., on the Teeswater River, 16 km NW of Walkerton. Pioneer Irish settler John Phelan built a dam and sawmill. In the 1860s, he and other Irish settlers petitioned the government for a post office, suggesting the name Emmett after the Irish patriot hanged for rebellion in 1803. Someone in the post office department with a knowledge of Irish history and a sense of irony, changed the name to Chepstow when the post office was established in 1865. Chepstow was the residence of Earl Strongbow, the first English invader of Ireland.

CHERRY VALLEY
Pop. 205. In Athol T., Prince Edward C., on C. Rds. 10 & 18, 10 km S of Picton. The first settler was Col. Henry Young, in 1783. The place was named by early settler Alva Stephens, who arrived in 1812. His inspiration may have been the wild cherry trees growing in the valley, or his hometown of Cherry Valley, New York. The post office was established as Cherry Valley in 1848.

CHESLEY

Pop. 1,790. In Elderslie T., Bruce C., on the North Branch of the Saugeen River and C. Rd. 10, 26 km N of Walkerton. The first settlers, in 1854, were Scots, and the place was known as Sconeville until 1868 when the post office named it Chesley without consulting the residents. Chesley was named after Solomon Chesley, an official in the Indian Office in London, England. Adam Scott Elliot was the founder of the settlement. In 1888 most of Chesley was destroyed by fire.

CHESTERVILLE

Pop. 1,456. In Winchester T., Dundas C., on the South Nation River and C. Rd. 7 just N of Hwy. 43, 64 km SE of Ottawa. George Hummel, a United Empire Loyalist, settled in 1817. The settlement was first known as Armstrong's Mills because of Thomas Armstrong's saw- and grist mill. A post office, called Winchester after the township, opened in 1845. In 1875 the first telegraph office opened. The first operator was Chester T. Casselman, and the residents decided to name their village after him.

CHIPPAWA

Pop. 5,134. Part of the City of Niagara Falls, Reg. Mun. of Niagara, at the Welland and Niagara rivers and on the Niagara Parkway, 5 km S of Niagara Falls. The village was the site of a French stockade before the British conquest of Canada in 1759, and during the American Revolution a British blockhouse known as Fort Chippewa stood here. Thomas Cummings, a Scot who had lived in Albany, New York, was the first settler and built a house in 1783 on the banks of the Welland River, then known as Chippewa Creek. In 1799 the settlement was called Fort Welland, and in 1835 the name was changed to Bridgewater. The post office, called Chippawa, opened in 1801.

The community was heavily damaged during the War of 1812. In 1813 a British and Canadian force crossed to the American side of the Niagara River from Chippewa and attacked the depot at Fort Schlosser. The successful raid inspired other raids along the frontier. Under cover of darkness on Dec. 29, 1837, volunteers commanded by Capt. Andrew Drew of the Royal Navy, captured the American schooner *Caroline*, which had been supplying Mackenzie's rebel forces on Navy Island in the Niagara River. The ship was set on fire and sunk in the Niagara River.

The Sir Adam Beck Hydro-Electric power project, begun in 1917, used an intake of water from the Niagara River at Chippawa through a cut made a century before for the first Welland Canal.

CHRISTIAN ISLAND

Pop. 435. On the S shore of Christian Island, Simcoe C., in Georgian Bay off Lake Huron near the entrance to Nottawasaga Bay, 20 km NW of

CCC

Midland and reached by a 5-km ferry trip operated only in summer. In 1649 a few French missionaries and Huron Indians, who had survived the massacre at Ste. Marie (now Midland), sought refuge on the island and built another mission known as Fort Ste. Marie II. A severe winter, followed by a failure of their corn crop, forced the missionaries and the Indians to return to Quebec. In 1830 many of the Indians in the county were gathered on a reserve in the Coldwater area. Within a few years, pressure from land-hungry settlers forced the government to move the Indians, some of whom were resettled on Christian Island, now an Indian reserve. The outline of Fort Ste. Marie II still can be traced in stones.

CHURCHILL

Pop. 350. In Innisfil T., Simcoe C., on Hwy. 11, 5 km W of Cook's Bay off Lake Simcoe and 56 km N of Toronto. The area was settled by the 1820s, and the community was known for a time as Gimby's Corners after early settler John Gimby. The presence of some rough characters inspired the local nickname, "Bully's Acre." When the post office opened in 1858 it was named Churchill, as church services at the time were held in the home of James Sloan, which was on a hill.

CLAREMONT

Pop. 620. Part of the Town of Pickering, Reg. Mun. of Durham, on C. Rds. 1 & 5, 46 km NE of Toronto. The community, settled in the early 1840s, was first called Noble's Corners because of Thomas Noble's grocery store. In 1851 a post office was opened and called Claremont. The name was suggested by W. H. Mitchell, who handled conveyancing for the settlers by walking to Toronto to register documents. Claremont, France was his ancestral home. Claremont was the birthplace of painter Tom Thomson whose work influenced the Group of Seven, formed in 1919, two years after Thomson drowned in Canoe Lake in Algonquin Park.

CLARENCE CREEK

Pop. 538. In Clarence T., Prescott and Russell C., on C. Rd. 8, 41 km NE of Ottawa. John Tyler was among the first pioneers, arriving in 1859. The post office was established as Clarence Creek in 1867. In 1935 the post office changed the name to LaFontaine, but the following year it was changed back to Clarence Creek. The community takes its name from the township, which was named in honour of Prince William Henry, duke of Clarence, son of George III.

CLARKSBURG

Pop. 538. In Collingwood T., Grey C., on the Beaver River 1.5 km from its mouth at Nottawasaga Bay off Georgian Bay at the Town of Thornbury and C. Rd. 13, 42 km E of Owen Sound. William Marsh settled in 1856.

In 1862 the post office was named after W. A. Clarke who built the first wool mill.

CLARKSON

Pop. 15,290. Part of the City of Mississauga, Reg. Mun. of Peel, on Lake Ontario and Hwy. 2 and the Queen Elizabeth Way, 26 km SW of Toronto. The first settlers were Thomas Marigold and Benjamin Monger, who arrived in 1808. Warren Clarkson and his brother Joshua later lived with the Mongers, and in 1819 Warren bought land and built a large house. In 1835 he built a store. In the 1850s he sold the right-of-way to the Great Western Railway, which named the station Clarkson's. The post office opened in 1875 with William Clarkson as postmaster and until 1919 all the postmasters were Clarksons.

CLIFFORD

Pop. 681. In Minto T., Wellington C., on Coon Creek and Hwy. 9 & C. Rds. 2 & 30, 85 km NW of Guelph. The first settler was Francis Brown, who located in 1854, having obtained a parcel of land from the Crown. When a post office was established in 1856, Brown became postmaster and named the village Clifford after a community in his native England. In 1867 the residents of Clifford celebrated Canada's birthday with a building bee, erecting the rafters of a grist mill, which was built by public subscription.

CLINTON

Pop. 3,091. In Goderich & Hullett ts., Huron C., on the Bayfield River and Hwys. 4 & 8 and C. Rds. 8 & 13, 20 km SE of Goderich. Jonas Gibbings and Stephen Vanderburg of Toronto settled in 1831, but William Rattenbury, who took over Vanderburg's tavern in 1844, is considered to be the town's founder. He laid out the building lots and called the place Clinton in honour of Lord Clinton on whose land in England his father had been a tenant farmer. The post office was named Clinton in 1853. Earlier, the settlement was also known as Vanderburg's, The Corners, Corners, and Rattenbury's Corners. Clinton native Dr. Robert Hamilton Coats was appointed in 1915 as Canada's first dominion statistician and controller of the census. He drafted the legislation that three years later established the Dominion Bureau of Statistics. Clinton has a unique museum in Sloman Park at the south side of town; the restored Canadian National Railway car is one of seven that travelled throughout Northern Ontario providing schooling to children in isolated areas. Teachers Fred and Cela Sloman of Clinton had living quarters in one end of the classroom car in which they spent nine months of the year and also raised their own five children.

COBALT

Pop. 1,481. In Coleman T., Timiskaming Dist., on Hwy. 11B, 140 km N of North Bay. Fred LaRose, who discovered the vein of silver that set off one of the greatest mining stampedes of all time, did not accidentally find it by throwing his prospector's pick at a curious fox. But LaRose did find the vein in 1903 and stake it and sell it to the Timmins brothers and their lawyer/financier partner Dave Dunlap for $30,000. News of the silver discovery brought Ontario's first provincial geologist, Dr. Willet G. Miller, to the site, and he christened the place Cobalt, an element of the iron group associated with native silver. In the first 10 years, Cobalt mines produced $300 million worth of metal, and the population reached 30,000. Dr. William Henry Drummond, author of the famous book of dialect verse, *The Habitant*, and four similar works, joined his brothers in a mining venture and died in Cobalt in 1907.

COBDEN

Pop. 991. In Ross T., Renfrew C., at the S end of Muskrat Lake and Hwy. 17 and C. Rd. 8, 125 km NW of Ottawa. French explorer Samuel de Champlain travelled through the area in 1613 and lost his astrolabe. In 1867 an astrolabe bearing the date 1603 was found near Cobden. There was a small settlement of lumbermen on the site in the 1820s, but Jason Gould, who arrived in 1849, is considered to be the founder of Cobden. He cleared a road from the Ottawa River to the southern tip of Muskrat Lake and established a steamship line up the lake and the Muskrat River to Pembroke, by-passing unnavigable rapids in the Ottawa River. When a post office was opened in 1851, Gould was the most prominent figure in the settlement and was asked to choose the name. He suggested Cobden to honour Richard Cobden, the British statesman who had been instrumental in having the corn laws repealed in England in the 1840s.

COBOCONK

Pop. 383. In Bexley and Somerville ts., Victoria C., on the Gull River and Hwy. 35, 1 km SE of its junction with Hwy. 48, 36 km N of Lindsay. The first sawmill was built at the townsite in 1851, and lumbering played an important role in the development of the community. Indians called the place Ko-ash-kob-a-cong, also spelled Quash-qua-be-conk and meaning "where the gulls nest" or "water falling over a smooth rock." When the post office was established in 1859 the name was anglicized. In 1873 the village was the northern terminus of the narrow gauge Toronto and Nipissing Railway. Railway officials renamed the station Shedden after the company president, but in 1881 the townspeople changed the name back to Coboconk.

COBOURG

Pop. 13,210. In Hamilton T., Northumberland C., on Lake Ontario at Factory Creek and Hwys. 2 & 45, just south of Hwy. 401, 114 km E of Toronto. The first settler was Eluid Nickerson, who arrived in 1798 and built a log cabin. The settlement was first known as Buckville, then Amherst, and then Hamilton, after the township. The pioneers also nicknamed it Hardscrabble. In 1822 the post office name was changed to Cobourg to commemorate the marriage of Princess Charlotte to Prince Leopold of Saxe-Coburg, Germany. (The extra "o" in Cobourg is believed to have been a mistake made by the clerk.) The town has a magnificent hall built between 1856 and 1860 when residents believed their town could be chosen capital of Upper Canada. Victoria Hall, one of Canada's most elegant buildings, serves as the Cobourg Town Hall and Northumberland County Court House. Hon. James Cockburn (1819-1883) practised law in Cobourg and represented the area in the legislature. He was a Father of Confederation as one of the delegates from Canada West at the Quebec Conference in 1864. Marie Dressler, Canada's first Oscar-winning actress, in 1930, was born Leila Marie Koerber in Cobourg in 1869. The house where she was born is now a museum filled with Dressler memorabilia.

COCHENOUR

Pop. 526. In Dome T., Kenora Dist., on Red Lake, 13 km N of Red Lake. The post office was established as Cochenour in 1951. The origin of the name is unknown.

COCHRANE

Pop. 4,370. In Glackmeyer T., Cochrane Dist., on Lake Commando and Hwys. 11 & 574, 83 km N of Timmins. The Indian name for the site was Little Lake Camping Grounds. In 1908 it was named Cochrane for Frank Cochrane, Ontario's minister of lands and forests in the early 1900s. The town was almost wiped out by forest fires in 1910, 1911, and 1916. Cochrane is the southern terminus of the Polar Bear Express excursion train to Moosonee, 300 km north on the Moose River estuary at James Bay. The 49th Parallel crosses Hwy. 11 about 6 km south of Cochrane and is marked by a plaque. (The line of latitude that forms the southern boundary of Canada's western provinces was the subject of bitter dispute between Canada and the United States during the first half of the 19th century.) Another plaque marks Niven's Meridian, which crosses Hwy. 11 about 3 km west of Cochrane. In 1896 the Ontario government set Alexander Niven the task of surveying a baseline from the Canadian Pacific Railway tracks due north to the Moose River. Two years later, Niven completed laying an astronomically straight line through 480 km of forests, lakes, swamps, and muskeg.

CODES CORNER

Pop. 250. In Pittsburgh T., Frontenac C., on the Cataraqui River and Hwy. 51 just N of Hwy. 401, 11 km NE of Kingston. No history of this community is available. The place was named after an early merchant named Code.

COLBORNE

Pop. 1,869. In Cramahe T., Northumberland C., on Keeler's Creek and Hwy. 2, 40 km SW of Trenton. Settled in 1789 by Joseph Keeler, a United Empire Loyalist from Rutland, Vermont. The first post office, in 1820, was called Cramahe after the township. In 1829 the name was changed to Colborne at the suggestion of Joseph Keeler's son, Joseph Jr. Colborne honours Sir John Colborne, lieutenant-governor of Upper Canada from 1828 to 1836. Old St. Andrew's Church is one of the oldest surviving Presbyterian churches in Ontario. It was built in the early 1830s. Renovations later in the century altered the building's classical Georgian lines and gave it a distinctly Italianate character.

COLCHESTER

Pop. 520. In Colchester South T., Essex C., on Lake Erie and C. Rds. 15 & 50, 29 km SW of Leamington. The area was settled in the late 1700s by United Empire Loyalists. In the 1860s Colchester became one of the busiest ports on the north shore of Lake Erie, but in 1890 the Lake Erie and Detroit River Railway bypassed the town by 8 km, diverting business to Harrow. The community was first called Sackville, but that name was changed to Colchester in 1831 after the township, named after the City of Colchester in England.

COLDSTREAM

Pop. 231. In Lobo T., Middlesex C., on the Sydenham River and C. Rd. 16, 16 km W of London. The pioneers in this area were mainly Quakers, who began arriving in 1834. Benjamin Cutler built a mill in 1837, and for a time the settlement was called Cutler's. Cutler and John Marsh donated land for the first Meeting House and Quaker Burying Ground in 1850, and by 1859 the Society of Friends had outgrown that small log house and built a larger brick building. A literary society called Olio was started in 1875 and was active for 25 years, founding the Coldstream library. The post office was established in 1856. The origin of the name is unknown.

COLDWATER

Pop. 1,057. In Medonte T., Simcoe C., on the Coldwater River and Hwy. 12, 19 km NW of Orillia. George Cowan, known to his French-Canadian employees as Jean Baptiste Constant, established an independent trading post on Matchedash Bay, 11 km northwest of present-day Coldwater, in 1770. His fur-dealing territory likely included most of present-day

Simcoe, Muskoka, and Haliburton. Coldwater was first inhabited by a band of Chippewa Indians under Chief John Aisance, who settled from 1830-38, calling the place Gissinausebing, meaning "cold water." In 1833 Chief Aisance built a grist mill to serve residents of the Coldwater reserve. Although the reserve was relinquished to European settlement in 1836 the mill was owned by Indians until 1849. The post office was established in 1835 as Coldwater.

COLLINGWOOD
Pop. 12,196. In Nottawasaga T., Simcoe C., on Nottawasaga Bay off Georgian Bay and Hwys. 24 & 26, 63 km E of Owen Sound. The first settler was George Carney, who arrived in 1835, when the place was described by the Tobacco Indians as "an impenetrable swamp." The place was first known to settlers as Hen-and-Chickens Harbour because of one large and four small islands in the bay. The locale had four other names connected with it in early years: Hurontario, New Village, Nattawa, and Old Village. In 1853 Collingwood was named for a township, formerly in Simcoe County, which in turn was named after the English admiral, Lord Cuthbert Collingwood. In 1933 a non-sectarian, non-political international organization, the Associated Country Women of the World, was formed largely through the efforts of Margaret Watt, a native of Collingwood. She was elected the first president of the association.

COLLINS BAY
Pop. 1,250. In Kingston T., Frontenac C., on Lake Ontario at the mouth of Collins Creek and Hwy. 33, 11 km W of Kingston. The area was settled in the 1780s by United Empire Loyalists led by Capt. Michael Grass. The settlement was named Collinsby and later Collins Bay in honour of deputy surveyor John Collins, who laid out the townsite. Collins Bay Penitentiary is one of a number of prisons in the vicinity.

COLUMBUS
Pop. 325. Part of the City of Oshawa in the Reg. Mun. of Durham on C. Rd.2, 9 km NW of Oshawa. The first settler was a Mr. Wilcockson. The community was first known as English Corners because most of the land was sold to people of some wealth, most of whom were English. When the post office was established in 1847, the community was named Columbus. The origin of that name is not known.

COMBER
Pop. 696. In West Tilbury T., Essex C., on Hwy. 77 & C. Rd. 48, 46 km SE of Windsor. The community had its beginnings in the 1840s when a post office was opened about 3 km east of the present site of the village. John Gracey, the first postmaster, named Comber after his hometown in Ireland.

CONCORD

Pop. 500. In Vaughan T., York C., part of the Town of Vaughan, on Hwy. 7, 21 km N of Toronto. The post office opened in 1854, and the first postmaster, John Duncan, named the place Concord—because the citizens couldn't agree on a name.

CONESTOGO

Pop. 502. In Woolwich T., Waterloo C., just W of the confluence of the Grand and Conestogo Rivers on C. Rds. 17 & 22, 16 km N of Kitchener. The first settler, in 1832, was David Musselman, after whom the place was named Musselman's Mills. In 1856 the settlement was renamed Conestogo by settlers from the Conestogo region of Pennsylvania.

CONISTON

Pop. 2,785. In Neelon T., Sudbury Dist., on Hwy. 17, 13 km E of Sudbury. Coniston is a company town founded by the Mond Nickel Co. in 1910 and now maintained by the International Nickel Co. as the site of a smelter. It was incorporated as the Town of Nickel Centre in 1973, but the name remains Coniston.

CONNAUGHT

Pop. 250. Part of the City of Timmins, Cochrane Dist., on the S shore of Frederick House Lake and Hwy. 610, 36 km NE of Timmins. A few kilometres east of Connaught is the hamlet of Barbers Bay where the Hudson's Bay Company established a trading post in 1785 called Frederick House after the second son of George III. The area was the scene of a massacre in the winter of 1812-13 when three company employees and a number of Indians were murdered over the fierce rivalry for precious furs. The post was abandoned in 1821. The post office was established in 1911 as Connaught Station, and in 1949 the name was changed to Connaught. The precise origin of the name is not known, but because many Irish people settled in the area in the 1800s, Connaught is likely named after a place in Ireland.

CONSECON

Pop. 268. In Hillier and Ameliasburgh ts., Prince Edward C., between Weller's Bay off Lake Ontario and Consecon Lake on Hwy. 33 and C. Rd. 1, 16 km SE of Trenton. In 1668, two Sulpician priests established a mission to serve the Iroquois bands migrating to the north shore of Lake Ontario. For a few years the Kente (Quinte) Mission was a significant outpost of French influence in the lower Great Lakes region. It was abandoned in 1680, mainly because of the growth of nearby Fort Frontenac. Matthias Marsh built the first grist mill in Ameliasburgh Township in 1804. In 1832 residents held a meeting and decided to call their community Marshton. Four years later, however, the post office opened as Consecon and the name came into common usage. Consecon derives from the Mississauga Indian word *con-con* (pickerel), a fish once found in abundance in Consecon Lake.

CONSTANCE BAY

Pop. 300. In West Carleton T., Reg. Mun. of Ottawa, on the Ottawa River, 42 km NW of Ottawa. The place was first named Sand Bay. It was later named Constance Bay, either after the daughter of early settler Hamnet Pinhey or an Indian trapper named "Constant."

CONSTANCE LAKE I.R.

Pop. 644. In Cochrane Dist., N of Hwy. 11, 32 km W of Hearst. The history of the place and the origin of the name are not known.

COOKSTOWN

Pop. 1,025. In Essa, Innisfil, Tecumseth, and West Gwillimbury ts., Simcoe C., on Hwys. 27 & 89, 21 km S of Barrie. The place was settled in 1826 by John Perry and first known as Perry's Corners. The name was then changed to Dixon's Corners for a tavern-keeper named Dixon. In 1847 the place was named Cooks Town, and subsequently Cookstown, for settler Thomas Cooke, who arrived in 1831.

COPPER CLIFF

Pop. 3,600. Part of the City of Sudbury, Reg. Mun. of Sudbury, on Hwy. 17, 11 km SW of Sudbury. The site of Copper Cliff was named in 1771 by Arctic explorer Samuel Hearne because of the rich copper deposits found in the area's cliffs. In 1884 prospector Tom Frood found a copper ore body, and in 1886 the first mine was established at Copper Cliff by Samuel J. Ritchie, owner of the Canadian Copper Company. When a high nickel content was discovered in the copper, Ritchie built a nickel smelter at Copper Cliff in 1888. In 1902 the Canadian Copper Company merged with the Orford Copper and Nickel Company of New Jersey to form International Nickel Company. In 1970 the company built the highest smokestack in the world; at 1,250 feet (381 m) it is as tall as the Empire State Building.

CORBEIL

Pop. 200. In East Ferris T., Nipissing Dist., on Hwy. 94, 13 km NE of North Bay. The first settlers were two brothers named Corbeil. The post office was established as Grit in 1900, but shortly after the Corbeil brothers built a sawmill to supply the Canadian Pacific Railway with railroad ties, the settlement's name was changed to Corbeil. The post office took the same name in 1906.

CORNWALL

Pop. 45,529. City in Stormont, Dundas, and Glengarry C., on the St. Lawrence River at the mouth of the Cornwall Canal and Hwys. 2 & 138 just S of Hwy. 401, 112 km SE of Ottawa and 110 km SW of Montreal. The city was founded about 1780 by United Empire Loyalists. The post office, called New Johnstown, was established in 1789 in what was then known as New France. The name likely came from an older Johnstown in the Mohawk Valley, former home of some of the settlers. In 1797 the name was changed to Cornwall in honour of Prince George, duke of Cornwall, eldest son of King George III. A canal starting at Cornwall around the Long Sault Rapids opened in 1843. It was in a Cornwall cotton mill that Thomas A. Edison installed his first plant for lighting by electricity. A bridge links Cornwall with New York State, just east of the Town of Massena.

Rev. John Strachan (1778-1867) came to Upper Canada from Scotland in 1799. He was appointed a missionary at Cornwall where he built the first Anglican church and established a school for boys. In 1812 he moved to York, now Toronto. An historic plaque in Cornwall recalls the Glengarry Fencibles, a fighting force raised from the Highland settlers of the area. The Fencibles distinguished themselves during the War of 1812 at the battles of Ogdensburg, Lundy's Lane, and Fort Erie.

CORUNNA

Pop. 7,500. In Moore T., Lambton C., on the St. Clair River opposite Stag Island and on C. Rd. 33, 9 km S of Sarnia. Corunna was surveyed in 1823 as a possible site for the capital of Upper Canada, but was considered unsafe because of its proximity to the United States. Among the first to settle, in 1836, was John Farquharson. The post office opened in 1852 as Corunna, named after the Battle of Corunna in Spain in 1809, where Sir John Moore's victory marked the turning point of Napoleon's power.

COTTAM

Pop. 750. In Gosfield North T., Essex C., on C. Rds. 27 & 34, 14 km N of Kingsville. Settled around 1818 after completion of the Talbot Road. When the post office opened in 1877, the postmaster, Major W. E. Wagstaff, named the settlement after a village in Yorkshire, England, where he had spent his childhood.

COUCHICHING I.R.

Pop. 422. In Rainy River Dist. on the W shore of Rainy Lake, 4 km N of Fort Frances. Couchiching is an Indian word meaning "at the edge of a whirlpool."

COURTICE

Pop. 365. In Reg. Mun. of Durham on Hwy. 2 and C. Rd. 34, 6 km NE of

Oshawa. A number of families named Courtice lived in the area. A plaque on the grounds of Ebenezer United Church at Courtice recalls The Bible Christian Church established in Upper Canada in the 1830s. The church was a small but fervent offshoot of Wesleyan Methodism and grew slowly because of the vast size of the teaching circuits. Ebenezer United Church formerly was a Bible Christian Church.

COURTLAND

Pop. 796. In Norfolk T., Reg. Mun. of Haldimand-Norfolk, on Hwy. 3, 7 km SE of Tillsonburg. The first settler was Lot Tisdale who arrived in 1823. When the London District was divided into townships, this place was the centre of Middleton Township, and named Middleton Centre. In 1861 a post office was petitioned and named Courtland because divisional courts, which had been held at nearby Fredericksburg (now Delhi), were moved to this community.

COURTRIGHT

Pop. 1,024. In Moore T., Lambton C., on the St. Clair River and Hwy. 80 and C. Rd. 33, 19 km S of Sarnia. Courtright is linked by ferry with St. Clair, Michigan. Land on the townsite was being farmed before 1800. The community was first called Sutherland's for an early settler who arrived in 1832. The post office opened in 1874, and the place was named Courtright for Milton Courtright, president of the Canada Southern Railway. Courtright was the western terminus of the rail line from St. Thomas.

CRAIGLEITH

Pop. 3,500. In Collingwood T., Grey C., on Nottawasaga Bay off Georgian Bay on Hwy. 26 and C. Rd. 19, 9 km NW of Collingwood. A post office called Craigleith opened in 1857, and two years later William Pollard started an oil extraction business unique in Ontario. For four years—until unable to compete with a cheaper product from SW Ontario—Pollard extracted oil from bituminous shales along the lakeshore. A plaque in adjacent Craigleith Provincial Park tells of a dramatic rescue of the crew of the *Mary Ward*, which went aground on a nearby reef on Nov. 24, 1872, with 27 people on board. Of two lifeboats launched, one capsized in the violent storm and eight men were lost. Nine who remained on board were rescued by Craigleith men who risked their lives in small boats.

CREDITON

Pop. 200. In Stephen T., Huron C., on C. Rd. 4, 6 km W of Hwy. 4, 43 km NW of London. Early settlers in the 1840s included Wesley Mitchell, William T. England, and Joseph Motz. The post office was established as Crediton in 1861. The origin of the name is not known.

CREEMORE
Pop. 1,203. In Nottawasaga T., Simcoe C., on the Mad River and C. Rd. 9, 27 km SE of Collingwood. The village is believed to be the site of the Jesuits' St. Jean mission to the Petun Indians and the place where Jesuit missionary Charles Garnier was killed by the Indians in 1649. Garnier was canonized in 1930. The first postmaster was appointed in 1849 and the place was named by Sen. James R. Gowan. Creemore is Gaelic, meaning "big heart."

CROW LAKE I.R.
Pop. 342. In Kenora Dist. on the SE shore of Lake of the Woods and Hwy. 71, 109 km S of Kenora. The post office was established as Crow Lake in 1937.

CRUMLIN
Pop. 293. In North Dorchester T., Middlesex C., on Hwy. 2, 8 km NE of London. The first settler was Robert Dreaney who came from Ireland in the 1840s and built a hotel and blacksmith shop on the Governor's Road. The settlement was first known as Dreaney's Corners. In 1869 Robert Dreaney became the first postmaster. He named the place after the British hometown of some of the settlers.

CRYSLER
Pop. 452. In Finch T., Stormont, Dundas, and Glengarry C., on the South Nation River and C. Rds. 12 & 13, 50 km SE of Ottawa. Among the early settlers, in 1802, were the McMillan and Cameron families, Moses St. Louis, and John Wright. The village is named for John Crysler, a United Empire Loyalist and member of the legislative assembly from 1808 to 1824. Crysler owned the land that is now the townsite and a farm on the St. Lawrence River where the Battle of Crysler's Farm was fought in 1813.

CRYSTAL BEACH
Pop. 2,526. Part of the Town of Fort Erie, Reg. Mun. of Niagara, on Lake Erie, 16 km SW of Fort Erie. In its heyday, the summer resort designed for Americans from nearby Buffalo, was nicknamed the "Atlantic City of the Great Lakes." In the early part of the 20th century, two of the finest steam vessels of their class ferried holidayers from Buffalo to the beach and amusement park. The community was settled in the 1780s and farmed by United Empire Loyalists. The place was named for the clear waters at the beach. In 1814, a small British fleet masquerading as supply craft embarked from Crystal Beach and captured two armed American schooners. This daring exploit was the last naval battle on the Great Lakes in the War of 1812. A summer post office was opened in 1896, and a year round post office has operated since 1908.

CUMBERLAND

Pop. 479. In Rideau T., Reg. Mun. of Ottawa-Carleton, on the Ottawa River, Hwy. 17 and C. Rd. 35, linked by ferry to Masson, Que., 26 km NE of Ottawa. Abijah Dunning and his four sons arrived from Massachusetts in 1801. Within a short time they acquired 3,000 acres (1,215 ha) of land holdings. The next settler was Amable Foubert, who in 1807 bought some of the Dunning land and opened a trading post. Cumberland was named for the township of which it was a part until the advent of regional government in 1969. The township was named after Prince Ernest Augustus, duke of Cumberland, fifth son of George III.

CUMBERLAND BEACH

Pop. 353. In Orillia T., Simcoe C., on the W shore of Lake Couchiching and Hwy. 11, 11 km N of Orillia. A summer post office was opened as Cumberland Beach in 1948. In 1961 it began operating year round. The origin of the name is not known.

CURRAN

Pop. 240. In North Plantagenet T., Prescott and Russell C., on C. Rd. 2, 32 km SW of Hawkesbury. One of the earliest settlers was Leon LaBelle, who arrived in 1857 and opened a general store. He later built a carriage shop and operated a hotel. The post office was established as Curran in 1858. The origin of the name is not known.

CUTLER

Pop. 210. In Algoma Dist. on the N shore of the North Channel of Lake Huron and Hwy. 17, 42 km SW of Espanola. The community's history and the origin of the name are not known.

DASHWOOD

Pop. 400. In Stephen and Hay ts., Huron C., on Hwy. 82 and C. Rd. 2, 61 km W of Stratford. Absolom Fried came from Waterloo County in 1860 and built a grist mill and a sawmill. The community was known as Friedsburg until 1871 when the post office was established as Dashwood. The origin of the name is not known.

DEALTOWN

Pop. 208. In Raleigh T., Kent C., on Lake Erie and Hwy. 3, 23 km SE of Chatham. The post office opened in 1831 as Ericus, a clerical error since the name was supposed to have been Erieus after Lake Erie. The error was corrected the following year, but then the post office closed for a time, and when it reopened in 1875 it was given the name Ouvry. Residents petitioned to have the name Erieus restored, but officials responded by naming the post office Dealtown, after Deal in England.

DEEP RIVER

Pop. 4,166. In Rolph T, Renfrew C., on the Ottawa River and Hwy. 17, 45 km NW of Pembroke. The Deep River townsite was selected in 1944 by the Canadian government as a community for the staff of the Chalk River Atomic Energy Plant then being built 9 km downstream. When the post office was established in 1945, Defence Industries Limited was designated the first postmaster. Deep River operated as a company town until 1956 when it was incorporated as a municipality, and residents elected a mayor and council.

DEER LAKE

Pop. 408. Indian reserve in Kenora Dist., on E end of Deer Lake, 183 km N of Red Lake.

DELAWARE

Pop. 240. In Delaware T., Middlesex C., on the Thames River, and Hwys. 2 & 81, 19 km SW of London. United Empire Loyalist Ebenezer Allan (1752-1813) settled in the area in 1794 on a 2,000-acre (810-ha) land grant. He built a grist mill around which a settlement grew, but his subsequent land transactions antagonized authorities and he was eventually imprisoned for counterfeiting money. He died shortly after his release in 1813. In 1820 the post office opened as Delaware, taking its name from the township. The name Delaware comes from an Indian tribe of that name, some of whom had been driven out of the United States and settled along the Thames River.

By the 1830s the original village around Allan's mill had been all but destroyed by a number of fires. The new village of Delaware was laid out in 1832 near the ruins of the first settlement. In 1842 Delaware was chosen as the township centre and a brick hall was built on the main road running through the settlement. By the 1940s the old town hall's location made it a traffic hazard. Vehicles often crashed into it when they failed to negotiate a sharp turn on Hwy. 2. The building was demolished, and council held meetings for a time in the former Presbyterian Church.

Prominent among past residents was Gideon Tiffany (1774-1854), one of the earliest printers in Upper Canada. He and his brother Silvester founded the province's first independent newspaper at Niagara in 1799. When it failed, he moved to Delaware Township where he became a major land owner and held public office.

DELHI

Pop. 4,043. In Delhi T., Reg. Mun. of Haldimand-Norfolk, on Big Creek and Hwys. 3 & 59, 18 km E of Tillsonburg. "The Tobacco Capital of Norfolk" was settled in the early 1800s by the Sovereen family and was first known as Sovereen's Corners. When Fred Sovereen laid out a townsite in 1828 he called the place Fredericksburg, but that name was in use elsewhere and the post office chose the name Middleton. In 1832 the first postmaster, Robert Decow, renamed the town Delhi after the city in India.

DELORO

Pop. 218. In Marmora T., Hastings C., on the Moira River and C. Rd. 11, 1 km N of Hwy. 7, 58 km NE of Peterborough. The name Deloro means "Valley of Gold." After gold was discovered at nearby Eldorado in 1866, shafts were sunk throughout the district, at least 20 on the site of the present community. In the late 1890s, Canadian Goldfields Ltd. and Atlas Gold and Arsenic Mining Co. bought properties at Deloro and began mining gold and arsenic, continuing until 1904. When silver was discovered at Cobalt in 1903, the Deloro Mining and Reduction Company built a silver refinery at Deloro. The first cobalt metal produced commercially in the world came from this plant. In 1961 the company closed its operations, demolished the plant, sold the company houses, and buried the arsenite refuse.

DELTA

Pop. 365. In Bastard and South Burgess ts., Leeds and Grenville C., on the SW shore of Upper Beverly Lake and Hwy. 42, 37 km W of Brockville. Abel Stevens, a United Empire Loyalist from Vermont, was granted land in the 1790s in the Beverly Lakes watershed and brought settlers into the area before the township was surveyed in 1796. For a time the settlement was known as Stevenstown, but by 1809 Stevens was operating a grist mill, and the place was called Stone Mills. Later the community was named Beverley after Chief Justice Sir John Beverley Robinson. When the post office opened in 1857 the name had to be changed because there already was a Beverley in Ontario. The name Delta was chosen because of its location between the two lakes. Dr. Lorne Pierce (1890-1961), born in Delta, was editor of *The Ryerson Press* from 1920 to 1960. He established an excellent collection of Canadian literature at Queen's University.

DESBARATS

Pop. 227. In Johnson T., Algoma Dist. on the North Channel of Lake Huron and Hwy. 17, 45 km SE of Sault Ste. Marie. The place is named for Montrealer George Desbarats, who in the 1840s obtained a licence to work mines on the shore of Lake Huron. The post office was established as Desbarats in 1895. Just west of Desbarats, Hwy. 17 passes through a large rockcut with prominent ripple marks carved into it. These were caused by shoreline waves about two billion years ago. Subsequent compression of the earth's crust tilted the sandstone formation to its present 60-degree angle.

DESERONTO

Pop. 1,774. In Tyendinaga T., Hastings C., on the Bay of Quinte, Hwy. 2 & C. Rd. 10, 28 km E of Belleville. The townsite was originally part of the Tyendinaga Indian Reserve, 2,000 acres (810 ha) of land granted to a band of Mohawks who helped the British during the American Revolution. Their chief, Capt. John Deserontyou, brought the Indians to the site in 1784. In 1835, John Culbertson, a grandson of Deserontyou, applied to the Mohawk chiefs for a parcel of land, on which he built a landing that became known as Culbertson's Wharf. The first post office, in 1851, was called Mill Point, and the first postmaster was James Bowen. In 1857 the name was changed to Bowen, but in 1859 it was changed back to Mill Point. In 1881 the community was named Deseronto to honour Chief Deserontyou. Christ Church, 3 km west of Deseronto on the Tyendinaga Reserve, was built by its Mohawk congregation to replace an earlier log chapel. It houses part of the communion plate given to the Chapel Royal at Fort Hunter, New York, by Queen Anne in 1712. The bell presented to the church in 1798 by George III has since been recast.

DINORWIC

Pop. 293. In Southworth T., Kenora Dist., at the narrows between Lake Dinorwic and Wabigoon Lake and on Hwys. 17 & 72, 28 km SE of Dryden. The community was established in 1897 by Church of England minister Rev. George Prewer. The name was given by General Superintendent

White of the Canadian Pacific Railway. It was taken from the Cree and means "white feather." The post office was established in 1897.

DOME

Pop. 468. Part of the City of Timmins, Cochrane Dist., on Hwy. 101, 4 km E of Timmins. The station on the Timiskaming and Northern Ontario Railway line was called Dome Mills until 1936 when the name was changed to Dome. The name derives from Dome Mines of the Porcupine District.

DONWOOD

Pop. 1,053. In Douro and Otonabee T., Peterborough C., on C. Rd. 4, 9 km NE of Peterborough. The names derives from an early church named Donwood Church.

DORCHESTER

Pop. 2,756. In North Dorchester T., Middlesex C., on the Thames River and C. Rd. 29, just north of Hwy. 401, 15 km E of London. William Reynolds is believed to have erected Middlesex County's first log cabin in 1794 just west of what is now Dorchester. A log tavern built in the 1820s was the first building on the actual townsite, which was first called Edwardsburgh. The first post office in 1855 was named Dorchester Station, shortened to Dorchester in 1861. The place was named in honour of Sir Guy Carleton, lord Dorchester, governor-in-chief of British North America from 1782 to 1783 and from 1786 to 1796. Dorchester's Donnybrook Fields was the site on Oct. 15, 1925, of the first public initiation into the Ku Klux Klan ever held in Canada. Both Klansmen and new members were masked in their white hooded robes. Hands on each other's shoulders, they circled the field three times to the tune of hymns played by a Klan band and then the new members (more than 100 residents of nearby London were reported to have joined) took the oath before an altar and flaming cross.

DORION

Pop. 491. In Dorion T., Thunder Bay Dist., on the W shore of Black Bay off Lake Superior on Hwy. 11 & 17, 73 km NE of Thunder Bay. Jack Stewart was the first settler in the area. He had been told by Indians of excellent fishing and trapping. The village takes its name from the township, which was named after Sir Antoine Aime Dorion, joint premier of United Canada in 1858 and 1863-64. Ouimet Canyon is about 10 km (6.25 mi) north of Hwy. 11 & 17 at Dorion. The canyon is a natural fault 329 feet (100 m) deep, 492 feet (150 m) wide and 2.4 km (1.5 mi) long. Viewing platforms are cantilevered out over the precipice for spectacular views up and down the canyon.

DOUGLAS

Pop. 262. In Bromley T., Renfrew C., on the Bonnechere River and Hwy. 60, 36 km W of Renfrew. The community grew up beside what was known as the Third Chute of the Bonnechere River, a 21-foot (6.4 m) waterfall over which log drivers had to shepherd their timber. Thomas Bell built a grist mill there in the 1840s and in 1853 Judge John G. Mallock had a townsite surveyed. When the post office was established the following year, Scottish settlers chose the name Douglas for their community.

DOWLING

Pop. 2,970. In the Reg. Mun. of Sudbury on Hwy. 144, 25 km NW of Sudbury. The first settler in the region was a Mr. Wilson from the Ottawa Valley. He was in the area helping clear the CPR right-of-way and thought it so beautiful that he and his wife moved there in 1891 and built a log house. The town and former township, now absorbed into the Reg. Mun. of Sudbury, is named after John F. Dowling, MPP for Renfrew South.

DRAYTON

Pop. 842. In Peel T., Wellington C., on the Conestogo River and C. Rds. 8 & 11, 53 km NW of Guelph. A Methodist preacher named Benjamin Jones settled in 1847. The first post office opened in 1849, and the first postmaster was Ezra Adams. The post office opened as Maryboro, but was also shown as Peel in the same year and then Peel or Maryborough until 1851 when the name was changed to Drayton. Drayton was the English home of Sir Robert Peel.

DRESDEN

Pop. 2,546. In Camden T., Kent C., on the Sydenham River, 28 km from its mouth in Mitchell Bay, Lake St. Clair, and Hwys. 21 & 78, 26 km N of Chatham. The first settler was Jared Lindsley, who came in 1825. The community was first called Fairport, but when the post office opened in 1852 it was named Dresden after a city in Germany. Prior to 1840, a number of fugitive slaves from the U.S. had settled in the township. In 1841, Rev. Josiah Henson, a Maryland-born former slave who had escaped to Canada in 1830, purchased 200 acres (81 ha) of land near what is now Dresden, with the help of abolitionists. Here he established a vocational school for fugitive slaves called the British American Institute. Henson was immortalized in Harriet Beecher Stowe's novel *Uncle Tom's Cabin*. His former house and other historic buildings are now a museum.

DRUMBO

Pop. 509. In Blandford-Blenheim T., Oxford C., on C. Rds. 3 & 29, just south of Hwy. 401, 24 km NE of Woodstock. Some land in the area had been granted by the Crown in 1811, but Squire Henry Mumo built the first log house on the site in 1811. The community was known as Windfall until a post office opened in 1854 named Drumbo after a town in Ireland. A fire in 1862 destroyed 50 business establishments and homes and another in 1864 wiped out a hotel, a shop, and a major store.

DRYDEN

Pop. 6,219. In Van Horne T., Kenora Dist., on Lake Wabigoon and Hwys. 17, 594, 601, & 665, 126 km E of Kenora. The town was founded by Hon. John Dryden, minister of agriculture in the provincial government. In 1897 he started an experimental farm and called the place New Prospect. In 1897 when the post office was opened, settlers changed the name to Dryden to honour its founder.

DUBLIN

Pop. 303. In Hibbert T., Perth C., on Carronbrook, Hwy. 8 and C. Rd. 10, 29 km NW of Stratford. The first settler was U. C. Lee, who opened a store for area farmers. Joseph Kidd settled a few years later in the community then known as Carronbrook after the stream that flowed through the settlement. When salt was discovered at Seaforth, about 11 km NW of Carronbrook, Kidd piped brine to Carronbrook, where he set up a saltworks employing up to 50 people and producing 200 barrels of salt a day. He also built a sawmill and a business block on the main street. The post office was established as Carronbrook in 1854. In 1878 the name was changed to Dublin because there were so many residents of Irish origin.

DUBREUILVILLE

Pop. 961. In Finan T., Algoma Dist., on Hwy. 519 and the Algoma Central Railway, 100 km N of Wawa. The community was founded in the early 1900s by Dubreuil Brothers Ltd., a lumbering company. The post office was opened in 1954 as Magpie Mine but was renamed Dubreuilville in 1961 after the company that founded the settlement. The first postmistress was Miss P. Dubreuil.

DUCLOS POINT

Pop. 212. In the Reg. Mun. of York on Lake Simcoe, 11 km N of Sutton. The community is at the northern tip of a narrow peninsula extending into Lake Simcoe south of Georgina Island. A summer post office was established in 1936. The origin of the name is unknown.

DUNDALK

Pop. 1,417. In Proton T., Grey C., on C. Rds. 8 & 9, 2 km S of Hwy. 10, 67 km SE of Owen Sound. The village was settled in the mid-1800s and first known as McDowell's Corners after an early settler. Later it was called May's Corners after James May whose large hotel burned down. When the post office opened in 1874, the community was named Dundalk after a place in Ireland, not a place in Scotland of the same name.

DUNDAS

Pop. 20,640. In Reg. Mun. of Hamilton-Wentworth on Hwy. 8, 6 km W of Hamilton Harbour at the west end of Lake Ontario and 3 km west of the City of Hamilton. The first settler, in 1787, was Anne Morden, a United Empire Loyalist widow. She and her children were granted most of the land that now comprises the north half of the Town of Dundas. In 1837 the Desjardins Canal was opened to link Dundas to the shipping trade on Lake Ontario. It contributed to the economic development of the area, but began to fall into disuse after the opening of the Great Western Railway in 1853. The place was first known as Coote's Paradise after a Capt. Thomas Coote, who frequently hunted waterfowl in a nearby swamp. The first post office, in 1814, was named Dundas after the Hon. Henry Dundas, British secretary of state for war and the Colonies. Dundas Town Hall, completed in 1849, is one of very few remaining municipal buildings in Ontario from the pre-1850 period. It was designed by a local contractor in the massive, unornamented Roman Classic style.

DUNGANNON

Pop. 277. In West Wawanosh T., Huron C., on C. Rd. 1, 17 km NE of Goderich. The place was laid out as a townsite in 1855 by William Mallough and named after his hometown in County Tyrone, Ireland. A post office had been opened in 1852 just south of the village and named Wawanosh after the township. After the townsite was surveyed, the post office was moved there and renamed Dungannon.

DUNNVILLE

Pop. 11,323. In the Reg. Mun. of Haldimand-Norfolk, on the Grand River 6 km from its mouth at Lake Erie and Hwy. 3 and C. Rd. 3, 31 km W of Welland. The place was settled by Solomon Minor in 1825. In 1829 the Welland Canal Company constructed a feeder canal from Dunnville to the Welland Canal; the company offered perpetual exemption from water rent to the first manufacturing enterprise that was operational when the canal was completed. Oliver Phelps began building a mill at Dunnville while a Mr. Keefer did the same at Thorold. Keefer's building was completed first, but Phelps had installed the machinery before a roof was put on, so when water was let into the canal, he was able to grind a bushel of wheat before water reached Keefer's mill. Phelps had won, but the canal company extended free water privileges to Keefer as well. The post office opened in 1830, and the place was named after Hon. Henry Dunn, receiver general of Upper Canada.

DUNROBIN

Pop. 370. In West Carleton T., Reg. Mun. of Ottawa-Carleton on C. Rd. 9, 32 km W of Ottawa. John Younghusband was the first settler, arriving in 1828. His son Henry bought a parcel of crown land and opened a store. In 1864 the post office was established as Torbolton, and Henry Younghusband became the first postmaster. In 1868 the name of the post office was changed to Dunrobin, the Scottish birthplace of Henry's mother.

DURHAM

Pop. 2,487. In Bentinck & Glenelg ts., Grey C., on the Saugeen River and Hwys. 4 & 6, 45 km SE of Owen Sound. In 1842 a Scotsman named Archibald Hunter led a group of settlers northward on the Garafraxa Colonization Road, which ran between Arthur and present-day Owen Sound. They built a log house near the present townsite. A post office called Bentinck, after the township, was opened in 1847. In 1857 Crown Lands Agent George Jackson changed the name to Durham after his hometown in England.

DUTTON

Pop. 1,058. In Dunwich T., Elgin C., on C. Rds. 8 & 13, just S of Hwy. 401. The settlement developed in the 1870s at the intersection of the Canada Southern Railway and the Currie Road, named for John Currie, a pioneer settler. The crossroads then was called Monkey Run. Selecting a name split the young community into three feuding factions. One group favoured the name Lisgar, after the incumbent governor general of Canada; another wanted Bennettville for George Bennett, who had surveyed and laid out the village plot, and the third group wanted Dutton, to honour the railway company's chief engineer. When the post office opened in 1873 it was named Dutton Station, but "Station" was dropped in 1881.

DYMOND

Pop. 1,136. In Dymond T., Timiskaming Dist., on the Wabi River and Hwy. 11, 4 km N of New Liskeard. The township at the head of Lake Timiskaming was subdivided in 1889 by T. B. Speight, who described the area as being "admirably adapted to agricultural purposes," with 90 percent of the land of excellent quality. C. B. Bowman, while surveying the area, met Jim Heard, a logger, who suggested Bowman name the new townships after Heard's team of oxen, Dymond and Bucke. He did. The Ontario government, concerned with the exodus of farmers to Western Canada in the late 1800s, opened up the area, and Crown Land Agent John Armstrong set up his office on the bank of the Wabi River. The community of Dymond takes its name from Dymond Township.

EAGLE RIVER
Pop. 319. In Aubrey T., Kenora Dist., on Hwy. 594, 1 km S of Hwy. 17, 29 km W of Dryden. The area was settled about the time the Canadian Pacific Railway line was being pushed west in the late 1880s. There are many summer homes in the area, a favourite haunt of sport fishermen. Eagle River once held the title for the world's largest muskellunge.

EAR FALLS
Pop. 1,824. In Patricia Portion of Kenora Dist. on the English River and Hwy. 105, 87 km N of Vermilion Bay on Hwy. 17. The community was developed in the late 1920s as the site of a large hydroelectric generating station. When gold was discovered in the Red Lake region in 1925, the Ear Falls area became the transportation hub of northwestern Ontario. Hudson was the closest connecting point from the Canadian Pacific Railway. Freight was transported by scows from Hudson to a place called Goldpines, immediately east of Ear Falls. There it was loaded onto larger scows and taken to the Red Lake area. In summer the scows, carrying up to 80 tons (81.28 tonnes) of freight, were pulled by boats. In winter, tractor trains pulled by horses, and later by Caterpillars, hauled the goods over the frozen lakes to their destination. In 1948 the highway was completed to Ear Falls, and the post office was established. Ear Falls is known as the Bald Eagle Capital of North America. The origin of the community's name is unknown.

EARLTON
Pop. 1,413. In Armstrong T., Timiskaming Dist., on Hwy. 11, 29 km NW of New Liskeard. The first pioneers moved into Ontario's "little clay belt" around 1900. This extremely fertile region supports beef and dairy herds. The community was named after George Earl Brasher, the first child born there, in 1904, son of postmaster Albert Edward Brasher.

EAST GWILLIMBURY
Pop. 16,513. Geographic T., York C., N of Whitchurch-Stouffville and S of Georgina. The Town of East Gwillimbury ceased to exist in 1971 when along with the communities of Holland Landing, Mount Albert, Queensville, and Sharon, it was annexed to the Township of East Gwillimbury. The town had dated back to the 1790s, when Lt.-Gov. John Graves Simcoe constructed a road north from Toronto to Lake Simcoe. The road was called Yonge Street in honour of Sir George Yonge, the secretary of war. Simcoe named the township after his wife, whose maiden name was Gwillim.

EAST YORK
Pop. 96,497. Borough, Mun. of Metropolitan Toronto, once a municipal

township in York C., and now one of five boroughs in the structure of Metropolitan Toronto. Surveyed in 1791 as one of 11 townships laid out along the shore of Lake Ontario from the Bay of Quinte to the Humber River. First known as Dublin Township, it was named York Township a few years later by Lt.-Gov. John Graves Simcoe in honour of the duke of York, second son of George III of England.

ECHO BAY

Pop. 541. In McDonald T., Algoma Dist., on Lake George, a part of the channel between Lakes Huron and Superior, on Hwys. 17 & 638, 24 km E of Sault Ste. Marie. A fur trading post existed on the site, which was also the scene of a battle between the French and English. First known as Ekoba, when the post office opened in 1889 it was renamed Echo Bay after a lake a few kilometres northeast where Indians interpreted the reverberation of sounds as voices.

EDEN

Pop. 222. In Bayham T., Elgin C., on Hwy. 19, 8 km SW of Tillsonburg. In 1817, Samuel Howie, a veteran of the War of 1812, obtained land in the area from Col. Thomas Talbot, cleared it and built a log house. The post office was established as Eden in 1854. The origin of the name is not known.

EDEN MILLS

Pop. 439. In Eramosa T., Wellington C., at the confluence of the Eramosa River and a branch of the Speed River on C. Rds. 29 & 37, 10 km NE of Guelph. David and Aaron Kribbs settled in the early 1840s and built a sawmill and grist mill. The place was known as Kribb's Mills until 1846 when the Kribbses sold the property to Adam L. Argo. Argo remodelled the mills and renamed the settlement Eden Mills. The origin of the name is not known.

EGANVILLE

Pop. 1,209. In Grattan T., Renfrew C., on the Bonnechere River and Hwys. 41, 60, & 512, 35 km S of Pembroke. In 1825 Gregoire Belanger became the first settler, but he left the following year. John Egan arrived in the early 1830s at what was then known as Donegal, and developed the townsite. When the post office opened in 1852 the place was named Eganville. The town was almost completely destroyed by fire in 1911.

ELGIN

Pop. 253. In South Crosby T., Leeds and Grenville C., on Hwy. 15, 32 km N of Gananoque. The area was settled in the early 1800s. In 1841, Mormons from the United States came to recruit followers in the area and started to construct a temple, but circumstances forced them to abandon it and move back to Utah. For many years thereafter the community was called Nauvoo after a Mormon community in Illinois. The post office was established in 1850 as Elgin after the eighth earl of Elgin, James Bruce, governor general of Canada from 1847 to 1854.

ELGINBURG

Pop. 212. In Kingston T., Frontenac C., on C. Rds. 3 & 9, 11 km N of Kingston. The place was first known as Scott's Corners. When the post office opened in 1853, residents requested the name Elgin, to honour the eighth earl of Elgin. Another community already had that name, so the name Elginburg was chosen.

ELGIN MILLS

Pop. 781. Part of the Town of Richmond Hill, Reg. Mun. of York on Hwy. 11 and C. Rd. 25, 24 km N of Toronto. The post office was established as Elgin Mills in 1900. The name honours James Bruce, eighth earl of Elgin, governor general of Canada from 1847 to 1854.

ELK LAKE

Pop. 356. In James T., Timiskaming Dist., on the Montreal River and Hwys. 65 & 560, 67 km NW of New Liskeard. The community was established by lumbermen and mine workers around 1907. For the first few years the only access to Elk Lake was by canoe in summer on the Montreal River, and in winter by a rough road connecting it to Charlton and Englehart. In 1913 a branch line of the Timiskaming and Northern Ontario Railway was opened between Earlton and Elk Lake. Railway chair Jacob Englehart drove a silver last spike at Elk Lake to mark the occasion. The settlement has been burned out a number of times, and after each fire the residents have returned, rebuilt their homes, and renamed the community. Thus the place has been known as Elk City, Bear Creek, Cookville, Smythe, and Elk Lake. In 1913 the government wanted to honour a man named Smythe and gave his name to this community. Residents refused to call their town anything other than Elk Lake and they tore down the "Smythe" signboard over the post office.

ELLIOT LAKE

Pop. 16,229. In Gunterman T., Algoma Dist., on Elliot and Horne Lakes and Hwy. 108, 29 km N of Hwy. 17 and 165 km W of Sudbury. In 1948 prospectors Aime Breton and Karl Gunterman discovered radioactive ore near Lauzon Lake in Long Township, south of the present town. In 1953 an ore body was discovered that became the Pronto Uranium Mine. By 1954 a road had reached the present townsite, and in 1955 the first mill was operational. A town was planned to accommodate up to 30,000 residents, but demand for uranium dropped and the population never exceeded 20,000. A post office, named for the lake on which the town is located, opened in 1956.

ELMIRA

Pop. 7,063. In the Reg. Mun. of Waterloo on C. Rds. 21 & 86, 19 km NW of Kitchener. First known as Bristow's Corners for Englishmen John and Edward Bristow, who settled in 1835. The post office opened in 1849 as West Woolwich, but the name was changed to Elmira in 1867 after the city in New York State. Toward the end of the 19th century, many German and Pennsylvania Dutch settlers arrived, some of them old-order Mennonites whose descendants still shun modern inventions such as motor cars. The numerous black, horse-drawn buggies and their passengers wearing traditional Mennonite clothing, attract many tourists.

ELMVALE

Pop. 1,564. In Flos T., Simcoe C., on the Wye River and Hwys. 27 & 92 and C. Rd. 19, 26 km NW of Barrie. First known as Four Corners and then Elm Flats and shown on some maps as Saurin, a name proposed by railway construction engineer James Saurin Murray. When the post office opened in 1859, the place was named Elmvale.

ELMWOOD

Pop. 378. In Brant T., Bruce C., and Bentinck T., Grey C., on C. Rd. 10, 34 km S of Owen Sound. The village straddles the boundary between Bruce and Grey counties and was named for a giant elm tree, which once stood at the intersection of Main and Queen streets. A post office was established in 1864.

ELORA

Pop. 2,991. In Nichol T., Wellington C., on the Grand River at Irvine Creek and C. Rds. 7 & 21, 24 km NW of Guelph. First known as Irvine Settlement and nicknamed "City of Rocks," the settlement was founded in 1832 by retired British officer Capt. William Gilkison. He named the townsite Elora after his brother's ship, which in turn had been named after the cave temples of India. Roswell Matthews had built a house at the site in 1817. He had been commissioned to build a mill, but after spring floods on the Grand River swept away a number of his efforts, he abandoned the project. The five-story limestone mill built in 1859 now is a posh inn. Charles Clarke (1826-1909), a long-time resident of Elora, was a prominent figure in the radical reform movement in Ontario. He played a leading role in drafting the Clear Grit platform in 1851, which included such policies as representation by population and the secret ballot.

EMBRO

Pop. 659. In West Zorra T., Oxford C., on the Thames River and Mud Creek and C. Rds. 6 & 33, 14 km W of Woodstock. The settlement was founded by Donald Matheson in the early 1830s and first known as

Edinborough and then Palmerston Depot. In 1836 the post office opened as Embro, an old form of the name Edinburgh.

EMBRUN

Pop. 1,883. In Russell T., Prescott and Russell C., on the Castor River and C. Rd. 3, 37 km SE of Ottawa. The place was settled about 1850 by French-Canadians from the parish of St. Jacques de l'Achigan in Quebec. The community was first called St. Jacques d'Embrun. In 1858 the post office opened as Embrun, named after a town in the *département* of Hautes Alpes in France.

EMO

Pop. 1,077. In Lash T., Rainy River Dist., on Rainy River and Hwys. 11 & 602, 37 km W of Fort Frances. The community came into being as a stopover for river boats bringing settlers into the area. The post office, opened in 1887, was called Emo River after a river in Ireland. A decade later the name was abridged to Emo.

ENGLEHART

Pop. 1,707. In Eventurel T., Timiskaming Dist., on the Blanche River near Kap-Kig-Iwan Falls and Hwy. 11, in a clay belt 39 km N of New Liskeard. Named after Jacob Lewis Englehart, chairman of the Timiskaming and Ontario Northland Railway, which created the town in 1906 as it laid track north from North Bay to link settlers at the head of Lake Timiskaming with Southern Ontario. The town's business district was razed in 1912, immediately rebuilt, and extensively burned again in 1922.

ENTERPRISE

Pop. 529. In Camden T., Lennox and Addington C., on C. Rd. 14, 35 km NW of Kingston. The place was first settled around 1830 by United Empire Loyalist Orin Jackson, who built a sawmill. The community was first known as Thompson's Corners after Robert Thompson, who opened the first store. When the post office was established in 1854, residents felt that their community should have a more suitable name. A visitor remarked that the hamlet was a "most enterprising place" and Thompson suggested that Enterprise should be its name. It was known locally as "Shirt-tail Corners" until the 1930s.

ERIEAU

Pop. 440. In Harwich T., Kent C., on Lake Erie along a sand spit at the entrance to landlocked Rondeau Harbour and C. Rds. 10 & 12, 21 km SE of Chatham. In 1793 Lt.-Gov. John Graves Simcoe envisaged the harbour's entrance as a possible site for border fortifications. He had his surveyors lay out a townsite farther north at the present location of Shrewsbury. Simcoe's plans were abandoned, and Erieau did not come into existence until almost 100 years later. J. J. Ross, manager of the Erie and Huron Railway, also recognized the possibilities of the natural harbour. The railway was constructed as a lumber line in the 1880s to link Lake Erie with Lake Huron, and Ross decided to have the line cross the marshland on the Lake Erie shore to the sand strip at the harbour's entrance. Thus, in 1886, Erieau became the southern terminus of what is now the Chesapeake & Ohio Railway. With rail access to the fine beach, summer cottages were built and resort facilities began to flourish.

ERIE BEACH
Pop. 229. In Harwich T., Kent C., on Lake Erie, 21 km SE of Chatham. The community was created in 1908 by the Chatham, Wallaceburg, and Lake Erie Railway, which shut down in 1830.

ERIN
Pop. 2,308. In Erin T., Wellington C., on a branch of the Credit River and Hwy. 24, 35 km NE of Guelph. The townsite was surveyed in 1819 immediately after Albion and Caledon had been named for England and Scotland. Erin is the poetic name for Ireland. Before the post office was established in 1832, the settlement was known as McMillan's Mills, often misspelled as McMullen's Mills.

ESPANOLA
Pop. 5,358. In Merritt T., Sudbury Dist., on the Spanish River and Hwys. 6 & 17, 70 km SW of Sudbury. The name derives from Espagnola, meaning Little Spain, or the English pronunciation of the French word for Spain—*Espagne*. The community came into being in 1899, when the Spanish River Pulp and Paper Company built a dam and mill at the site. At the onset of the Great Depression in the 1930s, the mill closed and the place became a virtual ghost town. During the Second World War, the mill was used as a camp for prisoners of war. After the war the mill was bought by an American company, which modernized it and began producing paper products.

ESSEX
Pop. 6,252. In Colchester North T., Essex C., on C. Rds. 8 & 34, 22 km SE of Windsor. The Talbot Colonization Road (now Hwy. 3) was surveyed through the area in 1810, and there was a small agricultural settlement at the present townsite in the 1830s. A village did not develop until 1873, when the New York Central System built a rail line between Windsor and Leamington. Because the village was near the centre of Essex County and at the corner of four townships, it was called Essex Centre when the post office opened in 1872. In 1891 the word "Centre" was dropped.

ETOBICOKE
Pop. 293,433. Borough in the Mun. of Metropolitan Toronto on the Humber River and Lake Ontario on the W side of Toronto. The name is

pronounced without the K and is an Indian name meaning "the place where the alders grow." French explorer Etienne Brûlé, the first white visitor, camped there with a party of Indians in 1615. Etobicoke was included in the 250,808-acre (101,577-ha) Toronto Purchase by Deputy Surveyor-General John Collins who paid £1,700 to three chiefs of the Mississauga Indians in 1787. By 1791, Jean Baptiste Rousseaux (1758-1812) had built a trading post at the mouth of the Humber River. Etobicoke became an organized township in 1792 and was completely settled by 1851. The post office was established in 1832. The Borough of Etobicoke was formed from the towns of New Toronto and Mimico, the Village of Long Branch, and the Township of Etobicoke. In 1967 it became one of the five boroughs of the Municipality of Metropolitan Toronto.

EUGENIA

Pop. 250. In Artemesia T., Grey C., on the W shore of Eugenia Lake, head of the Beaver River and C. Rd. 13, 53 km SE of Owen Sound. In the 1850s a deer hunter was reported to have found gold in the rocks near a 70-foot (23-m) waterfall. The stampede was on, but the "gold" turned out to be iron pyrites, also known as "fool's gold." Some of the would-be miners stayed on to try farming, and government surveyors laid out a village site. A French ex-soldier who was a member of the survey party suggested naming the place Eugenia after the Empress Eugenia, wife of Napoleon III. When the post office was established in 1862 it took that name.

EVERETT

Pop. 542. In Tosorontio T., Simcoe C., on C. Rds. 5 & 13, 32 km SW of Barrie. The settlement was established in 1868 and a post office called Everett opened in 1869. When the Hamilton and North Western Railway came through the area in 1878, the post office and business establishments moved 3 km west to be on the rail line. The community is believed to have been named by the first postmaster, Thomas Gordon, after his father's hometown in England.

EXETER

Pop. 3,767. In Usborne and Stephen ts., Huron C., on the Ausable River and Hwy. 4, 50 km NW of London. The James Willis family settled in 1832. In 1833 William McConnell built a sawmill on the river and a settlement formed, first known as Francestown (and sometimes misspelled Francistown). McConnell named the community Exeter after the town in Devonshire, England. The Rt. Hon. James G. Gardiner (1883-1962) was born near Exeter in Hibbert Township. He served as premier of Saskatchewan from 1926 to 1929 and from 1934 to 1935.

FALCONBRIDGE

Pop 839. In Sudbury Dist., on Hwy. 89, 13 km NE of Sudbury, part of the Town of Nickel Centre. The post office, opened in 1930, was named after Sir William Glenholme Falconbridge, justice of the High Court of Ontario and chief justice of the King's Bench from 1900 to 1920.

FAUQUIER

Pop. 841. In Shackleton T., Cochrane Dist., on Groundhog River and Hwy. 11, 96 km NW of Cochrane. First known as Alexandra. The post office opened in 1910 as Fauquier, to honour two brothers who built a section of the Canadian Transcontinental Railway (now the Canadian National Railway). The name has sometimes been misspelled Fanquier or Farquier.

FENELON FALLS

Pop. 1,755. In Fenelon T., Victoria C., on the Fenelon River between Sturgeon and Cameron Lakes and Hwys. 35A & 121, 22 km N of Lindsay. The community was founded in 1834 by Irish immigrants James Wallis and Robert Jameson, who built a sawmill at the 23-foot (7-m) waterfall. The place was first called Cameron's Falls, but when the post office opened in 1838 the name Fenelon Falls was chosen to honour Father Fenelon, Abbé François de Salignac, a Sulpician missionary who came to Canada in 1667 and founded a mission on the Bay of Quinte the following year. Wallis' former home, Maryboro Lodge, is now the Fenelon Falls Museum.

FENWICK

Pop. 1,000. Part of the Town of Pelham in the Reg. Mun. of Niagara, on C. Rd. 63, 12 km NW of Welland. The community was settled in the early 1800s and first known as Diffin's Corners. When the post office opened in 1853, the place was called Fenwick, likely after a British nobleman.

FERGUS

Pop. 6,757. In Nichol T., Wellington C., on the Grand River and Hwy. 8 and C. Rds. 19 & 21, 22 km NW of Guelph. The town is named after Scottish lawyer Adam Fergusson, who came to Canada in 1831 to explore colonization possibilities for the Highland Society of Scotland. He returned two years later with six of his seven sons and another lawyer, James Webster. He purchased 7,300 acres (2,956 ha) and laid out a townsite. The settlement was called Little Falls for a time but took the name Fergus when a post office opened in 1836. More than 200 19th-century buildings remain in the town and the annual Fergus Highland

Games, held on the second Saturday of August, are one of the largest and best-attended Highland Games in North America. The Fergus Curling Club, formed in 1834, has been in continuous operation longer than any other curling club in Ontario. The sport was played outdoors until 1879 when a covered rink was built. The pauper's grave of drunkard George Clephane draws visitors to Fergus from around the world. He is immortalized in the gospel song "The Ninety and Nine" written by his sister Elizabeth.

FESSERTON

Pop. 236. In Tay T., Simcoe C., on Matchedash Bay off Severn Sound off Georgian Bay and Hwy. 12, 34 km NW of Orillia. Benjamin Dusong, who came in 1840, was the first settler in the area. The place was first known as Bush's Point after another pioneer. When the Midland Railway of Canada was extending its line through the area in the 1870s, the railroad president, a Mr. Hugel, named the settlement Fesserton after one of his close friends. The post office was established in 1877.

FINCH

Pop. 459. In Finch T., Stormont, Dundas, and Glengarry C., on the Payne River and Hwy. 43 and C. Rd. 12, 30 km NW of Cornwall. In 1802, Allan McMillan, living on Lochaber Bay in the County of Invernesshire in Scotland, saw a map of Finch Township. In that same year he chartered a ship, the cost being met by each passenger from the McMillan and Cameron families paying £10 for passage fare. After a 13-week crossing, the ship reached Montreal in the autumn. The two families travelled from Montreal to Lancaster on foot and then walked through the bush to the settlements of Kirkhill and Laggan in Lochiel Township. The next spring, four members of each family walked to Finch, selected their lots, built their log houses, and then brought their families to their new wilderness homes. Unlike the settlers along the St. Lawrence, they received no rations or supplies for three years, and the land clearing was done without horses. Their group contained no half-pay army officers; what income they raised came from selling potash and oak barrel staves. (Half-pay officers received half pay as pensions because they had been wounded or because they remained available for recall to active service.) The community took its name from the township, which was named in honour of Lady Elizabeth Finch, a relative of David Murray, viscount Stormont of Perth, Scotland, after whom the county was named.

FINGAL

Pop. 358. In Southwold T., Elgin C., on C. Rds. 16 & 20, 14 km SW of St. Thomas. The community is the oldest village in Southwold Township and was named by Col. Thomas Talbot after Fingal's Cave in Scotland.

The first settler was Titus Cowle, who sold his land to Levi Fowler in the 1820s. In the 1830s Fowler laid out some of his land in village lots and opened a general store. He later went into partnership with Amasa Wood who, because of his habits of rising early and speaking loudly, was nicknamed the "Town Bell." A town hall was built in 1852, and Levi Fowler was the first reeve. There was so much quarrelling and fighting at the council meetings that the community was nicknamed the "Devil's Half Acre." In 1889 a smallpox epidemic wiped out half the population, which was then about 1,000. Nearby St. Thomas was then growing rapidly and attracting industry and settlers, and Fingal never recovered. Just outside the village is a unique architectural find, a double-walled aboriginal earthwork that shows no trace of European influence on its builders. The fort's origin and history remain a mystery.

FITZROY HARBOUR

Pop. 300. In West Carleton T., Reg. Mun. of Ottawa-Carleton at the foot of "the Chats," rapids on the Ottawa River and C. Rd. 5, 56 km NW of Ottawa. Charles Shirreff was the first settler, building a home in 1818 in anticipation that the "Huron Route," a waterway connecting east and west, would run through the Ottawa Valley. The next settlers did not arrive until 1823. When boats began to travel between Aylmer and the Upper Ottawa River, the community, first called the Chats, became known as Fitzroy Harbour after the township in which it was then located. Chats Falls, which once attracted visitors, was silenced in the 1930s by construction of the Chats Falls Generating Station and Power Dam. In 1960, Fitzroy Provincial Park was established nearby.

FLAMBOROUGH

Pop. 27,116. In the Reg. Mun. of Hamilton-Wentworth, on Hwy. 6, 11 km NW of Hamilton. In 1793 Augustus Jones surveyed a line through the area for the Dundas Road. John Green, the first settler, arrived in 1797 and built a grist mill. The place was known as Progress Town (which through usage became Progreston) before being named Flamborough after Flamborough Head in the Heights of Yorkshire.

FLESHERTON

Pop. 565. In Artemesia T., Grey C., on the Boyne River and Hwys. 4 & 10, 38 km SE of Owen Sound. The first settler was tavern owner Aaron Munshaw in 1849. The post office opened as Artemesia in 1851, but the place became known as Flesher's Corners after William Kingston Flesher acquired land in 1853 and built a large saw- and grist mill on the Boyne River, a tributary of the Beaver River. In 1867 the name was changed to Flesherton.

FLINTON

Pop. 200. In Kaladar T., Lennox and Addington C., on the Skootamatta River, 79 km N of Belleville. The place was first called Flint's Mills because of a sawmill built by Billa Flint. Flint was a senator and a prosperous Belleville merchant, who owned large tracts of timber in Kaladar Township. Aside from Flint's lumber camps, there was no settlement in the township until 1855 when the Addington Settlement Road was opened. When the settlement grew large enough to have a post office, in 1858, it was called Flinton.

FLORADALE

Pop. 209. In Reg. Mun. of Waterloo, on Canacagigue Creek on C. Rd. 19, 26 km NW of Kitchener. The place was first called Musselman after Jacob Musselman, a Pennsylvania German and one of the first settlers. In 1863 the post office was established as Flora. In 1876 the post office added "dale" to reduce confusion with Elora.

FOLEYET

Pop. 334. In Foleyet T., Dist. of Sudbury, on the Ivanhoe River and Hwy. 101, 98 km SW of Timmins. The settlement began when the Canadian Northern Railway established a divisional point at that location around 1912. Timothy Foley was a contractor on the railway, and Sír Donald Mann, a railway builder, wanted to name the new station after him. The name had already been given to another station so Mann proposed Foleyet. Floods in 1918 and 1960 caused extensive damage to the community, so in 1962 a concrete dam was built on the Ivanhoe River to prevent more such disasters.

FONTHILL

Pop. 6,000. Part of the Town of Pelham, Reg. Mun. of Niagara on Hwy. 20 and C. Rd. 63, 10 km NW of Welland. The place was first called Osborne's Corners after the first settler, but named Pelham after the township when the post office opened in 1836. The township was named after Henry Pelham, fifth duke of Newcastle. Most early settlers came either from England or Nova Scotia. Dexter D'Everardo was instrumental in persuading many families to move from Nova Scotia. In 1851 he was appointed the first county registrar. During the 1840s Pelham was called Temperanceville, but in 1856 the community was renamed Fonthill after Fonthill Abbey in England. In 1972 a tornado swept through Fonthill causing heavy damage.

FORDWICH

Pop. 425. In Howick T., Huron C., on the Maitland River and C. Rd. 30, 56 km N of Stratford. Arthur Mitchell, Joel Rogers, and W. G. Walker were the first settlers, arriving in 1854. The following year a post office named Lisadel was opened. In 1873 the name was changed to Fordwick, which was later modified to Fordwich after a village in Kent County, England.

FOREST

Pop. 2,555. In Warwick T., Lambton C., on Hwy. 21 and C. Rd. 12, 37 km NE of Sarnia. The community started with the completion of the Grand Trunk Railway line from Stratford to Sarnia in 1859 and still owes its status as a town to the railway. There had been scattered settlement in the area as far back as the 1840s, but the place became a pumping station for the railroad and was called Forest because of the heavy forest covering the area. A post office opened in 1862 as Forest, and the name remained even after the trees had been felled and the community became an agricultural centre. In 1888, when villagers sought town status, the community was just shy of the required population of 2,000. To get around this technicality, it was arranged to have one of the Grand Trunk Railway passenger cars wait at the station for one hour—just long enough to register the passengers and crew as residents of Forest.

FORMOSA

Pop. 321. In Culross T., Bruce C., on Stoney Creek and C. Rd. 12, 10 km SW of Walkerton. Early settlers were all of German or Alsatian descent and of the Roman Catholic faith. John B. Kroetsch built the first sawmill in the 1850s. The place was first named Stoney Creek for a small creek running through a rocky bed. When a post office was opened, the residents applied for the name St. Marys, but another place of that name existed. The unlikely alternative was Formosa, a Portuguese word meaning "majestic."

A brewery was founded in 1869, and the workers remained independent of trade unions through the 1950s and 1960s when major Ontario breweries were suffering long strikes. The resultant shortage of beer brought long lineups of thirsty customers to Formosa Springs Brewery, which then operated around the clock. In 1901 exploratory drilling for oil tapped into a gushing well from which pure, sparkling water still flows. Between 1875 and 1883 the huge, Gothic-styled Church of the Immaculate Conception was built. It was designed by Joseph Connolly of Guelph and has stained glass windows and five decorative carvings.

FORT ALBANY I.R.

Pop. 600. In the estuary of the Albany River on the W shore of James Bay, 131 km by air NW of Moose Factory. Trading was begun by Charles Bayly in 1675, and the first Hudson's Bay Co. trading post was built about 1679 on Bayly Island in the river's mouth. In 1684 the post was moved to the south bank of the river and then to Albany Island. Albany was seized by a French force under Pierre Chevalier de Troyes in 1686 and renamed Fort Ste. Anne. An attempt to re-establish the post in 1688 was defeated by the French, but it was finally recaptured by the English in 1693. Between the Treaty of Ryswick (1697) and the Treaty of Utrecht (1713) it was the only Hudson's Bay Co. post on Hudson or James bays.

FORT ERIE

Pop. 23,486. In the Reg. Mun. of Niagara on Lake Erie at the head of the Niagara River, border terminus of the Queen Elizabeth Way and Hwy. 3, the International Peace Bridge to Buffalo, New York, and the International Railway Bridge to Buffalo, 36 km SE of Niagara Falls. Originally a military post built in 1764 by Capt. John Montresor, it saw heavy action in the War of 1812 when it was taken by the Americans under Gen. Winfield Scott. In attempting to recapture the fort, British Commander-in-Chief Sir Gordon Drummond lost 1,400 men in two attacks. When the Americans retreated later that year they blew up the fort. It was restored in the 1930s by the Niagara Parks Commission and is now staffed in summer by students in period dress. When the first post office was established in 1801, all mail was dispatched under guard. As it grew, Fort Erie assimilated communities named Victoria, Victoriaville, Waterloo, International Bridge, Amagari, Bridgeburg, and Little Africa, a black settlement.

FORT FRANCES

Pop. 8,589. In Rainy River Dist. on the N bank of Rainy River as it leaves Rainy Lake and Hwy. 11 across from International Falls, Minnesota and 369 km W of Thunder Bay. Fort Frances, named after the wife of Sir George Simpson (a governor of the Hudson's Bay Company who visited the fort in 1830), is the oldest continuous settlement west of Lake Superior. Jacques de Noyon, an explorer, fur trader, and soldier, explored the Kaministiquia route to the Lake of the Woods in 1688 and was probably the first European to have travelled through the area. The first settlement was Fort St. Pierre, built in 1731 by Christophe de la Verendrye at Pither's Point, 3 km east of the present townsite. The fort was an important trading post, as it was the farthest point to which canoes could travel from Montreal and still return before freeze-up. It was occupied by six different trading companies before the Hudson's Bay Company took it over in 1821. In 1878 a canal was built linking Rainy Lake to Lake of the Woods. The post office, opened in 1876, had the distinction of being in three areas: first, the Northwest Territories, then when the boundary changed, in Keewatin, and after another boundary change, Ontario. The original fort, destroyed by fire in 1902, has been partially rebuilt as a tourist attraction.

FORT HOPE I.R.

Pop. 705. In Kenora Dist. on the N. shore of Eabamet L., 350 km by air NE of Thunder Bay. The reserve is home of the Fort Hope Indian band.

FORT SEVERN

Pop. 240. In Kenora Dist. on the Severn River, 16 km W of Hudson Bay and 765 km N of Geraldton or 770 km NW of Moosonee. A Hudson's Bay Company fort was established on the site in 1685 and called Churchill Fort. It was burned by the French, rebuilt in 1759 and renamed Fort Severn after the river on which it is located. It is still in operation.

FOURNIER

Pop. 225. In South Plantagenet T., Prescott and Russell C., on Paxton Creek, a branch of the South Nation River on C. Rds. 10 & 15, 66 km E of Ottawa. Bernard Lemieux settled in 1855. He came from Quebec and built a sawmill and a grist mill. In 1856 Cajetan Fournier opened a store. He became the first postmaster when the post office opened in 1856, and the place was named after him.

FOXBORO

Pop. 730. In Thurlow T., Hastings C., on the Moira River, Hwys. 14 & 62 and C. Rd. 5, 11 km NW of Belleville. Settled in 1789 by William Reed and Richard Smith and first named Smithville after either Richard Smith or blacksmith Smith Demorest, who made nails and, around 1800, built the first clapboard house in the settlement. The post office, opened in 1851, was named Smithville, but not surprisingly, there was already a Smithville, so in 1861 the name was changed to Foxboro.

FRANKFORD

Pop. 2,020. In Sidney T., Hastings C., on the Trent River at the mouth of Cold Creek and Hwy. 33 and C. Rd. 5, 12 km N of Trenton. In the 1820s Abel Scott built a grist mill on what was then known as Nine Mile Rapids, and the settlement was first called Scott's Mill or Cold Creek. For a time it was also known as Manchester, but when the post office opened in 1838 Sir Francis Bond Head named it Frankfort after himself. The name later changed to Frankford.

FRANKLIN BEACH

Pop. 358. In the Reg. Mun. of York on the S shore of Lake Simcoe and C. Rd. 78, 7 km NW of Sutton. The history of the community including the origin of its name is unknown.

FRASERVILLE

Pop. 880. In South Monaghan T., Northumberland C., on Hwy. 28, 15 km SW of Peterborough. The post office was established as Fraserville in

1876. The history of the community and the origin of its name are unknown.

FREELTON

Pop. 400. In the Reg. Mun. of Hamilton-Wentworth on Hwy. 6 and C. Rds. 97 & 504, 25 km NW of Hamilton. The community is named after its founder, Patrick Freel, who in 1840 built a hotel on the site. Before regional government changed boundaries, Freelton was at the junction of the townships of East Flamborough, West Flamborough, and Beverly. Freel's brother-in-law, Thomas Campbell, also built a hotel in Freelton. He named it Central Hotel because it was equidistant from Galt, Guelph, and Hamilton.

FRUITLAND

Pop. 300. Part of the Town of Stoney Creek, Reg. Mun. of Hamilton-Wentworth, on Hwy. 8, 8 km SE of Hamilton. The post office opened in 1894 and was named Fruitland because orchards abound in the region.

GGG

GALT

Pop. 48,205. Part of the City of Cambridge in the Reg. Mun. of Waterloo on the Grand River and Hwys. 8 & 24, 14 km SE of Kitchener. The former city of Galt, originally called Shade's Mills, had its beginnings when Scottish merchant William Dickson bought 92,000 acres (37,260 ha) of land including the confluence of Mill Creek and the Grand River. Dickson commissioned Pennsylvania carpenter Absalom Shade to develop a settlement at the site. When the post office opened, in 1825, it was called Galt to honour John Galt, a friend of Dickson and a commissioner of the Canada Company. The Galt Grammar School, familiarly known as "Tassie's," gained widespread recognition for its high academic standards under William Tassie, who was headmaster from 1853 to 1881. The school was among the first in the province to be made a collegiate institute. (See entries under Cambridge, Hespeler, Preston.)

GAMEBRIDGE

Pop. 362. In Thorah T. in the Reg. Mun. of Durham on the Talbot River and Hwy. 12, 30 km SE of Orillia. The post office was established as Gamebridge in 1869. The history of the community including the origin of its name is unknown.

GANANOQUE

Pop. 4,866. In Front of Leeds and Lansdowne ts., Leeds and Grenville C., on the St. Lawrence River at the mouth of the Gananoque River and Hwys. 2 & 32, 29 km E of Kingston. United Empire Loyalist Col. Joel Stone, who settled on his grant of 700 acres (283.5 ha) and built a mill in 1792, is considered to be the first settler. An Indian name, meaning "rocks rising out of the water" Gananoque had up to 52 different spellings until the post office opened in 1817. One of the first skirmishes of the War of 1812 took place at Gananoque. An American contingent under Capt. Benjamin Forsyth, having forced the retreat of the Canadian militia, attacked the settlement, seized the government stores, and burned the depot. Stone's wife was wounded by a random shot. In 1826, Charles McDonald who had become Stone's partner and married his daughter, built the largest flour mill in the province, which produced 25 percent of all the flour sent to Montreal.

Thousand Islands International Bridge is 15 km east of Gananoque at turnoff 661 from Hwy. 401. The structure was opened in 1938 by Prime Minister Mackenzie King and President Theodore Roosevelt. The international bridge system contains five separate bridges with connecting viaducts and highways, which together cover a distance of 13 km.

GARDEN RIVER I.R.
Pop. 588. In Algoma Dist., in the NW corner of North Channel of Lake Huron and the mouth of Garden River, 15 km east of Sault Ste. Marie.

GARDEN VILLAGE
Pop. 300. In Pedley T., Nipissing Dist., on the N shore of Lake Nipissing W of Dokis Point, 7 km SE of Sturgeon Falls. The history of the community and the origin of its name are unknown.

GARSON
Pop. 6,180. Part of the towns of Nickel Centre and Valley East, Reg. Mun. of Sudbury on Hwy. 541, 13 km NE of Sudbury. The community came into being while the Emery Lumber Company was harvesting timber in the 1880s. The town was first called Happy Valley. When the post office opened in 1907, it was named after Lincoln MPP William Garson, an Orkney Islander who immigrated in 1887.

GEORGETOWN
Pop. 17,600. Part of the Town of Halton Hills, Reg. Mun. of Halton, on the Credit River and Hwy. 7, 46 km W of Toronto. The settlement was first known as Hungry Hollow. When the post office opened in 1851 it was named Georgetown after either the British monarch George III, or George Kennedy, the first settler, who came to the area in 1821. In 1888 John Roaf Barber installed a dynamo in the Credit River to augment the power of his paper mill. He was the first person in Canada to use hydroelectric power for industrial purposes.

GEORGINA
Pop. 22,587. Township in the Reg. Mun. of York, 80 km N of Toronto. Georgina was created by regional government in 1986. The name is from a former township, which was named after King George III.

GERALDTON
Pop. 2,528. In Ashmore T., Thunder Bay Dist. on Hwy. 584, 6 km N of Hwy. 11, 270 km NE of Thunder Bay. The town name is an abridged compound of FitzGerald and Errington, two men who financed mines when gold was discovered near Kenogamisis Lake in 1931. The post office opened as Geraldton in 1933. (Before the post office opened, the settlement was known as Oklend [sometimes misspelled as Oklene] and Little Longlac.) During peak production 12 mines were in operation, and when the last mine closed in 1971, more than $156 million in gold had been produced.

GILFORD
Pop. 329. In West Gwillimbury T., Simcoe C., 2 km W of the W shore of Cook's Bay off Lake Simcoe, 22 km SE of Barrie. The history of the community and the origin of its name are not known.

GLEN CAIRN

Pop. 7,238. In the Reg. Mun. of Ottawa-Carleton, 20 km SW of Ottawa on C. Rd. 49. The residential community was created in 1974 by the Glen Cairn Development Company.

GLENCOE

Pop. 1,801. In Mosa and Ekfrid ts., Middlesex C., on Hwy. 80, 48 km SW of London. The area was settled by William Sutherland, who began farming in 1853. It was first known as Mosa Station after the township, but when the post office was established in 1856 it was named by surveyor A. P. Macdonald after Glencoe in Scotland.

GLEN MILLER

Pop. 500. In Sidney T., Hastings C., on C. Rd. 4, 6 km N of Trenton. The post office, established in 1877, was named Gordon Mills. In 1884 the name was changed to Glen Millar, later spelled Glen Miller. The community is situated in a glen and is believed to have been named after Alexander Miller, a mill builder who retired there.

GLEN MORRIS

Pop. 310. In South Dumfries T., Brant C., on the Grand River, 12 km SW of Cambridge. The site was settled in 1823 by pioneers from Scotland and New York State. In 1831 mill owner John Dawson built a bridge across the Grand River, and the settlement became known as Dawson's Bridge. In the 1840s the community was called Middleton because it was in the centre of a ring of villages formed by Ayr, Paris, and St. George. In 1851 the post office opened under the name Glen Morris after then-postmaster general James Morris, during whose administration the postage rate for a letter was reduced from 16 cents to five cents.

GLEN ROBERTSON

Pop. 360. In Locheil T., Stormont, Dundas, and Glengarry C., on C. Rds. 10 & 23, 43 km NE of Cornwall. The post office was established as Glen Robertson in 1874. The land where the railroad station was built was owned by a Mr. Robertson, whose son David Robertson later became warden of the county. The community is believed to have been named after Mr. Robertson.

GLEN WALTER

Pop. 590. In Charlottenburgh T, Stormont, Dundas, and Glengarry C., on the St. Lawrence River and Hwy. 2, 10 km NE of Cornwall. The post office was established as Glen Walter in 1874. The history of the community and the origin of the name are not known.

GLEN WILLIAMS

Pop. 1,100. Part of the Town of Halton Hills on the Credit River, 56 km W of Toronto. The community was originally known as Williamsburg after Charles Williams who built a mill there in 1825. When the post office was established in 1852 the name was changed to Glen Williams.

GLOUCESTER

Pop. 93,121. A township in the Reg. Mun. of Ottawa-Carleton, bounded on the east by Prescott and Russell C., on the south by Russell T., on the west by the Rideau River, and on the north by the Ottawa River. Bradish Billings from New England was the first settler, arriving in 1809. The township was named after William Frederick, the second duke of Gloucester, a nephew of George III.

GODERICH

Pop. 7,348. In Goderich T., Huron C., on Lake Huron at the mouth of the Maitland River and Hwys. 8 & 21, 100 km N of London. Samuel de Champlain was the first European visitor, in 1618, when the Indian settlement there was called Menesetung. The site was chosen by John Galt, founder of the Canada Company, as the terminus of the Huron Road, which he built from Guelph. Dr. William "Tiger" Dunlop supervised the building of the town in 1828, naming it after Viscount Goderich, chancellor of the exchequer when the British government sold the land to the Canada Company. A central park, where the courthouse is located, is a perfect octagon, and eight streets radiate out from the eight angles. With an uncharacteristic lack of tact, Queen Elizabeth II once called Goderich, which sits on a high bluff overlooking Lake Huron and the Maitland River Valley, "the prettiest town in Canada." A plaque at Cobourg and Lighthouse Streets in Goderich recalls "The Great Storm of 1913." The storm raged for three days in November; 244 lives were lost, and 19 vessels were destroyed. Lake Huron bore the brunt of the storm's fury and extensive salvage operations were conducted along the length of the county's shoreline.

GOGAMA

Pop. 800 In Jack and Noble ts., Sudbury Dist., on Minisinakwa Lake and the Minisinakwa River and Hwy. 144, 112 km S of Timmins. The place was a railway point on the Canadian Northern Railway (now the Canadian National Railway) until Arthur L'Abbé settled there in 1917. The post office, opened in 1919, was called Gogama, an Indian word meaning "jumping fish."

GOLD CENTRE

Pop. 400. Part of the City of Timmins in Cochrane Dist., 3 km SE of Timmins. About 50 dwellings were erected around 1927 for workers of the Gold Dale Mine claim. The mining rights now are controlled by Central Porcupine Mines. (See entry under Timmins.)

GOLDEN LAKE

Pop. 236. In North Algona T., Renfrew C., on the E shore of Golden Lake and Hwy. 60 and C. Rd. 30, 39 km SW of Pembroke. The community started in the early 1800s as an outpost of the Hudson's Bay Company. One of the company's best traders, John McLean, raced on snowshoes up the frozen Bonnechere River to make contact with the Indians ahead of the independent traders. When the post office was established in 1873, the community was named after early settler John Golden.

GOODWOOD
Pop. 348. In Uxbridge T., Reg. Mun. of Durham, on Hwy. 47 and C. Rd. 21, 39 km NW of Whitby. Early settlers included T. Robinson and Henry Stapleton, who emigrated from England in 1825 and 1833 respectively. In 1850 William Todd applied to operate the post office. The story goes that he drew cards with a Michael Chapman to choose a name for the community. Chapman won and named the place Goodwood after a town in England. Mr. Todd appears to have lost more than the name choice; Michael Chapman ran the post office for the next 40 years.

GORE BAY
Pop. 819. In Gordon T., Manitoulin Dist., on the North Channel of Lake Huron and N shore of Manitoulin Island on Hwy. B540, 60 km W of Little Current. The Indians called the place Pushk-dinang, meaning "barren hill" and referring to a sheer wall of grey limestone on the east side of the bay. The first settler was Williard Hall in the 1850s. When a post office opened in 1874, it was named Gore Bay after a steamship, the *Gore*, which had become frozen in the ice of the North Channel in the 1850s.

GORE'S LANDING
Pop. 243. In Hamilton T., Northumberland C., on the S shore of Rice Lake and C. Rd. 18, 16 km NW of Cobourg. Permanent settlement began in the area in the 1840s and the community enjoyed a boom when it became the northern terminus of a plank road from Cobourg to Rice Lake, completed in 1848. F. W. Barron Boys' School was opened by a former headmaster of Upper Canada College. In St. George's Anglican Church, which replaced an earlier church in 1908, is a battle flag used at Admiral Nelson's victory at Trafalgar in 1805. Before 1848 the community was known as Claverton but was usually called Tidy's Tavern for David Tidy, who operated a tavern there. When the post office was established in 1848, it was named Gore's Landing after Thomas S. Gore, a British navy captain who owned land in the area in 1845.

GORRIE
Pop. 414. In Howick T., Huron C., on the Maitland River and Hwy. 87 and C. Rd. 28, 17 km E of Wingham. The first settlers on the site were the Creer brothers who arrived in 1854. In 1856 James and Nathaniel Leech purchased mill sites and their grist and flour mills, built the same year, soon became the most important in the area. In 1857 the Leeches laid out

the village site. The name on the plans was Howick Village, but everyone called the place Leechville. When the post office was established that year the Leech brothers named the settlement Gorrie after a place near their parents' home in Ireland.

GRAFTON

Pop. 549. In Haldimand T., Northumberland C., on Hwy. 2 near Lake Ontario, 12 km E of Cobourg. The hamlet was settled by United Empire Loyalists from Vermont and Massachusetts around 1798. It was called Newcastle when the post office opened in 1814. In 1832 the name was changed to Haldimand, and in 1858 it was changed again to Grafton after a town in Massachusetts. During the War of 1812, the home of the first settler, Eliakim Barnum, was accidentally burned by British troops. Barnum rebuilt his house on the same site and today the building, now a museum, is one of Ontario's finest remaining examples of Loyalist-style architecture.

GRAND BEND

Pop. 660. In Bosanquet T., Lambton C., on Lake Huron at the mouth of the Ausable River and Hwys. 21 & 81, 69 km NW of London. The Ausable River originally flowed to within 200 metres of Lake Huron and then made an abrupt bend and flowed 21 km south, parallel to the lakeshore, emptying into Lake Huron at Port Franks. In 1832 a man named Brewster built a mill at the point of the "grand bend" in the river. The settlement that grew up there was called Brewster's Mills. In 1845 a group of French-Canadians fleeing a famine in Quebec, settled in the area which they called Aux Croches, meaning "crooked tongs" and referring to the twisting river. From the time it was built, settlers complained that Brewster's mill dam caused flooding of their farmlands. In 1860 a group of angry farmers destroyed the mill and dam, but the flooding continued.

In 1872 a post office was established called Grand Bend. The Canada Company, which held the land as part of the Huron Tract, solved the flooding problem by cutting a straight channel across the series of loops in the river from the village of Port Franks to the big loop in the river at Grand Bend. The diversion also destroyed the natural harbour at Port Franks. In 1891 a channel was cut from the big loop in the river at Grand Bend to Lake Huron, and the community began to develop as a popular summer resort. Grand Bend was originally in Huron County, but when Huron stayed dry after repeal of the Canada Temperance Act in Ontario, Grand Bend businessmen felt temperance would hurt their tourist trade, so they seceded to Lambton County. The businessmen were right—providing alcohol further boosted the town's popularity. While the year-round population is only 660, there are often 20,000 holidayers in and around the town on summer weekends. The popular Pinery Provincial Park is 8 km south of Grand Bend off Hwy. 21.

GRAND VALLEY

Pop. 1,204. In East Luther T., Dufferin C., on the Grand River and Hwy. 25, 20 km SW of Orangeville. The first settlers, in 1836, were Richard Joice, Samuel Stuckey, and Richard Ponsford. The place was originally known as Luther and kept that name when the post office was established in 1860. It was also known locally as Little Toronto. In 1883 the villagers changed the name of their community to Grand Valley.

GRANTON

Pop. 326. In Biddulph T., Middlesex C., on C. Rds. 17 & 59, 28 km N of London. Brothers Alexander, William, and James Grant and William Levitt and George Foreman settled the place around 1842, but the community grew slowly until the arrival in the 1860s of the Grand Trunk Railway. At that time a name was needed for the settlement and the issue divided the residents. The Grant brothers suggested Granton; Levitt and Foreman favoured Amwik, an Indian word for "beaver." At an open meeting, residents drew lots out of a hat to make the final decision. Amwik was drawn but was rejected by both the post office and the railway. A Mr. Christie, local superintendent of the railway, had come from a village in Scotland named Granton, so the Grant brothers got their wish. Residents remained unhappy over the choice, and for years the north side of the railway tracks was known as Granton and the south side was called Amwik.

GRASSY NARROWS

Pop. 367. In Kenora Dist. on the English River system and Hwy. 671, 77 km NE of Kenora. The Ojibway name for the place was Iskapiciwan, meaning "dried-up stream." A Hudson's Bay post operated in the area in 1840. The post office was established as Grassy Narrows in 1960.

GRAVENHURST

Pop. 8,624. In Dist. Mun. of Muskoka at the S end of Lake Muskoka on Hwy. 169 and C. Rds. 17 & 18, 18 km S of Bracebridge. Explorers passed through the area in 1826, but there was little settlement until completion of the Muskoka Road in 1858-1859. The town is nicknamed "Gateway to Muskoka." James McCabe, who built a tavern at the site in 1859, is considered to be the first settler. Lumbering was the major industry, and by the 1870s there were 17 mills and the settlement was nicknamed Sawdust City. The place was variously known as McCabe's Landing, McCabe's Mills, and McCabe's Bay, but when the post office opened in 1862 postmaster James McCabe selected the name Gravenhurst from the book Bracebridge Hall by Washington Irving. In 1864 the postmaster general of Canada referred to the same book to name nearby Bracebridge.

Dr. Norman Bethune, remembered for his heroic work in Spain and

China as a field surgeon and medical educator, was born in the manse of Knox Presbyterian Church in 1890. Today the home is a museum and a shrine of sorts for Chinese visitors to Canada. The R.M.S. *Segwun*, last of a fleet of steamships that once provided transportation through the Muskoka Lakes, still operates in summer out of Gravenhurst. The ship was built in Scotland and reassembled in Gravenhurst in 1887.

GREELY
Pop. 561. In Reg. Mun. of Ottawa-Carleton, on Hwy. 31, 18 km SE of Ottawa. Settled in 1850 by Adam and Sam Rossiter and first known as Rossiter's Corners. The post office was established in 1885 as Greeley, probably after General Greely, an Arctic explorer in the 1880s. The spelling later changed to Greely.

GREENSVILLE
Pop. 998. In Reg. Mun. of Hamilton-Wentworth on Glen Creek and Hwy. 8, 4 km NW of Dundas. The community was known as Franklin Corners and Joyce's Corners until the post office was established in 1853 as Greensville after William Green who settled in 1799. A half mile (.8 km) west of Greensville was Crook's Hollow, where James Crook operated Upper Canada's first paper mill. Crook built the mill in 1826 because of the growing domestic market and the high tariff imposed on imported paper. The mill operated until it was destroyed by fire in 1875. In 1860 Greensville was the home of Ontario's largest distillery, which was converted to a malt house in 1870.

GREENBANK
Pop. 284. In Scugog T., Reg. Mun. of Durham, on Hwys. 7 & 12, 34 km N of Whitby. The first settler was E. Bassingthwait who came from Lincolnshire, England, in 1832. The place for decades was known as Smithtown, the name painted in large letters on the first hotel, owned by Richard Smith. In 1855 the post office was opened as Greenbank after the hometown of Mr. Bassingthwait.

GRIMSBY
Pop. 16,996. In the Reg. Mun. of Niagara, on the S shore of Lake Ontario at Forty Mile Creek and Hwys. 8 & QEW, 26 km SE of Hamilton. United Empire Loyalists began a settlement in 1783, when the place was known as The Forty because of its location at the mouth of Forty Mile Creek. It was also called Butlersburg for Col. John Butler, a United Empire Loyalist whose troops were early settlers. A town meeting held on April 5, 1790 at present-day Grimsby, which was then called Township # 6, marked the beginning of local self-government in what is now Ontario. Such matters as the height of fences and the registration of livestock brands were discussed at the meeting. St. Andrews Anglican Church, completed in 1825, was the third church built on the site by a congregation formed

almost 40 years earlier. Many early settlers are buried in the churchyard. The post office was established as Grimsby in 1816 after Great Grimsby in England.

GUELPH

Pop. 80,786. In Guelph T., Wellington C., at the confluence of the Speed and Eramosa Rivers and Hwys. 6 & 24, 20 km NE of Kitchener. The settlement was founded in 1827 by John Galt, who laid out the radial street pattern and named the place after the family name of George III of England. Galt was more popular with the settlers he helped to locate in the Huron Tract than with his business colleagues, and in 1829 he was discharged. Among settlers Galt helped was a group of Scottish emigrants unable to adapt to the tropical climate of South America. They were called the La Guayra Settlers after their original destination in Venezuela, and Galt helped them settle in and around Guelph. No other place in the Commonwealth has the name Guelph, hence its nickname—"The Royal City." By law, all buildings erected on Main Street must be constructed of local grey limestone.

Guelph is the home of the Ontario Veterinary College and the Ontario Agricultural College. The Ontario Veterinary College was founded in Toronto in 1862 and was the first Canadian institution to offer courses in veterinary medicine. The College moved to Guelph in 1922. The Ontario Agricultural College opened in a Guelph farmhouse in 1874. The home of Col. John McCrae, a physician who died in France during the First World War—and who wrote the immortal lines of *In Flanders Fields*—is now a museum. Guelph was also the home of two architects who designed many churches across Ontario. Henry Langley (1836-1907) designed more than 70 churches and numerous residential, commercial, and public buildings. Joseph Connolly (1840-1904) also designed several churches, primarily for the Irish Roman Catholic community. Edward Johnson (1878-1959), born in Guelph, made his operatic debut in Italy in 1912 as Eduardo di Giovanni. He sang leading tenor roles in major opera houses in Europe and North America, and from 1935 to 1950 was general manager of the Metropolitan Opera Association in New York.

GULL BAY I.R.

Pop. 421. In Thunder Bay Dist. on the W shore of Lake Nipigon and Hwy. 527, 185 km N of Thunder Bay. Originally called Nipigon House. The post office was established in 1960 as Gull Bay.

HHH

HAGERSVILLE

Pop. 2,402. Part of the Town of Haldimand, Reg. Mun. of Haldimand-Norfolk, on Hwy. 6 and C. Rd. 20, 37 km NW of Hamilton. The town is named after the first settlers, Charles and David Hager, who arrived in 1842 and built a hotel.

HAILEYBURY

Pop. 4,744. In Bucke T., Timiskaming Dist., on the W shore of Lake Timiskaming and Hwys. 11B & 558, 8 km N of Cobalt. The Hudson's Bay Company established a post near the townsite in 1873. C. C. Farr, a chief agent of the company, was commissioned to define the Ontario-Quebec border between the head of Lake Timiskaming and James Bay. In 1885 Farr was struck by the beauty of a birch and poplar grove on a slope beside the lake and bought the land from a man named Louis Sirouin. The Indian name for the place was Matabanick, meaning "the place where the trail comes out." Farr built a log cabin on his land in 1887, and as a settlement grew, he named it Haileybury after the exclusive public school he had attended in England.

HALDIMAND

Pop. 18,211. In Reg. Mun. of Haldimand-Norfolk. The town came into existence in 1974 with the formation of the Reg. Mun. of Haldimand-Norfolk composed of the former town of Caledonia, the former villages of Cayuga and Hagersville; the former townships of North Cayuga, Oneida, Seneca, and South Cayuga; the former police villages of Canfield and Fisherville, and parts of Rainham and Walpole Townships. The town is named after Sir Frederick Haldimand, governor-in-chief of Canada from 1778 to 1786.

HALIBURTON

Pop. 1,878. In Dysart T., Haliburton C., at the head of Lake Kashagawigamog and mouth of Drag Creek, and at Hwys. 118 & 121 and C. Rd. 19, 85 km E of Bracebridge. Charles A. Stewart was the first resident, in 1864. He was the land agent for the Canadian Land and Emigration Company of London, England. The company had bought several wilderness townships in the area for colonization, totalling 360,000 acres (145,800 ha). The settlement was named in honour of Judge Thomas Chandler Haliburton, first chairman of the company, a noted Canadian humourist and historian, and author of the *Sam Slick* stories.

HALLEBOURG

Pop. 401. In Kendall T., Cochrane Dist. on Hwy. 11, 13 km E of Hearst.

Early settlers called the place Holleywood. The post office was established as Hallewood in 1922. In 1935 the post office name was changed to Hallebourg after Bishop Halle, first bishop of the Diocese of Hearst, in 1910.

HALTON HILLS

Pop. 34,189. Town in the Reg. Mun. of Halton, 49 km W of Toronto. Created in 1974 by the amalgamation of the towns of Acton and Georgetown, part of the Town of Oakville, and part of the Township of Esquesing. Halton was named after Maj. William Halton, secretary to Francis Gore, lieutenant-governor of Upper Canada.

HAMILTON

Pop. 307,160. In the Reg. Mun. of Hamilton-Wentworth at the W end of Lake Ontario. The city is on the south side of Hamilton Bay, a triangular-shaped landlocked harbour bounded on the lake side by a sandbar, which is crossed by the Queen Elizabeth Way, a highway from Toronto to Fort Erie. In 1813 a heavily armed American fleet attacked the British squadron off York (now Toronto). After a running battle, the British managed to bring their ships over the sandbar to the safety of the harbour. The city, nicknamed "the Steel City" because it is Canada's largest steel producer, is built on a sloping plain between the harbour and the Niagara Escarpment, which rises steeply to a height of 250 feet (76.2 m) and is called "the Mountain." The first recorded visit to the site was by French explorer René Robert de la Salle in 1669.

In 1784 the British government bought land from the Mississauga Indians to provide home sites for United Empire Loyalists, who had been forced to leave the United States after the American Revolution. Robert Land, the first settler, arrived in 1778. The city was known first as Burlington Bay and then as King's Head after an inn erected for travellers by order of Lt.-Gov. John Graves Simcoe. It was then named after George Hamilton who bought land in 1813, and the name Hamilton stuck when the post office opened in 1825. George Hamilton was the son of Robert Hamilton, founder of Queenston and a member of the legislative council of Upper Canada.

Hamilton has produced two great runners. William Sherring (1877-1964) won an Olympic gold medal in Athens in 1906 by defeating 55 other runners on a 26-mile (41.6-km) course. The Around-the-Bay Marathon, one of the oldest long-distance races in North America, was renamed in his honour. Bobby Kerr (1882-1963) first gained prominence as a sprinter in the local Coronation Games in 1902. For more than a decade he dominated short distance races in Canada and in 1908 won a gold medal at the London Olympics. The Co-operative Union of Canada was founded in Hamilton in 1909. It is a national cooperative association to coordinate local cooperatives and unions. Hamilton is the home of the Tiger Cats football team, the Canadian Football Hall of Fame, the Royal Botanical Gardens, Canadian Warplane Heritage Museum, Dundurn Castle, the residence of Sir Allan Napier MacNab (Canada's pre-Confederation prime minister) and McMaster University.

HAMMOND

Pop. 806. In Clarence T., Prescott and Russell C., on C. Rd. 21, 35 km E of Ottawa. The post office opened here in 1895, and the first postmaster, W. F. Empey, named the place after a Mr. Hammond who owned a large pork packing company in Chicago.

HAMPTON

Pop. 719. In Darlington T., Durham C., on Bowmanville Creek and C. Rd. 4, 9 km N of Bowmanville. The community was settled in 1840 by Henry Elliott, who built a mill and after whom the place was called Elliott's Mills. In 1848 the name was changed to Millville. That name was later changed to Hampton, part of the name Kilkhampton, the home of the Elliotts in North Cornwall, England.

HANMER

Pop. 4,944. Part of the Town of Valley East, Reg. Mun. of Sudbury, 11 km NE of Sudbury. The first settlers were French-Canadian farmers, who arrived in the spring of 1898. Jacob Proulx, Henry Beaulieu, Napoleon Labelle, and Joseph Chartrand had between them two horses and one cow, but they persevered and eked out a living from the land. The community slowly grew, and in 1903 the post office was established as Hanmer after early settler Gilbert Hanmer, a farmer from Brant County.

HANOVER

Pop. 6,327. In Bentinck T, Grey C., on the Saugeen River and Hwy. 4, 61 km S of Owen Sound. The first settler, in 1848, was innkeeper Abraham Buck after whom the settlement was named Buck's Bridge and Buck's Crossing. Subsequent names were Adamstown and Slabtown. When the post office opened in 1856, the place was named Hanover for the province of Hanover in Germany. In 1906 Noah Brusso (1881-1955) of Hanover became the first Canadian to win the heavyweight championship of the world. Brusso, who had exceptional muscle coordination, boxed under the name Tommy Burns.

HARRISTON

Pop. 1,940. In Minto T., Wellington C., on the Maitland River and Hwys. 9 & 89, 72 km NW of Guelph. The town is named after Joshua and George Harriston, who were the first to settle on the site. They built a sawmill in 1856.

HARROW

Pop. 2,395. In Colchester South T., Essex C., on Hwy. 18, 15 km W of Kingsville. The community was first called Mungers or Mungers Corners after a pioneer family. The first postmaster, in 1857, was J. Munger. The name Harrow, after Harrow-on-the-Hill, Middlesex, England, was chosen by John O'Connor, member of Parliament and later postmaster general. Harrow is the site of a large Canada Department of Agriculture research station.

HARTY

Pop. 950. In Idington T., Cochrane Dist. on Hwy. 11, 25 km NW of Kapuskasing. The post office was established as Harty Station in 1927. In 1952 the name was shortened to Harty. The community is named after Hon. William Harty, commissioner of public works for Ontario from 1884 to 1899.

HARWOOD

Pop. 231. In Alnwick T., Northumberland C., on the S shore of Rice Lake and C. Rds. 15 & 18, 17 km N of Cobourg. Cattle breeder and dealer S. C. Curtis, who arrived in 1832, was one of the first settlers. By the 1850s the community was a prosperous lumber town with two large sawmills and known as Sully or Sully's Landing. In the early 1850s the Cobourg and Peterborough Railway built a line from Cobourg, via Harwood and Tick Island, across the widest part of Rice Lake to Hiawatha and on to Peterborough. The bridge across Rice Lake was about 5 km in length and at the time was one of the longest railway bridges in North America. It was also one of the most poorly planned. In the winter of 1853, just after it had opened, it was severely damaged by ice. Nearly every winter the damage increased and repair costs mounted. When the Prince of Wales visited the area in 1860, he was not permitted to cross Rice Lake on the infamous bridge; the following winter the bridge disintegrated and floated down the lake. In 1854 the post office was established and named Harwood after the first postmaster, Euphrasia Vivian Harwood.

HASTINGS

Pop. 1,008. In Asphodel T., Peterborough C., and Percy T., Northumberland C., on both banks of the Trent River and Hwy. 45 and C. Rd. 2, 38 km E of Peterborough. United Empire Loyalists settled on the south side of the river mouth in 1795, and Indians lived on the north side until 1818. James Crooks built a mill on the river in 1827 and laid out a settlement he called Crooks' Rapids. In 1852, the first postmaster, H. Fowlds, renamed the community to honour Francis Rawdon-Hastings, the marquis of Hastings.

HAVELOCK

Pop. 1,271. In Belmont T., Peterborough C., on Hwys. 7 & 30, 35 km NE of Peterborough. The first mill was built in 1840 by Jehiel Breckenridge. When a post office was established in 1859, the place was named Havelock to honour Sir Henry Havelock, a British war hero of the Indian Mutiny.

HAWKESBURY

Pop. 9,400. In West Hawkesbury T., Prescott and Russell C., on the Ottawa River and Hwys. 17 & 34, 94 km NE of Ottawa, linked to Grenville, Que., by highway and railroad bridges. Nathaniel Treadwell opened the area—first known as Le Chenal—for settlement in the 1790s, and Thomas Mears was the first to settle. In 1804 he bought two islands in the Ottawa River from Treadwell and built a dam and grist mill. The narrow channel was called Chenaille Ecarte (lost channel) by French-Canadian settlers, a name that was corrupted by the English to "Snye Carty." The place eventually became known as "the Snye." During the Napoleonic War, when the ports of Europe were closed to Britain, two Irish brothers named Hamilton came to the area and set up a lumber-exporting business and a sawmill in 1807. They soon had four mills and the largest lumber business in Canada. The place became known as Hamilton's Mills. The post office opened in 1819 as Hawkesbury after Charles Jenkinson, lord Hawkesbury (1727-1808), a British statesman.

HAWK JUNCTION

Pop. 333. In Algoma Dist. at the junction of the Michipicoten branch and the main line of the Algoma Central Railway and Hwy. 547, 26 km NE of Wawa. The post office was established in 1923, and in the same year the community was destroyed by a forest fire. The town was rebuilt and is a shipping point for iron from the Helen mine in the Michipicoten area.

HEARST

Pop. 5,239. In Kendall T., Cochrane Dist., on the Mattawishkwia River and Hwy. 11, 97 km NW of Kapuskasing. The settlement, first known as Grant, started in the early 1900s as a maintenance point on the transcontinental railway and the northern terminus of the Algoma Central Railroad from Sault Ste. Marie. In 1911 the name was changed to Hearst to honour Sir William Howard Hearst, premier of Ontario from 1914 to 1919.

HEIDELBERG

Pop. 597. In Wellesley and Woolwich ts., Reg. Mun. of Waterloo, on C. Rds. 15 & 16, 11 km NW of Waterloo. The first settlers, in 1832, were French but they were followed by Germans, many of them Mennonites, from the Baden region. They called the place Heidelberg, its approved name since the post office was established in 1854.

HENSALL

Pop. 1,155. In Hay T., Huron C., on Hwys. 4 & 83, 58 km N of London.
Brothers George and James Petty from Hensall in Yorkshire, England,
founded the place they called Hensall, in 1851. They attracted the Huron
and Bruce Railway to the community by offering free land for a station
and yard, and they built a pork packing plant, which was ready to operate
when the railroad arrived.

HEPWORTH

Pop. 391. In Amabel T., Bruce C., on Hwys. 6 & 70 and C. Rd. 8, 21 km
NW of Owen Sound. William Spencer and William Plows were the first
settlers in the area, arriving from England in 1862. William Plows laid
out his farm for a townsite, which he called Epworth after the English
village from which he and Spencer came. Because of Plows' accent, he
pronounced "Epworth" as "H'epworth," and when the post office was
established in 1866 the name came with the "H." Around the turn of the
century, the community was thriving with five sawmills in operation.
Business slowed as the forests of the Bruce Peninsula were gradually
decimated. A river flows beneath Hepworth and can be heard through
several sink holes in the village. The stream's source is Skinner's Marsh
east of Hepworth, which emerges west of the community as Spring
Creek.

HESPELER

Pop. 9,945. Part of the City of Cambridge, Reg. Mun. of Waterloo, on the
Speed River and Hwy. 24, 10 km N of Galt and 14 km S of Guelph. The
community started when Abram Clemens, a United Empire Loyalist
from Pennsylvania, bought land in the area. By 1830 Michael Bergey had
built a sawmill and foundry, and the place was known as Bergeyville. In
1851 the post office was established as New Hope, but in 1858 the name
was changed to Hespeler after the town's leading citizen, Jacob Hespeler.
Hespeler, originally from Baden-Baden, Germany, moved to New Hope
from nearby Preston in 1845. He built a grist and flour mill, a distillery,
and a wool mill and became the first postmaster and the first reeve.

HEYDEN

Pop. 240. In Aweres T., Algoma Dist., on Hwy. 17, 14 km N of Sault Ste.
Marie. The history of the community and the origin of the name are not
known.

HIGHGATE

Pop. 451. In Orford T., Kent C., on C. Rds. 19 & 20, 2 km S of Hwy. 401,
64 km SW of St. Thomas. Brothers John, James, and Joseph Gosnell from
Ireland settled in 1822. Relatives followed, and the community became
known as the Gosnell Settlement. Around 1850 Anthony Atkinson set

up an unofficial post office, to which he brought mail from nearby Duart. When the government established a post office in 1865, he became postmaster and named the community Highgate after a suburb of London, England. American sculptor Evelyn Beatrice Longman attended Highgate Public School while she lived in the village with her grandparents. In 1916 she designed the logo for the American Bell Telephone Company.

HILLIARDTON
Pop. 292. In Hilliard T., Timiskaming Dist., on the Blanche River, 18 km N of New Liskeard. The community was settled in the late 1890s by lumbermen, trappers, and farmers. The post office opened in 1903 as Ironwood. The following year the name was changed to Hilliardton after Thomas Hilliard, an inspector of high schools and member of provincial parliament.

HILLSBURGH
Pop. 1,267. In Erin T., Wellington C., on a branch of the Credit River and Hwy. 25, 34 km N of Guelph. The village was founded in the late 1840s and named Hillsburgh when the post office was established in 1851.

HILLSDALE
Pop. 387. In Medonte T., Simcoe C., on Hwy. 93, 28 km SE of Penetanguishene. Patrick Murphy, a retired soldier, settled in 1829. The community developed at the point where the Gloucester Road left the Penetanguishene Road, halfway between Kempenfeldt Bay and Penetanguishene. When the post office was established in 1867, the place was named after Alexander Hill, a prominent tavern-keeper.

HILTON BEACH
Pop. 205. In Hilton T., Algoma Dist., on the E side of St. Joseph's Island on the North Channel of Lake Huron and Hwy. 548, 61 km SE of Sault Ste. Marie. The post office was established as Marksville in 1879 after the first postmaster, John Marks, who was also the customs officer. In 1921 the name of the post office was changed to Hiltonbeach. In 1956 the spelling was changed to Hilton Beach.

HOCKLEY
Pop. 232. In Adjala T., Simcoe C., on the Nottawasaga River and C. Rd. 1, 44 km NW of Brampton. The post office was established as Hockley in 1863 after Thomas Hockley, a local mill operator during the last half of the 19th century.

HOLLAND LANDING
Pop. 2,172. In East Gwillimbury T., Reg. Mun. of York, on the E branch of the Holland River just E of Hwy. 11, 54 km N of Toronto. John Evesin

began operating a sawmill in 1808, and the place was surveyed in 1811 by a Mr. Wilmot. It was known as Beverly, St. Albans, the Landing, Lower Landing, Old Soldier's Landing, and Steamboat Landing before the post office was established in 1831 as Holland Landing. The name honours Maj. Samuel Holland, surveyor general of the province of Quebec in the late 18th century. Samuel Lount was a prosperous farmer at Holland Landing and a reform politician. He was in joint command of Mackenzie's rebel forces when they were defeated at Montgomery's Tavern in 1837. Lount was convicted of treason and executed at Toronto the following year. Holland Landing is situated near a market gardening area settled mainly by Dutch immigrants, who drained 8,000 acres (3,240 ha) of black muck and turned it into agricultural black gold. When Hurricane Hazel struck in 1954, Holland Marsh disappeared under 20 to 30 feet (6 to 9 m) of floodwater, which also destroyed the nearby Dutch village of Ansnorveldt, causing losses in the millions of dollars. With aid from all levels of government, the marsh was pumped out and produced crops the following summer.

HOLLY
Pop. 201. In Innisfil T., Simcoe C., on Hwy. 27, 7 km S of Barrie. The post office was established in 1874 as Holly, named for his hometown by W. C. Little, MP.

HOLSTEIN
Pop. 265. In Egremont T., Grey C., on C. Rd. 109, 76 km NW of Guelph. Egremont Township was organized in 1850, but Holstein did not become a village until 1855. The place was first called Rosemont, but when the post office opened in 1863, postmaster N. D. McKenzie, a former schoolteacher, chose the name Holstein. Prussia had recently marched against Denmark for control of the duchies of Schleswig and Holstein, and McKenzie's choice is believed to have been influenced by that historic event.

HONEY HARBOUR
Pop. 558. In Georgian Bay T., Dist. Mun. of Muskoka, on the E coast of Georgian Bay off Lake Huron, facing the Inside Passage through the 30,000 Islands and at the N terminus of C. Rd. 5, 54 km NW of Orillia. First visited by a party of surveyors in 1780, the community did not develop until Didace Grise built the Royal Hotel. The post office was established in 1910 as Royal Honey Harbour, and in 1912 the Royal was dropped. The origin of the name is not known.

HORNEPAYNE
Pop. 1,848. In Wicksteed T., Algoma Dist., on Hwy. 631, 103 km N of White River and 69 km S of Hwy. 11, at a point 63 km W of Hearst. When

the Canadian National Railway came through the district in 1916, the place was called Fitzback. In 1920 the name was changed to honour R. M. Horne-Payne, the British financial advisor to Sir William Mackenzie, one of the builders of the line. It is a railway divisional point and has a large pulp and paper company.

HOYLE

Pop. 231. Part of the City of Timmins, Cochrane Dist., on Hwys. 101 & 610, 24 km NE of Timmins. Hoyle Township, surveyed in 1904, has since disappeared into the City of Timmins. When the post office was established in 1915, the community of Hoyle took its name from the township, which was named after William H. Hoyle, MPP for the North Riding of Ontario.

HUDSON

Pop. 458. In Vermilion Additional T., Kenora Dist. on the S shore of Lost Lake and Hwy. 664, 21 km W of Sioux Lookout. The community was first known as Rolling Portage. When the post office was established in 1932, it was named Hudson after a surveyor who worked for the Canadian National Railway. Western Canada Airways, based at Hudson in 1926, was one of the first airlines in Canada.

HUNTSVILLE

Pop. 12,320. In the Dist. Mun. of Muskoka on the Muskoka River between Vernon and Fairy Lakes, just SE of the intersection of Hwys. 11 & 60, 35 km N of Bracebridge. The first documented "visitor" to the area was William Cann, who came to hunt, and the first settler was James F. Haines, who built a home at the east end of Hunter's Bay. The township was surveyed in 1869, and in the same year an army officer, Capt. George Hunt, settled at what was then known as Fairy Lake Junction. Hunt was a teetotaler, who divided his land and sold lots with a "no drinking" clause written into the deeds. It is said this is why Huntsville grew on the west side of the Muskoka River where there are difficult hills, rather than on Hunt's flat lots on the east side. George Hunt was the first postmaster and named the place after himself when the post office opened in 1870. In 1894 fire destroyed the business district and many homes. Huntsville Pioneer Village, a museum and tourist attraction, first opened in 1961. It's now called Muskoka Pioneer Village and has 14 historic buildings on a 33-acre (13.36-ha) site. In 1873 a Wesleyan Methodist congregation built a square-timbered church about 6 km south of Huntsville on Madill Church Road. The church, named after John Madill who donated the land, is one of the area's many tourist attractions.

HURKETT

Pop. 266. In Stirling T., Thunder Bay Dist., on Black Bay off Lake Superior and Hwy. 582, 82 km NE of Thunder Bay. The community was known as Wolf Station when it became a stop on the Canadian Northern Railway main line. In 1910 the name was changed to Hurkett Station. When the post office was established in 1919, it was named Hurkett. The origin of the name is not known.

HURON PARK

Pop. 1,074. In Stephen T., Huron C., just W of Hwy. 4, 7 km S of Exeter. A military post office was established as RCAF Centralia in 1952. By 1966 the place was no longer an armed forces base and the name was changed to Huron Park, taking the name from the county. The post office became the civilian post office of Huron Park.

HUTTONVILLE

Pop. 500. Part of the City of Brampton, Reg. Mun. of Peel, on the Credit River and C. Rd. 1, 6 km SW of Brampton. When the settlement was established in 1820, it was called Wolf Pack and sometimes, Wolf Den. A decade later it was nicknamed "Bully Hollow" for an Alex Burnett who lived there. In 1848 a Mr. Brown arrived and built a mill; the place became known as Brown's Mills. In 1855 James P. Hutton bought the mills and the name changed to Hutton's Mills. When Hutton named his home, Fountain Valley, locals called the community by that name. In 1873 the post office was established as Huttonville, honouring mill owner James P. Hutton.

III

IGNACE

Pop. 2,499. In Ignace T., Kenora Dist., on the N shore of McNamara Lake and Hwy. 17, 107 km SE of Dryden. The place was first recorded by Sir Sandford Fleming as a station on the proposed route of the Canadian Pacific Railway's transcontinental line. It was named by the railway builder after his guide, Ignace Mentour, who led a cross-Canada surveying expedition in 1872. The first house was a surveyor's house built by the government in 1875. Indians settled around it to provide services for the surveyors and railroad workers. The first non-Native settler was Albert McGillie in 1879. The first mining patent in the area was granted to Capt. S. V. Halstead in 1889. He established the Maple Leaf Gold Mining Company and opened the Black Fox Mine. The gold rush of the 1890s brought many prospectors to the area, and Ignace became headquarters for the U.S. Gold Mining Company. At one time, a large settlement of railway boxcars nearby was nicknamed "Little England" because of its many English residents. Lumbering and tourism are now the major industries. One attraction on White Otter Lake, 25 km south (by boat or float plane) is a four-story log "castle" built single-handedly of one-ton (1.016-tonne) logs by diminutive James Alexander McQuat. How he managed to erect the structure between 1903, when he was 57, and 1912, baffles engineers.

ILDERTON

Pop. 418. In London T., Middlesex C., on C. Rds. 16 & 20, 16 km NW of London. The first settlers arrived in 1824 and included William McAndless, Edward Charlton, Robert Little, William Lipsett, and Samuel Paisley. In 1864 the first postmaster, George Ord, named the community Ilderton after his hometown in England.

INGERSOLL

Pop. 8,253. In North Oxford and West Oxford ts., Oxford C., on the Thames River and Hwy. 19 and C. Rd. 9, 32 km E of London. The town is named after Maj. Thomas Ingersoll, a member of a wealthy Massachusetts family, who brought settlers to the Niagara Peninsula in 1793 after being promised 80,000 acres (32,400 ha) of land. The British government revoked its promise, and Ingersoll settled instead at the point on the Thames River trail where Indians used to cross to Brantford to see their chief, Joseph Brant. The community was first known as Oxford-Upon-The-Thames and later as Ingersollville. In 1822 the post office opened as Oxford. In 1852 the name was changed to Ingersoll. The major's eldest daughter, Laura, married United Empire Loyalist James Secord, a sergeant in the First Lincoln Militia. During the War of 1812, Laura Secord walked 32 km through the bush from her home at Queenston to warn a British commander of an impending American attack. Major Ingersoll left the area in 1805 to settle at what is now Oakville near Toronto, but his son Charles returned in 1817 and laid out the townsite.

Ingersoll made the news in 1857 when a great hoax was pulled there. Rumours of an alligator-like creature in the village pond attracted 10,000 people to watch attempts to capture it. Supervising the operation was an eminent scientist from the United States, who alienated the local people by remaining aloof from them. There was reported to be great delight when he finally brought up a monster—the stuffed carcass of a cow. In 1866 Ingersoll cheese producers manufactured a 7,300-pound (3,311-kg) cheese. It was 21 feet (6.4 m) in circumference and was exhibited at the New York State Fair and in London, England.

INGLESIDE

Pop. 1,446. In Osnabruck T., Stormont, Dundas, and Glengarry C., on the St. Lawrence River and Hwy. 2, 24 km W of Cornwall. The community was established as a result of the flooding of the St. Lawrence River shore in 1957 by the St. Lawrence Seaway project and represents the union and relocation of the former communities of Aultsville, Farran's Point, Dickinson Landing, and Wales. During the planning stages it was known as New Town No. 1. (New Town No. 2 was Long Sault.) Before their sites were inundated, Aultsville was on the St. Lawrence shore on Hwy. 2, 29 km west of Cornwall; Wales was 19 km west of Cornwall and 1.5 km north of the former shoreline. (Wales received its name in 1860 after a visit by the Prince of Wales;) Farran's Point and Dickinson Landing were, respectively, 24 and 18 km west of Cornwall on the former shoreline.

INGLEWOOD

Pop. 400. Part of the Town of Caledon, Reg. Mun. of Peel, on the Credit River 1 km W of Hwy. 10, 19 km NW of Brampton. The place was settled in the 1830s but wasn't named on any map until the Credit Valley Railway arrived in 1879. The community was first called Riverdale after Riverdale Woollen Mills, which burned twice before being replaced by a stone building in 1871. When the railway arrived, officials wanted to change the name to avoid confusion with another Riverdale village in Ontario. Residents disliked the proposed name of Sligo Junction, and the matter was referred to Hon. Thomas White, MP for Cardwell in Sir John A. Macdonald's cabinet. He chose the name Inglewood after a village of the same name in England.

INNERKIP

Pop. 822. In East Zorra T., Oxford C., on the Thames River and C. Rd. 29,

9 km NE of Woodstock. When the post office opened in 1853 the name was changed from Melrose because there was one already. Innerkip was suggested by resident Mrs. Hugh Barwick, who came from a village of the same name in Renfrewshire, Scotland.

INVERARY

Pop. 227. In Storrington T., Frontenac C., on C. Rds. 10 & 12, 15 km N of Kingston. The area was settled around 1812 by United Empire Loyalists attracted by land grants of 200 acres (81 ha). The community first took its name from the township in 1841, but in 1856 early settler James Campbell, on whose land most of the settlement was built, suggested the name Inveraray after that town in Scotland. The second "a" in the name was later dropped. Few would question that Inverary's most versatile businessman in the late 1800s was Robert A. Marrison. He was a carriagemaker and blacksmith, a piano salesman, apiarist, and undertaker.

INVERHURON

Pop. 404. In Bruce T., Bruce C., on Lake Huron and C. Rds. 15 & 20, 15 km NE of Kincardine. The townsite was laid out in 1851, and the first settler was William Gunn from Glasgow who came in 1852. The place was named Inverhuron from the Gaelic word *inver* meaning "confluence," because the settlement was on Lake Huron at the mouth of a small river called the Little Sauble. Because of its fine harbour it soon became a port of call for lake steamers and a trans-shipment port for grain, bark, cordwood, and lumber. In 1882 fire destroyed three warehouses filled with 30,000 bushels (10,920 hl) of grain, and the town never regained its commercial importance. The community is just south of Inverhuron Provincial Park. Immediately north of the park is the Douglas Point Nuclear Power Station and the heavy water plant of the Atomic Energy Commission of Canada.

INWOOD

Pop. 200. In Brooke T., Lambton C., on C. Rd. 8, 58 km SE of Sarnia. In the early 1870s, James Courtright, nephew of the president of the Canada Southern Railway, recognized the timber potential of the land through which his uncle's railroad ran. He and his partners, Holmes and Moore, (the bridge contractors on the new railroad), bought a 95-acre (38.4-ha) site which they subdivided into village lots. In 1873 the three men built a stave mill and sawmill, which turned out tens of thousands of board-feet of lumber until it closed in 1898. The community that grew up around the mill was named by C. H. Moore after Inwood, a town on the Hudson River in New York State. Three of the streets commemorate the names of the founding partners. In 1899 a fire destroyed many businesses and houses, most of which were rebuilt.

IPPERWASH BEACH

Pop. 500. In Bosanquet T., Lambton C., on the W shore of Lake Huron, 16 km N of Forest. The name means "upper wash." The summer resort community is on a sandy beach, which was Stoney Point Indian Reservation until 1937 when the government moved the Indians into the nearby Kettle Point Indian Reserve and created Ipperwash Provincial Park.

IRISH LAKE

Pop. 200. In Artemesia T., Grey C., 5 km SW of Hwy. 10, 45 km SE of Owen Sound. The post office was established as Irish Lake in 1889. The history of the community and the origin of the name are not known.

IRON BRIDGE

Pop. 762. In Gladstone T., Algoma Dist., on the Mississagi River and Hwys. 17, 546, & 554, 26 km NW of Blind River, about 112 km E of Sault Ste. Marie. When the post office was established in 1886 the name requested by residents was Tally Ho. This was rejected by the post office, which called the place Iron Bridge because the first non-wooden bridge in the area had just been built across the Mississagi River. The iron bridge was dismantled, sold, and replaced by a cement bridge in 1949.

IROQUOIS

Pop. 1,144. In Matilda T., Dundas C., on the N bank of the St. Lawrence River and Hwy. 2, 18 km NE of Prescott. The village was the largest residential and business community along the St. Lawrence River to be entirely relocated during construction of the St. Lawrence Deep Waterway during the early 1950s. Its original location was across the Galop Canal from Iroquois Point, a headland famous in legend and history as a camping ground of the Iroquois Indians. The point's proximity to the Canadian-U.S. mid-river boundary line caused it to be selected as the Canadian terminus of the international dam built to control water levels for the waterway. A new canal, cut through the headland to avoid the dam, turned Iroquois Point into a small island. The relocated town of Iroquois is north of the original site. United Empire Loyalists settled the place in 1776. The post office, established in 1789 in what was then New France, was called Matilda. In 1812 the first British fort on the site had not been completed, or named. A second fort was built on the riverbank in 1814, but U.S. troops did not attack, so the fort was nicknamed "Fort Needless." In 1856 the post office name was changed to Iroquois.

IROQUOIS FALLS

Pop. 5,895. In Calvert T., Cochrane Dist., on the Abitibi River and Hwys. 67 & 577, 50 km SE of Cochrane. The first white men in the area were French soldiers under the command of Chevalier Pierre de Troyes on their way to attack the Hudson's Bay Company posts at James Bay in 1686. The legend of the falls is that Iroquois Indians attacked a peaceful Huron tribe, killed all the men, and captured the women. The Iroquois then went to sleep in their canoes, tied to the riverbank near the falls. During the night, the captives cut the canoes loose, and the Iroquois were swept over the 14-foot-high (4.26-m) waterfall to their deaths. In 1912, Montreal businessman Frank Harris Anson financed two young men on a gold prospecting trip to northern Ontario. No gold was found, but the men told Anson of the great potential of the Iroquois Falls area for a pulp and paper industry. The first campsite was established beside the falls that same year. In 1913, with financing from Chicago, the Abitibi Pulp and Paper Mills came into being, and work started on the first planned town in northern Ontario, which has come to be nicknamed "Northern Ontario's Original Model Town." The company owned the land, the houses, and the stores, and all the residents of Iroquois Falls were Abitibi employees. When the workers formed a union in 1915, one of their first aims was to get control of their own town, to which the company agreed. In 1916 one of the worst forest fires in Canadian history swept across this part of northern Ontario, wiping out six towns and 1,000 square miles (2,590 sq km) of farmland and bush, and killing 223 people. The residents of Iroquois Falls were evacuated to the company mill, which escaped the fire. Most of the town was destroyed and had to be rebuilt. The lowest measured temperature in Ontario was -73 degrees Fahrenheit (-57.5 degrees Celsius) at Iroquois Falls on Jan. 23, 1935.

ISLAND GROVE

Pop. 644. In North Gwillimbury T., York C., on the S shore of Lake Simcoe opposite Snake Island, 10 km W of Sutton. The post office was established as Island Grove in 1911. The origin of the name is not known.

JJJ

JACKSONS POINT

Pop. 622. In Georgina T., York C., on the south shore of Lake Simcoe on C. Rd. 78, 70 km N of Toronto. First known as Bourchier's Point after James O'Brien Bourchier, the postmaster at nearby Georgina. The settlement was later named after John Mills Jackson, who settled there in 1812.

JAFFRAY MELICK

Pop. 3,651. In the Dist. of Kenora, N of Kenora, incorporated as a township in 1908. The history of the community and the origin of its name are not known.

JANETVILLE

Pop. 608. In Manvers T., Durham C., on McDermid's Creek and C. Rd. 5, 32 km SW of Peterborough. The first settlers were Capt. John Burn and Henry Irwin who built a sawmill in the early 1800s. A group of settlers arrived from Ireland in 1832, among them Neil McDermid. When the post office was established here in 1862, his daughter, Janet, became the first postmaster, and the postal station was named after her.

JARVIS

Pop. 1,398. Part of the City of Nanticoke, Reg. Mun. of Haldimand-Norfolk, on Hwys. 3 & 6, 17 km NE of Simcoe. The community began when the Hamilton and Port Dover Plank Road was being built in the mid-19th century. James Shearman, the first settler, built a log shanty and a blacksmith shop beside the road. He also kept a supply of liquor available to slake the thirsts of the construction crews and later opened a tavern. W. C. Shannon was the second settler. He tended the tollgate on the plank road. Much of Jarvis was destroyed by fire in the mid-1870s, but by the end of the decade it had been rebuilt. The post office was established in 1851 and named Jarvis after Lt.-Col. William Jarvis, aide-de-camp of Lt.-Gov. John Graves Simcoe. Several streets in Jarvis are named after his daughters.

JASPER

Pop. 252. In Kitley T., Leeds and Grenville C., on Irish Creek and C. Rds. 16 & 17, 45 km NW of Brockville. In 1806 a Mr. Haskins built a grist mill in the tiny settlement then called Albune. In 1820 Gideon Olmstead bought the mill, and the community became known as Olmstead's Mills. In 1830, construction of the Rideau Canal raised the water level in Irish Creek and destroyed the waterfall, which had supplied power for the mill. That closed the mill but allowed Irish Creek to be used for rafting timber. The community became known as Irish Creek and took that name when the post office was established in 1863. In 1864 the post office was renamed Jasper. The origin of the name is not known. In the 1860s Jasper was the closest community of any size to the hamlet of Plum Hollow where people from far and wide sought to learn their fortunes from "the Witch of Plum Hollow." The "witch" was Mrs. Elizabeth Barnes, who had been born in County Cork, Ireland. She was a good and kind woman and well respected. She had been left to raise a family of nine and (because she had a highly developed sense of prophecy) turned to fortune-telling.

JEANETTE'S CREEK
Pop. 252. In Tilbury East T., Kent C., on C. Rds. 2 & 36, 27 km SW of Chatham. The post office was established as Jeanette's Creek in 1891. The history of the community and the origin of its name are not known.

JOGUES
Pop. 415. In Cochrane Dist. on Hwy. 583, 16 km SW of Hearst. The community was founded between 1908 and 1912 and became a meeting place for Indians engaged in the fur trade. The settlement is named after the first parish priest, Father Isaac Jogues.

JOHNSTOWN
Pop. 692. In Edwardsburgh T., Leeds and Grenville C., on the St. Lawrence River and Hwy. 2, 5 km NE of Prescott. In the 17th century the place was an Indian campground and a favourite resting spot for French *voyageurs*. In 1760 the last stand of the French in Canada took place on nearby Chimney Island (then Isle Royale). Capt. François Pouchot and 300 men held Fort de Lévis against Gen. Jeffery Amherst and 10,000 troops in an effort to delay the British troops and give French troops enough time to retreat to Montreal. Pouchot surrendered in August, and the British went on to gain control of Canada. Two decades later, after the American Revolution, Americans who had remained loyal to the British Crown moved to Canada. The first United Empire Loyalists landed at the Johnstown site in 1784 and were surprised to find Chevalier François-Thomas de Verneuil de Lorimier and his brother Guillaume, living on land granted to them there. Johnstown, named to honour United Empire Loyalist leader Sir John Johnson, grew rapidly and was made the administrative centre of the eastern district in 1793. But for a shallow harbour the town might have become an important centre.

JORDAN
Pop. 227. Part of the Town of Lincoln, Reg. Mun. of Niagara, on Twenty Mile Creek and C. Rd. 81, 8 km W of St. Catharines. The first settlers, in the 1780s, were United Empire Loyalists, including some members of

the famed Butler's Rangers who fought for the British in the American Revolution. In 1784 the British government bought the land in the Jordan area from the Indians and granted it to the Loyalists and soldiers. In 1799 Mennonite settlers from the United States, including Amos Albright and Jacob and Abraham Meyer, bought some of the land from Colonel Butler, and by 1800, 25 families had moved to the area and formed Canada's first Mennonite settlement. Ball's Falls, a nearby scenic spot where Twenty Mile Creek drops over the Niagara Escarpment, was the site of one of Jordan's earliest industries. Here Mr. Ball built the first mill, which was protected by soldiers during the War of 1812. The settlement was first called Twenty Mile Creek and then St. Mary's. When the post office opened in 1840, the community was given the biblical name Jordan, presumably by William Bradt, an early merchant, magistrate, and post-master.

JORDAN STATION

Pop. 400. Part of the Town of Lincoln, Reg. Mun. of Niagara, 1 km S of the Queen Elizabeth Way, 10 km E of St. Catharines. The first Mennonites known to have settled in Canada took up land west of the mouth of Twenty Mile Creek in 1799. By the end of the century, a settlement of about 25 families from Pennsylvania was established near present-day Vineland and Jordan. In 1801 the first Mennonite congregation in Canada was organized. Jordan Station began as Bridgeport, named after the Great Western Railway bridge, which crossed the Jordan River near its mouth. When the post office was established in 1870, the community was renamed Jordan Station. Around the turn of the century, area farmers switched from grain to fruit-growing. The first cannery opened in 1912, and for a time there were three large fruit shipping establishments, the last of which closed in 1958.

KAGAWONG

Pop. 201. In Billings T., Manitoulin Dist., on Manitoulin Island on Mudge Bay off North Channel of Lake Huron and Hwy. 540, 45 km SW of Little Current. Kagawong, an Indian name meaning "where mists rise from the falling waters," was the name given to the community when the post office opened in 1876. Before that, the place had been called Mudge Bay. A generating station near Bridal Veil Falls once provided hydroelectric power for all of Manitoulin Island, but only the foundations of the plant remain. Tourists now visit Kagawong to enjoy the beauty of the falls, which drop from Kagawong Lake and flow through Falls Park.

KAHSHE LAKE

Pop. 400. Part of the Town of Gravenhurst, Dist. Mun. of Muskoka, on the S shore of Kahshe Lake and Hwy. 11, 20 km SE of Gravenhurst. A summer post office was opened as Kahshe Lake in 1915. Kahshe is a short form of the Indian name for the place—Kah-she-she-bog-a-mog—the meaning of which is not known.

KAKABEKA FALLS

Pop. 298. In Oliver and Conmee ts., Thunder Bay Dist., on the Kaministikwia River and Hwys, 11, 17 & 590, 22 km W of Thunder Bay. The site was known to the earliest fur traders who faced a gruelling portage around the 154-foot (46.9-m) waterfall. There is now a provincial park surrounding the falls and guard-railed lookout decks on both sides of the falls and gorge. Kakabeka means either "the river with short bends and many islands," or "the place where there is always plenty of game."

KANATA

Pop. 30,295. In the Reg. Mun. of Ottawa-Carleton, 24 km NW of Ottawa. The community was created by regional government in 1978, and the electors of the municipality voted on the name. Kanata is the Indian name for Canada and means "a collection (or cluster) of huts."

KAPUSKASING

Pop. 10,830. In Dist. of Cochrane on the Kapuskasing River and Hwy. 11, 118 km W of Cochrane. In the early 1900s, when the Transcontinental Railway was being pushed west, the place where the line crossed the Kapuskasing River was known as MacPherson. In 1914 the federal government established an internment camp for enemy prisoners of war. By the following year, there were 1,200 prisoners and 250 troops in the camp and 600 acres (243 ha) had been cleared. The camp operated until

1920 when the last prisoner of war was repatriated; the graves of 32 German prisoners may be seen in a small cemetery near the public cemetery. In 1917 the town took its present name from an Indian word meaning "the divided waters," or "bend in the river."

KARS

Pop. 500. In Reg. Mun. of Ottawa-Carleton on the W bank of the Rideau River and the N shore of Stevens Creek, on C. Rd. 13, 37 km S of Ottawa. North Gower Township was surveyed in 1791-93, and the first settlers were Irish squatters John and Ellen O'Callaghan in 1815. In 1820 two men named Merrick and Stevens scouted the area for its lumbering potential, but that venture ended when Stevens drowned in the creek that bears his name. In 1829 James Lindsay built a commercial wharf, known as Lindsay's Wharf. In 1856 Provincial Land Surveyor H. O. Wood was hired to survey a village site, which he named Wellington. A place by that name already existed in Ontario, so the name was changed to Kars when the post office opened that year. The name honours the people of Kars, Turkey, for defending their city against the Russians in 1855 during the Crimean War.

KASABONIKA I.R.

Pop.402. In Kenora Dist. on a peninsula in the S end of Kasabonika Lake, 580 km NE of Thunder Bay. The name is an abbreviation of the Indian name Kaussaubonikauk, meaning "the narrow place; the small, narrow, shallow waterbed." In Cree the name means "the lake with many islands."

KASHECHEWAN I.R.

Pop. 850. In Cochrane Dist. on the N shore of the Albany River near its mouth on the W shore of James Bay, 12 km NW of Fort Albany and 120 km NW of Moosonee. The Kashechewan Indian Band lives on the reserve, which was named when a post office was established in 1963. The name is a Cree word for "swift current."

KEARNEY

Pop. 575. In Perry and Bethune ts., Parry Sound Dist., on the S branch of the Magnetawan River and Beaver Lake, on Hwy. 518, 8 km NE of Hwy. 11, 25 km N of Huntsville. First settled by the O'Neils, Kearneys, and Murphys in the late 1870s and first known as Old Kearney. The post office was established as Kearney in 1879 after early settler Patrick Kearney. In 1908 the Scott Act, which allowed local option on the sale of liquor, threatened the community's two licensed hotels. The community's businessmen successfully petitioned the government for town status, thereby exempting Kearney from a liquor plebiscite. That ruling remains, making Kearney one of the smallest towns in Ontario.

KEARNS

Pop. 301. In Timiskaming Dist. on the N shore of Larder Lake and Hwy. 66, 2 km W of the Quebec border and 43 km E of Kirkland Lake. The place was first settled in 1937 by employees of the Kerr-Addison Gold Mine, who wanted to build their own homes. The community was first known as Chesterville after the Chesterville mine, but was renamed Kearns in 1939 after J. T. Kearns, founder of the Chesterville-Larder Lake Gold Mining Company.

KEENE

Pop. 207. In Otonabee T., Peterborough C., on Indian River near the N shore of Rice Lake and C. Rds. 2 & 34, 17 km SE of Peterborough. The first settlers were Thomas and Andrew Carr, who arrived in 1820, but Keene's founder was the energetic John Gilchrist. In 1819 he became the first doctor in Ontario to be issued a licence to practise "physic surgery and midwifery." In 1825 Gilchrist built a grist mill on the Indian River, followed by a distillery and homes for his workers. In 1829 he opened the settlement's first store. The community was originally known as Gilchrist's Mills, but when the post office was established Gilchrist renamed the place Keene after his hometown in New Hampshire. The Keene Curling Club, organized in 1861 by Thomas Miller, is one of Ontario's oldest. One of Keene's tourist attractions is the nearby Serpent Mounds Provincial Park. Excavations have revealed that the earth mounds, in the shape of a 200-foot-long (60.9-m) serpent and eggs, were built by the Hopewellians, a tribe of Indians who lived in the area about 2,000 years ago. The serpent-shaped mounds are unique in Canada.

KEEWATIN

Pop. 1,974. In Pellat T., Kenora Dist., on the N shore of Lake of the Woods and Hwys. 17 & 596, 5 km W of Kenora. The name is an Ojibway word meaning "north wind." When the post office was established in 1880, the place was called Keewatin Mills because of the flour mills there. The name was soon abridged.

KEJICK

Pop. 271. In Kenora Dist. on the N shore of Shoal Lake, 14 km S of Hwy. 17, 49 km W of Kenora. The post office was established as Kejick in 1962. The name was chosen by area Indian bands to honour an old Indian by that name, who had been decorated for his service to Canada in one of the Great Wars.

KEMPTVILLE

Pop. 2,491. In Oxford T., Leeds and Grenville C., on Kemptville Creek, a tributary of the Rideau River and Hwy. 43 and C. Rds. 18 & 44, 41 km

S of Ottawa. In 1812 Lyman Clothier settled and built a mill. The community, first known as the Branch, then became known as Clothier Mills. In 1828 the settlers wanted a more dignified name and chose Kemptville in honour of Sir James Kemp, lieutenant-governor of Nova Scotia in 1820 and governor general of Upper and Lower Canada in 1828. The Hon. G. Howard Ferguson (1870-1946) was born in Kemptville and practised law there before entering provincial politics in 1905. Following his term as Ontario's ninth premier, from 1923 to 1930, he served as Canadian high commissioner to the United Kingdom. In the early 1930s a 43-kilometre plank road was built to connect Kemptville with steamship traffic landing at Prescott on the St. Lawrence River.

KENOGAMI LAKE
Pop. 220. In Eby and Grenfell ts., Timiskaming Dist., on the SE shore of Kenogami Lake and Hwys. 11 & 66, 11 km SW of Kirkland Lake. The post office was established in 1912 and took the name of the lake, which is an Indian word meaning "long water." On Hwy. 11 about 14 km NW of Kenogami Lake, a provincial plaque marks the height of land, or watershed, which figured prominently in several boundary disputes during the 19th century. The line wends an erratic course of 2,240 km across Ontario.

KENORA
Pop. 9,373. In Kenora Dist. on the N shore of Lake of the Woods on Hwys. 17, 598, & 658, 52 km E of the Manitoba border. Intense rivalry between two fur-trading companies ended in 1821 when the Hudson's Bay Company and the North West Company amalgamated as Hudson's Bay Company. In 1836 a trading post was built on Old Fort Island. In 1861 the post was moved to the mainland, and around it grew the community of Rat Portage, so named because it was on a muskrat migration route between Lake of the Woods and the Winnipeg River. Following acquisition in 1869 by the Dominion of Canada of the territories of the Hudson's Bay Company, the western and northern boundaries of the province of Ontario became a matter of ongoing dispute. The matter was finally settled at present-day Kenora in 1884. In 1905 the Maple Leaf Flour Company told the town it wouldn't build a plant in a place where the word "rat" would have to appear on its flour bags. The town changed its name that year. Kenora comes from the first two letters of Keewatin, Norman, and Rat Portage. Keewatin and Norman are nearby communities. In 1907, in a best-of-three challenge, the Kenora Thistles hockey team defeated the Montreal Wanderers to win the Stanley Cup. Competition rules were less formal in those days, and two months later the Wanderers re-challenged the Thistles and won back the cup.

KESWICK

Pop. 8,119. In Georgina T., Reg. Mun. of York on the E side of Cook's Bay off Lake Simcoe, 64 km N of Toronto. First known as Medina, sometimes spelled Madina, the post office was established in 1835 as Keswick and originally located at Roache's Point which later became Roche's Point. Roche's Point is 2.5 km northwest of Keswick. The origin of the name is not known.

KETTLE POINT I.R.

Pop. 1,000. In Bosanquet T., Lambton C., on Lake Huron, 18 km N of Forest. The place is named for strange, kettle-shaped rock formations caused by wave action. The reserve was formed by treaty in 1827.

KILBRIDE

Pop. 600. In Nelson T., Halton C., on C. Rd. 25, 10 km S of Milton. The first settler was Thomas Simpson, who arrived in the late 1820s. In 1856 the first postmaster, William Panton, named the place Kilbride for a village in County Wicklow, Ireland.

KILLALOE

Pop. 611. On the Brennan River in Haggarty T., Renfrew C., on Hwy. 60, 40 km SW of Pembroke. James Bonfield, who bought land there in 1850, named the place after his hometown in County Clare, Ireland. A local nickname for the place was "Fort McDonnell" because a large rock formation on the east side of the Brennan River created the appearance of a fortified town, and William McDonnell owned the sawmill there.

KILLARNEY

Pop. 445. In Rutherford T., Manitoulin Dist., on a peninsula opposite George Island on the N shore of Georgian Bay and Hwy. 637, 67 km SW of Hwy. 69, 44 km SE of Sudbury. In 1820 fur trader Etienne Augustin Robert de la Morandiere moved to the site, then known as Shebahonaning. He planted crops and imported cattle. The remote settlement continued to grow despite the fact that until Hwy. 637 was opened in 1962, the only access to the community was by water. A post office was established as Shebahonaning in 1853, but the name was later changed to Killarney. Lord and Lady Dufferin visited the place in 1882, and she is said to have remarked that the rugged beauty of the area reminded her of Killarney. It is believed that this remark accounts for the change of name.

KILWORTHY

Pop. 200. In Morrison T., Ontario C., 2 km W of Hwy. 11, 29 km NE of Orillia. The post office was established in 1876 as Lethbridge. In 1886 the name was changed to Kilworthy. The origin of the name is not known although the place likely was named by early Irish settlers after a place of the same name in Ireland.

KINCARDINE

Pop. 5,734. In Kincardine T., Bruce C., on Lake Huron at the mouth of the Penetangore River and Hwys. 9 & 21, 80 km SW of Owen Sound and 52 km N of Goderich. The first settlers landed from a schooner in 1848, and by the following year a mill was in operation. The community was first called Penetangore after the river. In 1857 the name was changed to that of the township in which it was located and which honoured James Bruce, earl of Elgin and Kincardine and governor general of Canada from 1847 to 1854.

KING CITY

Pop. 3,513. In King T., Reg. Mun. of York on the E branch of the Humber River and on C. Rd. 11, 35 km N of Toronto. Nathaniel Pearson Crossley was the first settler, in 1836. The place was first called Spring Hill because of many springs in the area, but that name was changed to King when the post office was established. In 1953 the post office name was changed to King City. Nearby is Lake Marie Estate, former summer home of Sir Henry Pellatt, builder of Toronto's 98-room Casa Loma. The name King is believed to be that of a foreman on the railroad line that reached the community in 1853.

KINGFISHER LAKE I.R.

Pop. 240. In Kenora Dist. on the S shore of Kingfisher Lake, 504 km N of Thunder Bay.

KING KIRKLAND

Pop. 315. In Lebel T., Timiskaming Dist., on Hwy. 66, 6 km E of Kirkland Lake. The community was founded in 1932 by people who wanted to live outside Kirkland Lake. Most were employees of the Murphy and Morris-Kirkland mines, which closed in the 1950s, but many found new employment in the Upper Canada Mine and other regional mines. The origin of the name is not known.

KINGSTON

Pop. 57,382. In Frontenac C., on Lake Ontario at the head of the St. Lawrence River and the mouth of the Cataraqui River and Hwys. 2, 15, 33, 38, & 401, 75 km E of Belleville. In 1671, fur trader René Robert Cavelier, Sieur de la Salle recommended the building of a fort and fur-trading post at the site of present-day Kingston, then called Cataraqui, an Indian word for "rocks standing in water." Two years later Count Frontenac, governor of New France, met with local Indian chiefs to assure them his intentions were peaceful. He then built Fort Frontenac, appointing LaSalle as commander. The following year, LaSalle was granted the fort and surrounding lands as a seigneury. In 1756 the fort was used by French commander-in-chief Montcalm to attack the British during the Seven Years War for control of Canada. In 1758 the fort was captured by the British under Col. John Bradstreet. The walls were destroyed, the garrison withdrew to Montreal, and French rule at Cataraqui ended.

In 1783 surveyor John Collins laid out the town plot of Kingston, and the following year a group of United Empire Loyalists arrived to build homes. They named the place King's Town after George III, but the name soon contracted to its present form. Because of its location at the head of the St. Lawrence River where goods were changed from river to lake boats, Kingston soon became an important trading centre. In 1792 it became the seat of government of Upper Canada. Lt.-Gov. John Graves Simcoe did not feel Kingston was a suitable site for a capital, so he named Newark (now Niagara-on-the-Lake) as capital, and then York (Toronto). During the War of 1812, Fort Henry was built at Kingston at enormous cost to the British. Thanks to errors in American strategy, Kingston was overlooked in the war, and today the magnificent fort is one of Ontario's premier tourist attractions. In 1841 Kingston became the capital of United Canada—the name given newly united Upper and Lower Canada— and in 1843 the town began building a grand domed limestone hall. The hall was no sooner completed than the government moved the capital to Montreal. Another of Kingston's many historic buildings is Bellevue House where Canada's first prime minister, Sir John A. Macdonald, lived for a year.

A plaque in Confederation Park recalls The King's Royal Regiment of New York also known as the Royal Greens and Sir John Johnson's Corps. The loyalist regiment was raised in 1775 from the Highland Scottish and other settlers on Johnson's estates in New York. The "Royal Yorkers" was the largest loyalist corps in the Northern Department (the old province of Quebec) during the American Revolution. When the regiment was disbanded, many of the men settled in townships border- ing the St. Lawrence River. Rev. John Stuart (1740-1811), the first resident Anglican priest in Upper Canada, settled at Cataraqui in 1785 and ministered to native and loyalist settlers in the Quinte area and as far west as the Grand River (Kitchener area). A plaque at St. Paul's Church recalls Molly Brant (1736-1796). Her Indian name was Degonwadonti, and she was higly respected by her fellow Mohawks and governing officials. She was born in the Ohio Valley and played a leading role in persuading the Iroquois Confederacy to support Britain during the American Revolution. She fled to Canada in 1777, living first at Niagara and later on land granted to her at Cataraqui. Kingston native Sir Oliver Mowat (1820-1903) was Ontario's third premier, and held the office for almost 25 years, from 1872 to 1896. He also served as postmaster-general of the Province of Canada and lieutenant-governor of Ontario.

In 1847 the potato famine brought a wave of immigration to North America and with it, a major outbreak of typhus. In Kingston, 1,400 people died of the disease. The first optical astronomical observatory in Ontario was established in Kingston in 1855 after a solar eclipse aroused public interest in astronomical study. The observatory produced barometric readings, fixed meridians for surveying purposes, and provided a time service as well as recording astronomical observations. The city is also known for Royal Military College of Canada, Queen's University, and Kingston Penetentiary.

KINGSVILLE

Pop. 5,332. In Gosfield South T., Essex C., on Pigeon Bay of Lake Erie and Hwy. 2 and C. Rd. 29, 45 km SE of Windsor. Thomas Curtis was the first recorded settler in the Kingsville area, in the late 1780s, although some French families had settled there earlier because of the site's proximity to the French post at Detroit. The town is named after Col. James King, the first person to build a house at the site on the shore of Pigeon Bay. Near Kingsville is the former home of conservationist pioneer Jack Miner, who from 1910 to 1940 lectured on conservation and convinced kings and presidents of the need for it. In recognition of his efforts, he was awarded the Order of the British Empire in 1943. His estate is now a wildlife sanctuary and a stopping point for flocks of tens of thousands of Canada geese on their spring and fall migrations. Kingsville is one of two ports on the Ontario shore from which summer ferry service connects with Pelee Island and Sandusky, Ohio.

KINMOUNT

Pop. 267. In Sommerville T., Victoria C., on Burnt River and Hwys. 121 & 503, 57 km N of Lindsay. John Hunter built the first mill, in 1861. The place was first called Burnt River after the river that flows through it. When the post office was established it was named Kinmount. A fire in 1890 almost wiped out the entire community. The Lindsay fire brigade, alerted by telegraph, arrived within 50 minutes by railway, but at least 12 businesses and stores were lost. In 1928 the Burnt River flooded the town, causing widespread damage. Guests at the hotel were rowed to the railway station. The origin of the name is unknown.

KIRKLAND LAKE

Pop. 11,300. In Teck T., Dist. of Timiskaming, on Hwy. 66, 90 km N of New Liskeard. In 1911, prospector Bill Wright headed east from Swastika, skirted the shore of an unnamed lake, panned rock, and discovered gold. He and his brother-in-law founded the Wright-Hargreaves Mine. Six months later, Harry Oakes staked a claim on the south shore of the same lake. His claim, the Lake Shore Mine, developed the deepest mining shaft on the continent. The first producing mine was Tough Oakes, which sparked a gold rush that led to the incorporation of Swastika, Chaput Hughes, and Kirkland Lake into the Township of Teck in 1919. The place was named after the lake, (now filled in by mine tailings), which was named by L. V. Rorke of the Department of Mines after his secretary, Miss Winnie Kirkland of Toronto. From 1911 through 1927 there were so many gold mines along a strip of land on the south shore of the lake that the area was called The Golden Mile. It is said that the streets of Kirkland Lake are paved with gold, and to some extent that's true. A construction crew building the road was instructed to take material from a ballast rock pile. By mistake, they took material from an ore storage pile. By the time the error was noticed the ore had been covered by concrete and its recovery wasn't worth the expense. Kirkland Lake is said to have produced more professional hockey players than any other place in the world.

KIRKTON

Pop. 204. In Usborne T., Huron C., and Blanshard T., Perth C., on Hwy. 23 and C. Rds. 6 & 24, 27 km SW of Stratford. The region was surveyed in the early 1830s by the Canada Company and first settled by the Kirk, Hazlewood, and Hanna families. When the post office was opened in 1856, the community was named Kirkton, likely after the Kirk family. In the 1860s, Timothy Eaton (1834-1907) operated dry goods stores in Kirkton and nearby St. Marys. He moved to Toronto in 1869 and opened a store that used a cash system instead of barter and credit; the rest is North American merchandising history.

KITCHENER

Pop. 152,771. In the Reg. Mun. of Waterloo on the Grand River and Hwys. 7, 8, & 86, just N of Hwy. 401, adjacent to the City of Waterloo, 18 km SW of Guelph. Kitchener and Waterloo could be one city but for their different names, and they are often referred to as "K-W." Early settlers, in the late 1790s, called the place Sand Hills because of sand dunes at the site and later, Mount Pleasant. A few years after Mennonite Benjamin Eby settled in 1807, the community was renamed Ebytown. Eby became Canada's first Mennonite bishop, and for 40 years he was minister of Canada's first Mennonite church. By 1830 immigrants were coming from Germany, and Ebytown was renamed Berlin in 1841 in honour of their homeland. In 1916, when the First World War was being fought and anti-German sentiment ran high in Canada, the name was changed to Kitchener after Lord Kitchener of Khartoum, a British war hero who drowned at sea that year.

Joseph Schneider is considered by many to have been the founder of Kitchener. He arrived in 1807 and started a meat-packing plant which continues to this day. The second house he built at Kitchener, in 1820, is the city's oldest building and is now a museum. William Lyon Mackenzie King (1874-1950) was born in Kitchener and began a public service career as a specialist in labour relations. He was prime minister of Canada from 1921 to 1926, 1926 to 1930, and 1935 to 1948. King spent his teenage years in a 10-room house in Kitchener called Woodside, which is now a museum in Woodside National Historic Park maintained by Parks Canada.

KLEINBURG

Pop. 1,360. Part of the Town of Vaughan in the Reg. Mun. of York on a branch of the Humber River and C. Rd. 7, just E of Hwy. 27, 18 km NW of Toronto. The community is named after the first settler, John Nicholas Klein, who arrived in 1837. For years the name was misspelled as Klineburg. On the community's outskirts is the McMichael Art Gallery with a major collection of Group of Seven paintings and Native and Inuit art.

KLUEYS BAY

Pop. 350. In the Town of Gravenhurst, Dist. Mun. of Muskoka on the NW shore of Kahshe Lake, 8 km SE of Gravenhurst. A summer post office was established in 1922 and was named after the first postmaster, William Kluey.

KOMOKA

Pop. 1,152. In Lobo T., Middlesex C., on C. Rd. 16, 16 km W of London. The community was settled in the 1830s by Scottish families, most of the Campbell clan. The post office was established in 1853 as Lobo Station, but in 1856 the name was changed to Komoka, an Indian word believed to mean "place where the dead lie."

LAC SEUL I.R.

Pop. 519. In Kenora Dist. on Lac Seul, an extension of the English River, 40 km NW of Sioux Lookout. The lake has hundreds of bays and inlets and an area of 416 square miles (1,077 sq km). Fort Lac Seul trading post was established in 1815. Seul is a French word meaning "alone" or "by oneself."

LAC STE. THERESE

Pop. 213. In Casgrain T., Cochrane Dist., at the N terminus of Hwy. 583, 13 km N of Hearst. The post office was established as Lac Ste. Thérese in 1935. The place was named after a Roman Catholic parish of the same name and a French Catholic saint.

LAFONTAINE

Pop. 269. In Tiny T., Simcoe C., on C. Rd. 26, 10 km W of Midland. The place was first known as St. Croix because of the many crosses erected there by Father Jean Louis Hennepin, a missionary sent from France to Canada in 1675. The second time the place was settled was in the 1830s when disbanded French-Canadian soldiers came to take up grants of land they had been assigned. They named the community Lafontaine to honour Sir Louis Hippolyte LaFontaine, joint premier of United Canada from 1848 to 1851, with Robert Baldwin. Lafontaine survived well into the 20th century as the only Ontario settlement of any size where English was not spoken, but by the 1940s most residents were bilingual.

LAKE DALRYMPLE

Pop. 200. In Carden T., Victoria C., on Dalrymple Lake, 30 km NE of Orillia. The history of the community and the origin of its name are not known.

LAKEFIELD

Pop. 2,359. In Douro T., Peterborough C., on the Otonabee River just below Katchewanooka Lake and Hwy. 28, 13 km N of Peterborough. One of the first settlers, in 1831, was half-pay British army officer Col. Samuel Strickland who directed the laying out of a road along the Otonabee River. (Half-pay officers received half pay as pensions because they had been wounded or because they remained available for recall to active service). Strickland was joined by two sisters, Catherine Parr Traill and Susanna Moodie, each of whom had married half-pay officers. Strickland wrote a book titled Twenty-seven Years in Canada; his sister, Catherine, wrote Backwoods of Canada, and their sister Susanna wrote Roughing it in The Bush. The three books are considered to be important Canadian literature. The place was first called Nelson's Falls after John Nelson who had settled in the area in 1819, and later Thompson's Rapids, Herriot's Falls, North Douro, and Selby. In 1875 the post office was established as Lakefield, reflective of the area's topography. Lakefield Preparatory School is a private school for boys whose pupils have included His Royal Highness Prince Andrew. Novelist and children's book author Margaret Laurence (1926-1987) did much of her writing here.

L'AMABLE

Pop. 225. In Dungannon T., Hastings C., on Hwy. 62, 10 km SE of Bancroft. This is one of the few places in Ontario that has a post office with a different name from the town. Green Corners is the name of the community and L'Amable is the name of the post office. The place is believed to have been named for an Indian family that operated a trap line in the area or for an Indian chief who drowned in the lake in 1873.

LAMBETH

Pop. 3,056. In Westminster T., Middlesex C., on Dingman Creek, a tributary of the Thames and Hwys. 2, 4, & 81, 8 km SW of London. Abraham Patrick, who built his home in 1811 on land he had bought from Col. Thomas Talbot, was probably the community's first resident. The place was first known as Hall's Mills and then Junction or The Junction because it was at the junction of the Longwoods and Talbot Roads. When the post office opened in 1840, the community was named Westminster. In 1857 the post office changed the name to Lambeth after a place in England.

LANARK

Pop. 784. In Lanark T., Lanark C., on the River Clyde and Hwy. 511 and C. Rd. 12, 14 km NW of Perth. The first house at what settlers called New Lanark, was built by David Bowers in 1820. More than 3,000 settlers, many of them unemployed weavers from Scotland and discharged soldiers, were established on recently surveyed townships in this area during 1820 and 1821. The government set up a depot on the site of the present village to serve as the centre of a military settlement in the newly surveyed surrounding townships. Most of the settlers of the Lanark area were immigrants from the Scottish counties of Lanark and Renfrew. When the post office was established in 1823, the place was called Lanark.

LANCASTER

Pop. 751. In Charlottenburgh and Lancaster ts., Stormont, Dundas, and Glengarry C., 1.5 km N of Lake St. Francis (a widening of the St. Lawrence River and Raisin River) on Hwys. 2 & 34, just N of Hwy. 401, 24 km NE of Cornwall. The settlement was founded by United Empire Loyalists in 1787 and first known as New Lancaster, then Kirktown, and finally Lancaster after George III, one of whose titles was duke of Lancaster. Three major fires in the 1920s destroyed many of the community's historic buildings, but the 1825-vintage Moose Head Inn survived. It was a stagecoach inn and in its early years was also used as a courtroom. During later renovation of the basement under the courtroom, a keg of deteriorated gunpowder was discovered; it had been placed directly under the judge's chair.

LANGSTAFF
Pop. 1,095. Part of the Town of Vaughan and part of the Town of Markham, Reg. Mun. of York on Hwys. 7 & 11, just N of Toronto. Named after John Langstaff, who settled in the area in 1808 and was the first teacher in the local school.

LANGTON
Pop. 406. In Norfolk T., Reg. Mun. of Haldimand-Norfolk on Hwy. 59 and C. Rd. 28, 21 km SW of Simcoe. The place was first known as North Walsingham, and a post office opened under that name in 1854. In 1862 the name was changed to Langton to honour John Langton, auditor general of Canada from 1867 to 1878. The community grew rapidly in the 1870s when the excellent forests of the region were exploited. When the supply of timber was exhausted, that industry was replaced by tobacco growing. In 1945 Langton opened the first central public school in Ontario built by a municipality.

LANSDOWNE
Pop. 538. In Front of Leeds and Lansdowne T., Leeds and Grenville C., on C. Rds. 3 & 34, 16 km NE of Gananoque and 6 km NW of the Thousand Islands International Bridge. The community was settled in the 1780s by United Empire Loyalists. Among the first arrivals were the Findlay family and the family of Oliver Landon. The large size of these families contributed significantly to Lansdowne's early growth; by 1818 Oliver Landon had nine sons and three daughters, and 59 other family members lived in the area. The place was named after Maj.-Gen. William Petty Fitzmaurice, earl of Shelbourne, who was created marquis of Lansdowne in 1784.

LANSDOWNE HOUSE
Pop. 229. In Kenora Dist. on the S shore of Attawapiskat Lake, 280 km NW of Geraldton. The post office was established as Lansdowne House in 1953. The history of the community and the origin of its name are not known.

LAPPE
Pop. 600. In Gorham T., Thunder Bay Dist. on Hwys. 589 & 591, 19 km N of Thunder Bay. The post office was established as Lappe in 1936. The history of the community and the origin of its name are not known.

LARDER LAKE

Pop. 1,084. In Hearst T., Timiskaming Dist., on the NW shore of Larder Lake and Hwys. 66 & 624, 29 km E of Kirkland Lake. The community was settled in 1906 after an Indian staked a gold claim beside the lake. A gold rush began, and within months 4,000 claims had been staked. The community was named after the lake. Larder is an Indian word meaning "stockpile," and the lake, which abounded in fish, could always be relied upon to provide food. The lake is only 11 km by 5 km, and a commercial fishery in the 1920s soon depleted the fish stock.

LA SALLE

Pop. 14,629. In Sandwich West T., Essex C., on the Detroit River and Hwy. 18, 14 km S of Windsor. The post office was established in 1889 as Petite Coté and changed its name to LaSalle in 1924 to honour French explorer Robert René de La Salle who passed through the area in 1679. During prohibition LaSalle carried on a prosperous liquor-exporting business. When prohibition was repealed the community's prosperity declined and its population decreased.

LATCHFORD

Pop. 347. In Coleman T., Timiskaming Dist., on Bay Lake and the Montreal River and Hwy. 11, 130 km NW of North Bay. The place was well known to Indians and explorers because it was on the Montreal River system, but the first settlement of any kind was a Hudson's Bay Company trading post built on nearby Fiddler's Island in 1888. It burned down in 1905. No settlement developed until the arrival of the Timiskaming and Northern Ontario Railway. When the rail line was being built, silver was discovered in Cobalt, 14 km north. Latchford prospered on the heels of the great silver boom as the jumping off place for prospectors headed north. By 1907 the population was over 1,000. Major fires in 1908, 1910, and 1911; the end of transient prospectors, and the First World War, dealt the community a series of blows from which it never economically recovered. The community was named after Hon. Francis R. Latchford, minister of works, who turned the first sod for the railway in North Bay in 1902 and drove the last spike at Moosonee 30 years later. By covering a culvert over Latchford Creek with a wooden structure, Latchford claims the World's Shortest Covered Bridge. It is 11 feet, 3 inches (3.4 m) long.

LAVIGNE

Pop. 200. In McPherson T., Nipissing Dist., on the W shore of Lake Nipissing and Hwy. 64, 30 km SW of Sturgeon Falls. The community was founded around the Visitation Parish Church built in 1914 and named after Father Lavigne, the first parish priest.

LEAMINGTON

Pop. 12,764. In Mersea T., Essex C., on Pigeon Bay of Lake Erie and Hwys. 3, 18, & 77, 53 km SE of Windsor. The community had its beginnings in the early 1800s after the Talbot Road was laid out by Col. Thomas Talbot. It was first called Wilkinson Corners, and when the post office was to be established in 1854, mill owner William Gaines suggested the name Gainesborough. There already was such a place in Ontario, so Gaines proposed Leamington for his native town in England. Natural gas and oil were discovered in the area, but by 1904 the wells had petered out. Point Pelee National Park is just southeast of Leamington. The park has the smallest dry land area of any Canadian national park but draws more than half a million visitors each year. Point Pelee juts into Lake Erie like the spout of a funnel and is a migratory flyway for birds and butterflies, at the tip of which they rest before or after crossing the lake. More than 700 species of plants have been identified in the tiny park, and 347 species of birds have been spotted. On a clear night in August of 1845, two steamships, the Kent and the London, sighted each other and signalled but failed to alter course and collided. The London attempted to tow the badly damaged Kent to Point Pelee, but the Kent sank with an estimated loss of 10 lives. Leamington is one of two ports on the Ontario shore from which summer ferry service connects with Pelee Island and Sandusky, Ohio.

LEASKDALE

Pop. 358. In the Reg. Mun. of Durham, on C. Rd. 1, 45 km NW of Whitby. The post office was established in 1857 and named after the first postmaster, George Leask. Lucy Maud Montgomery (1874-1942), author of Anne of Green Gables lived in the Presbyterian manse in Leaskdale from 1911 to 1926 during which time she wrote 11 novels including two of the Anne books and the Emily series.

LEFAIVRE

Pop. 239. In Alfred T., Prescott and Russell C., on the Ottawa River and C. Rds. 15 & 24, linked by ferry service with Montebello, Que., 18 km W of Hawkesbury. The place was first known as Presaults Wharf. The post office was established in 1877 and named Lefaivre after the first postmaster, Hercules Lefaivre.

LEFROY

Pop. 500. In Innisfil T., Simcoe C., 5 km E of Hwy. 11, 21 km SE of Barrie. The first settler was Henry Grose, who came to the area in 1832 from Cornwall, England. The community's name honours Sir John Henry Lefroy, who was in charge of the magnetic observatory in Toronto from 1844 to 1853. In the 1860s, Albert Kirkpatrick, who ran the general store, published a monthly leaflet for farmers in which he boasted of his store:

"We sell everything Eatons sell and some which they don't." This referred to matches, tobacco, and playing cards, which founder Timothy Eaton had forbidden to be sold in his store.

LEVACK

Pop. 1,994. Part of the Town of Onaping Falls, Reg. Mun. of Sudbury, off Hwy. 144, 38 km NW of Sudbury. The community lies on the northern rim of the Sudbury Basin and surrounds the Levack Mine of International Nickel Company. The post office was established in 1914 as Levack. The name honours Mary Levack, Scottish-born mother of Sir Oliver Mowat, premier of Ontario from 1872 to 1896.

LIGHTHOUSE COVE

Pop. 350. In Dover T., Kent C., on Lake St. Clair at the mouth of the Thames River and C. Rd. 39, 25 km SW of Chatham. The lighthouse was built in 1872 and is a popular tourist attraction.

LIMEHOUSE

Pop. 230. In Reg. Mun. of Halton Hills on the W branch of the Credit River, 23 km SW of Brampton. Limehouse was first known as The Rock and was later named Fountain Green, but when the post office was established in 1857 it was named Limehouse for the limestone that abounded in the area. In the 1850s, lime kilns were built to produce quicklime which, when mixed with water, formed mortar. In the 1880s, the Bescoby Lime Works employed more than 100 men on three shifts, producing 75,000 bushels (27,300 hl) of lime a year from six kilns.

LIMOGES

Pop. 1,085. In Cambridge T., Prescott and Russell C., on C. Rd. 37, just N of Hwy. 417, 40 km E of Ottawa. The post office was opened as South Indian in 1883. In 1926 the post office name was changed to Limoges. The origin of the name is not known.

LINCOLN

Pop. 14,335. Town in the Reg. Mun. of Niagara. The town was created in 1970 by regional government by the amalgamation of the Town of Beamsville, the Township of Louth, and the police villages of Campden, Jordan, Jordan Station, and Vineland. It was named after the former county of Lincoln of which it was once a part. Lincoln County was created in 1792 by Col. John Graves Simcoe, first lieutenant-governor of Upper Canada. It was named after Lincolnshire, England.

LINDSAY

Pop. 15,265. In Ops T., Victoria C., on the Scugog River and Hwys. 7, 35, & 36 and C. Rd. 17, 43 km W of Peterborough. The Township of Ops was surveyed in 1825 by Col. Duncan McDonnell. He found a layer of rich clay loam covering the limestone bed of the area, and because of the excellent agricultural potential of the area he named the township after Ops, wife of Saturn and goddess of plenty and fertility in ancient Rome. Patrick Connell settled that year although American William Purdy and his sons, Jesse and Hazard, are considered to be founders of Lindsay. The townsite was then a portage place across the Scugog River which the Indians called Onigahning. Settlers called it Portage Place, and after Purdy built a mill in 1828 the place was known as Purdy's Mills or Purdy's Rapids. When the post office was established in 1836, the place was called Lindsay after a surveyor's assistant, who was accidentally shot in the leg in 1825 and subsequently died of infection. In 1861 a fire destroyed four hotels, two mills, the post office, and 83 other buildings. Character actress Marie Dressler made her debut at Lindsay's opera house in 1897 at the age of five. Ernest Thompson Seton (1860-1946) lived his childhood on a farm near Lindsay. He was an amateur naturalist and freelance illustrator and combined those interests to produce about 40 books of stories about North American wildlife. In 1958 promoters staged Canada's first bullfight in Lindsay. It was to be bloodless, and the matadors were armed only with wooden swords, but protests flooded in from across the country. The promoters lost a bundle because hundreds of spectators gained entrance without paying admission.

LINWOOD
Pop. 504. In the Reg. Mun. of Waterloo on C. Rds. 5 & 17, 22 km NW of Waterloo. Thomas Ransom and John Brown were the first settlers, in 1846. The post office was established in 1858 and named Linwood by a Mr. Hutton, a school teacher. The "Lin" part of the name is from "lyn," a Welsh word meaning "pool."

LION'S HEAD
Pop. 496. In Eastnor T., Bruce C., on Whippoorwill Bay off Georgian Bay, 5 km E of Hwy. 6, 35 km NW of Wiarton. George Moore, Richard Tackaberry, and John Richardson were among the first settlers, in 1871. The place was first known as Point Hangcliffe and later took its name from the same steep cliff across the bay, on which a rock formation resembling the head of a lion may be seen from certain angles. Lion's Head is on the Bruce Trail; its sandy beach and protected harbour make it a busy tourist centre in summer.

LISLE
Pop. 441. In Tosorontio T., Simcoe C., on C. Rd. 12, 40 km SW of Barrie. Local landowner Thomas Crosbie had named the community Forestlea, but when the Grand Trunk Railway arrived in 1878 the station was named New Airlie. There was already a village named Airlie nearby, so a new name was chosen to avoid confusion. Lisle was chosen from a popular song of the day, Annie Lisle.

LISTOWEL

Pop. 5,083. In Wallace and Elma ts., Perth C., on the Middle Maitland River and Hwys. 23 & 86, 54 km NW of Kitchener-Waterloo. The first settler was John Binning, who bought land in 1852 from a man named Henry in exchange for a rifle. In 1855 residents held a meeting and decided to name their community Mapleton. The same year, William Gibson opened a store nearby and called it Windham. When an application for a post office was approved in 1856, the government rejected both proposed names for the community and called the place Listowel after the town of Listowel in Kerry County, Ireland. An early storekeeper in Listowel was John Livingstone, brother of African explorer and missionary, Dr. David Livingstone.

LITTLE BRITAIN

Pop. 377. In Mariposa T., Victoria C., on C. Rds. 4 & 6, 12 km SW of Lindsay. Harrison Haight settled in 1834 and built the township's first mill. Robert Ferguson Whiteside built a store in 1853 in which a meeting was held the following year to choose a name for the community. The first name suggested—by a James Metherell—was Margaretville, after his mother. Whiteside, in whose store the post office was to be located, decided the name should be Elm Grove. But there turned out to be four other Elm Grove post offices in Ontario, so the post office assigned the name Little Britain after a township in Pennsylvania.

LITTLE CURRENT

Pop. 1,400. In Howland T., Manitoulin Dist. on the NE tip of Manitoulin Island and Hwys. 6 & 540, 128 km SW of Sudbury. The place was known by the Indians as Waibejewung—"where the waters flow back and forth"—descriptive of winds causing a slight current through the narrow channel between the island and the mainland. French fur traders knew the place as La Petit Courant which translates as "the little current." The settlement was originally a Hudson's Bay Company fur-trading post built in 1856. A post office, called Little Current, was established in 1865, but in the 1870s settlers also called it Shaftesbury.

Archaeological digs on Manitoulin Island have produced traces of human habitation over 30,000 years old, the oldest known on the North American continent. Who those people were, where they came from, and where they disappeared to, remains a mystery. The first recorded European resident of Manitoulin Island was Father Joseph Poncet, who established a mission in 1648 about 16 km south of Little Current to serve the island's Algonkian-speaking people. The mission was abandoned in 1650 following the destruction of the Huron nation by the Iroquois.

LIVELY

Pop. 3,465. Part of the Town of Walden, Reg. Mun. of Sudbury on Hwy. 17 and C. Rd. 55, 11 km SW of Sudbury. The International Nickel Company (INCO) built the community in 1951 to accommodate employees of its nearby Creighton Mine. The place was named after longtime INCO employee Charles E. Lively.

LONDESBOROUGH

Pop. 214. In Hullett T., Huron C., on Hwy. 4 and C. Rd. 15, 23 km SE of Goderich. For a time the settlement was named Wright's Corners after R. Wright, the first settler, who came before 1850. Later it was also known as Hagyard's Corners after Thomas Hagyard, another early settler. When the post office opened in 1861, the community was named Londesborough by Thomas Hagyard, who had previously lived on the estate of Lord Londesborough in Yorkshire, England.

LONDON

Pop. 281,745. In Middlesex C. at the forks of the Thames River and Hwys. 2, 4, 22, and 401, 173 km SW of Toronto. London's nickname is "The Forest City" and it has more than 50,000 trees on city property and 1,500 acres (607.5 ha) of parks, including 1,000 acres (405 ha) along the Thames River. Archaeological excavations in London have revealed that a Neutral Indian village existed on the site about 1500 AD. In 1793 Col. John Graves Simcoe chose the site for the capital of Upper Canada and named it after the British capital city. Simcoe was overruled by a superior and York, now Toronto, became the capital. Eldon House, the oldest remaining house in London, was built in 1834 by retired naval officer Capt. John Harris. It is now a museum. London's oldest building is the Old Courthouse, built between 1827 and 1829, with additions in 1878 and 1911. It is modelled after Malahide Castle in England and in 1980 was rescued from the wrecker's ball and given a $2.5 million facelift. It is now the home of Middlesex County Council and the 1st Hussars Museum. The oldest known wrought iron bridge in Ontario was built in 1875 to replace a wooden structure. Blackfriars Bridge is still in use. In 1881 London was the scene of one of the worst marine disasters in Canada. On May 24 the overloaded excursion steamboat Victoria overturned and sank in the Thames River. About 200 of the 600 passengers were drowned. The University of Western Ontario was founded in London in 1878. The city has been called a microcosm of Canadian life and is so "typically Canadian" it is often used as a test market for new products; if something will sell in London, it's likely to sell anywhere in Canada.

LONGLAC

Pop. 2,133. In Oakes T., Thunder Bay Dist. at the N end of Long Lake and Hwy. 11, 213 km W of Hearst and 296 km NE of Thunder Bay. The region was well known to fur traders by the mid-1700s and was a centre of commerce by 1800. From 1814 until their merger in 1821, the Hudson's Bay Company and the North West Company operated separate trading posts a short distance apart on Long Lake in bitter competition with each other. Permanent settlement did not take place until after 1900. Canadian Northern Railway employees Mr. Ruel and A. J. Hills suggested the name Longuelac for the railway station. The post office, established in 1919, took the name Longlac.

LONG LAKE I.R.

Pop. 300. In Thunder Bay Dist. 2 km NW of the N end of Long Lake, and 2 km W of the Town of Longlac, 215 km W of Hearst and 294 km NE of Thunder Bay. Long Lake Band #58 owns the reserve.

LONG POINT

Pop. 275. In Reg. Mun. of Haldimand-Norfolk on Lake Erie and Hwy. 59, 48 km SW of Simcoe. The place was first recorded in 1670 when Sulpician missionaries Dollier de Casson and Galinee portaged across the peninsula near the present community. From that time on, the portage was used steadily until a storm in 1833 broke a navigable passage through the neck of land. From 1802 until 1816 the place was called Charlotteville and was capital of the London District and defended by Fort Norfolk. In 1816 the courthouse burned and the capital was moved inland to what is now Vittoria. Hwy. 59 continues east past Long Point to the entrance to Long Point Provincial Park, popular with naturalists because of its sand dunes and marsh areas and because it—like Point Pelee farther west—is another migratory flyway for birds and butterflies.

LONG SAULT

Pop. 1,227. In Cornwall T., Stormont, Dundas, and Glengarry C., on the St. Lawrence River and Hwy. 2, 14 km W of Cornwall. The community was established as a result of the flooding of the St. Lawrence River shore in 1957 by the St. Lawrence Seaway project and represents the union of the former communities of Mille Roches and Moulinette. During the planning stages it was known as New Town No. 2. (New Town No. 1 was Ingleside.) Before widening of the river, Moulinette (French for "little mill") was on the St. Lawrence shore on Hwy. 2, 11 km west of Cornwall. Mille Roche (French for "thousand rocks," which could be seen at the foot of rapids in the St. Lawrence) was 8 km west of Cornwall on Bergin Lake, part of the Cornwall Canal.

L'ORIGNAL

Pop. 1,970. In Longueuil T., Prescott and Russell C., on the Ottawa River and C. Rd. 24, just N of Hwy. 17, 7 km W of Hawkesbury. In 1674 a large tract of land along the Ottawa River was granted as a seigneury to François Prévost, mayor of the town of Quebec. It became known as the

Longueuil Seigneury when it passed to Paul Joseph LeMoyne de Longueuil in 1778 upon his marriage to the heiress of the seigneury. In 1796 Longueuil sold the property to New York land speculator Nathaniel Hazard Treadwell. Settlement of the area started in 1798 when Treadwell erected saw- and grist mills on Mill Creek and built roads. The place was named after Pointe a Orignal, a river crossing for elk. (The translation of "orignal" in Canada is "elk," though elsewhere it means "moose.") The name of this settlement was often misspelled. For a time even the post office cancelled letters as "Original." A courthouse, designed in the United Empire Loyalist neoclassical style and completed in 1824, is the oldest remaining courthouse in Ontario.

LORNE PARK

Pop. 7,470. Part of the City of Mississauga, Reg. Mun. of Peel on Lake Ontario 24 km W of Toronto. Some properties in what is now Lorne Park were deeded as early as 1811, but there was little development until the railroad arrived in the 1850s and the place became a summer resort. It was named after Sir John Douglas Sutherland Campbell, marquess of Lorne, governor general of Canada from 1878 to 1883.

LOWBANKS

Pop. 244. Part of the Town of Dunnville, Reg. Mun. of Haldimand-Norfolk on Lake Erie and C. Rd. 3, 16 km W of Port Colborne. The community was settled in the early 1800s, and the post office was established as Lowbanks in 1865. It is a popular summer resort for people from Buffalo and Hamilton. At one time there were two telephone companies in Lowbanks, which resulted in bizarre "long distance" charges for telephone calls between some neighbouring homes and buildings. The community was so named because the Lake Erie shoreline here has low banks as opposed to the high banks in Sherbrooke Township where there is a community named Highbanks.

LOWVILLE

Pop. 245. Part of the City of Burlington in the Reg. Mun. of Halton on Twelve Mile Creek and C. Rd. 1, 15 km NW of Burlington. The post office was opened as Lowville in 1847. In 1869 the community was divided into Upper and Lower Town by Twelve Mile Creek. The parts were called Upper Lowville and Lower Lowville. The community was named Lowville because of its position below the Niagara Escarpment.

LUCAN

Pop. 1,740. In Biddulph T., Middlesex C., on Hwy. 4 and C. Rds. 13 & 47, 27 km NW of London. In 1829 a group of fugitive slaves from Cincinnati, Ohio, purchased 800 acres (324 ha) of land in the area with help from Ohio Quakers. They established one of the earliest black settlements in

Upper Canada and soon were joined by other groups from New England. They called the place Wilberforce Colony after the British abolitionist William Wilberforce. By 1833 there were 32 families in the colony. However, a series of bizarre murders and the suicide of Mrs. Wyatt, a religious fanatic, caused the Quakers to disperse during the early 1840s. For a time the place was known as Marysville after the sheriff's wife, Mary Macdonald. In 1857 the post office was established as Lucan, named after Lucan in Ireland. Near Lucan was the homestead of an Irish immigrant family named Donnelly, which between 1847 and 1880 was involved in one of the bloodiest feuds in Canadian history. The feud ended in 1880 with the massacre of five members of the family. The subsequent trial, in London, acquitted those charged with the murders.

LUCKNOW
Pop. 1,042. In Kinloss T., Bruce C., on Nine Mile River and Hwy. 86 and C. Rd. 1, 18 km NW of Wingham. Eli Stauffer, a German from Waterloo County, accepted a government offer in 1856 of 200 acres (81 ha) of land to anyone who would build a mill on Nine Mile River, (which empties into Lake Huron at Port Albert). The founder of the settlement is considered to be James Somerville of Dunfermline, Scotland, who laid out the village lots in 1858. The community took its name from Lucknow in India, which was much in the news during the bloody Indian Mutiny of 1857-1858.

LYNDEN
Pop. 451. In Flamborough T., Reg. Mun. of Hamilton-Wentworth on C. Rd. 299, 27 km W of Hamilton. Barnabus Howard was among the first to build a home in the area, some time before 1835. In the early 1840s Benomy VanSickle erected the first sawmill, after which the place was known as VanSickle. By 1889 there were 16 sawmills in the Lynden area. Native son Silas Bishop, who grew to a height of seven feet six inches (2.28 m) toured as a giant with the Barnum Circus. (Angus McAskill, the Cape Breton giant (1825-1863) was seven feet nine inches [2.36 m] tall.)

LYONS
Pop. 294. In South Dorchester T., Elgin C., on Clear Creek and Hwy. 73 and C. Rd. 48, 8 km N of Aylmer. Until 1860 the settlement was called Hale's Corners after William Hale, who had established an inn at the site. The origin of the name is unknown.

MacTIER

Pop. 631. In Freeman T., Muskoka Dist. on C. Rd. 11 just off Hwy. 69, 40 km SE of Parry Sound. In 1909 the post office was established as Muskoka Station. In 1915 its name was changed to MacTier. The origin of the name is unknown.

MADAWASKA

Pop. 264. In Murchison T., Renfrew C., on the Madawaska River and Hwy. 60, 28 km W of Barry's Bay. The post office was established in 1900. Madawaska is an Algonquin Indian name, which means "there is a bay at the river junction."

MADOC

Pop. 1,200. In Madoc and Huntingdon ts., Hastings C., on Deer Creek near Moira Lake and Hwys. 7 & 62 and C. Rd. 12, 71 km NE of Peterborough. Donald MacKenzie founded the settlement and built a saw- and grist mill on Deer Creek. The place was called MacKenzie's Mills for two decades until the name was changed to Hastings, after the county, Ontario's second largest. The county was named in honour of the family of Francis Rawdon-Hastings (1754-1826) a military leader who distinguished himself during the American Revolution. His family took its name from the town of Hastings in Sussex, England, and he was created marquess of Hastings in 1817. When the post office opened in 1836 it was called Madoc. The name is derived from Madoc ad Owaiin Gwynedd, a legendary Welsh prince said to have discovered America in 1170. In 1866 gold was discovered in Madoc Township, and Canada's first gold rush made the settlement a boom town. Twenty-five mounted police were stationed here to keep order. Most of the gold mines failed because of the high cost of extracting the ore, but prospectors also discovered copper, lead, marble, quartz, talc, and lithographic stone.

MADSEN

Pop. 200. In Baird T., Kenora Dist., on Hwy. 618, 11 km SW of Red Lake, 212 km NW of Dryden. The community was established in 1938 by the opening of Madsen Red Lake Gold Mine. The post office opened as Madsen later in the same year.

MAGNETAWAN

Pop. 238. In Chapman T., Parry Sound Dist. on the Magnetawan River and Hwys. 510 & 520, 56 km NE of Parry Sound. Lt. F. H. Baddeley of the Royal Engineers explored the area in 1835. Settlement did not start until the Nipissing Road was cut by the Dodge Lumber Company from

Rousseau to Magnetawan in 1873. By 1879 there was daily steamboat service from Magnetawan to Burk's Falls and from Magnetawan to the foot of Ahmic Lake. The routes were joined by a lock at Magnetawan in 1885. The post office was established as Magnetawan. The original spelling was Maganetawan and the Indian word meant "swiftly flowing water," an apt name for a river that drops 800 feet (243.8 m) on its journey from Algonquin Park to Georgian Bay at Byng Inlet. In 1872 the government adopted an immigration policy that offered subsidized steamship fares and free inland transportation to European settlers. Elise von Koerber was one of several special agents appointed, and by 1877 she had brought several hundred Swiss to this region of Canada.

MAIDSTONE

Pop. 248. In Sandwich South T., Essex C., on C. Rd. 34, 18 km SE of Windsor. Settlement in the area did not begin until 1828 when the Middle Road from Charing Cross to the St. Clair River had been surveyed and the area opened to settlement. The post office was established in 1837 as Maidstone, taking its name from the township, which had been named after the county town of Kent in England.

MAITLAND

Pop. 635. In Augusta T., Leeds and Grenville C., on the St. Lawrence River and Hwy. 2 and C. Rd. 15, 8 km NE of Brockville. In 1758 the French built a star-shaped fort on the site of what is now Maitland. At Pointe au Barril (or Baril) on the outskirts of Maitland, a plaque marks the former site of a shipyard where the last ships to defend the river for France were built. The six-acre (2.4-ha) shipyard, built by the French shortly after the British captured Fort Frontenac in 1758, was surrounded by a 12-foot-high (3.65-m) wall of upended logs. In 1759 the last two French warships, the *Iroquoise* and the *Outaouaise*, were launched. The first civilian community was founded by Ziba Phillips in 1818 and named Oswegatchie. The place was also known as Johnstown and Lower Selma. When the post office was established in 1828, it was named Maitland after Sir Peregrine Maitland, lieutenant-governor of Upper Canada from 1818 to 1828. One of the oldest churches in the Anglican Diocese of Ontario is the Gothic Revival-style St. James', started in 1826 and consecrated in 1830.

MALACHI

Pop. 300. In Kenora Dist. on Canadian National Railway, 74 km NW of Kenora. The post office was established in 1911. The history of the community and the origin of its name are unknown.

MALLORYTOWN

Pop. 700. In Front of Yonge T., Leeds and Grenville C., on Hwy. 2 and C. Rd. 4, 20 km SW of Brockville. Founded in 1790 by Vermont native and

United Empire Loyalist Nathaniel Mallory and his 13 children. When the post office was established in 1852 its name honoured the pioneer family. Mallorytown Landing is 3 km south on the St. Lawrence River. A cairn marks the site of Bridge Island, which was fortified and garrisoned in 1814 to protect the vital supply line from Lower Canada.

MALTON
Pop. 32,750. Part of the City of Mississauga, on Hwys. 7 & 410, 24 km NW of Toronto. First settled by Samuel Moore in 1823, and named Malton, after an English town, by Richard Halliday in the 1830s. The name remained when the post office was opened in 1856. Toronto Airport opened just south of here in 1937 and for years was known as Malton Airport. The name was changed to Toronto International Airport and later to Lester B. Pearson International Airport, honouring Lester Bowles Pearson, prime minister of Canada from 1963 to 1968.

MANILLA
Pop. 270. In the Reg. Mun. of Durham, on Hwys. 7 & 46, 24 km SW of Lindsay. The first settler was S. Patterson who came in 1827. The place was originally called Ham's Corners because Jacob Ham had the first store. Later the settlement was called Coulthard's Corners and then Monticello. In 1836 the post office opened as Mariposa even though the settlement was still known as Coulthard's Corners. In 1857, a public meeting held to decide on a new name for the post office agreed the name Manilla would also be used for the community. The origin of the name is unknown.

MANITOUWADGE
Pop. 3,507. In the Dist. of Thunder Bay, on Manitouwadge Lake at the N terminus of Hwy. 614, 58 km N of Hwy. 17 at a point 52 km NW of White River. The discovery of a copper-zinc-silver ore body in 1953 touched off one of the biggest staking rushes in the history of Canadian mining—more than 10,000 claims were staked during the first winter. In 1954 the Department of Mines built an access road into the area. Most of the claims were staked in the winter and the hopeful prospectors had to wait until spring to find out if their claims would pay off; most did not. The Ojibway name means "cave of the great spirit."

MANITOWANING
Pop. 473. In Assignack T., Manitoulin Dist., on Manitoulin Island at the foot of Manitowaning Bay off Georgian Bay on Hwy. 6, 51 km S of Little Current. The Manitowaning Indian Treaties of 1836 and 1862, between chiefs of the Ojibway and Ottawa nations and the Government of Canada, were signed here. The treaty of 1836 designated the entire island as a reserve for Indians wishing to settle there. The 1862 treaty opened

Manitoulin, exclusive of the eastern peninsula, to general settlement. The eastern peninsula remains the Wikwemikong Indian Reserve, believed to be North America's only unceded Indian reserve and therefore, in theory at least, not a part of Canada. The first permanent Anglican church mission on Manitoulin Island was established in 1838 as an outpost of the Diocese of Toronto. Between 1845 and 1849 the small Indian congregation, led by Rev. F. A. O'Meara, built St. Paul's Church, the oldest remaining church in the Manitoulin-Algoma area. Manitowaning is Indian for "home of the great spirit," in this case the precise home of the good spirit Gitchie Manitou.

MANOTICK

Pop. 261. In the Reg. Mun. of Ottawa-Carleton, on the Rideau River and C. Rd. 8, 17 km S of Ottawa. The settlement dates to 1860 when Moss Kent Dickinson and Joseph Currier built a flour mill around which a small industrial complex formed, including a sawmill and textile mill. Part of the community is on an island in the Rideau River. The post office was established in 1864 and named Manotick, an Indian word meaning "long island." The mill and some of its original machinery has been restored to working order by the Rideau Valley Conservation Authority. It is now called Watson's Mill and is open to the public.

MAPLE

Pop. 2,500. Part of the Town of Vaughan, Reg. Mun. of York on C. Rd. 25, 29 km N of Toronto. The place was settled in the early 1800s and first called Noble's Corners or Nobleville after the first postmaster, Joseph Noble, in 1852. In 1855 the name was changed to Maple. One of the earliest Lutheran congregations in Upper Canada was formed in Vaughan Township in 1806 by German-speaking settlers from Pennsylvania. The present church, which dates from 1860, was the site of the founding of the Canada Synod of the Lutheran Church in 1861. William Maxwell Aitken was born in Maple in 1879, the third son of Rev. William Aitken and Jean Noble. He became an industrialist, newspaper publisher, and philanthropist. He was knighted in 1911, created a baronet in 1916 and the following year was raised to the peerage as Baron Beaverbrook of Beaverbrook, New Brunswick and Cherkley, Surrey, England.

MARATHON

Pop. 4,140. In Dist. of Thunder Bay, on Peninsula Harbour of Lake Superior and Hwy. 626, 3 km S of Hwy. 17, 92 km W of White River. Although the area was well known to fur traders in the late 1700s, construction of the Canadian Pacific Railway brought the settlement into being around 1883. At the peak of the project, an estimated 12,000 men using 5,000 horses worked out of the community then known as

Peninsula Harbour. The first permanent store was built there just after the turn of the century by a man named McCoy, and a post office was established as Peninsula in 1917. In 1944, when Marathon Paper Mills of Wisconsin was building a pulp mill, residents asked the post office to rename their community Everest. Postal authorities, believing this name could be confused with Everett, Ont., named the place Marathon after the parent company of the mill.

MARKDALE
Pop. 1,234. In Glenelg T., Grey C., on the Rocky Saugeen River and Hwy. 10 and C. Rd. 12, 38 km SE of Owen Sound. The first settlers were George Walker and Joseph Price, in 1846. The place was first known as East Glenelg and then Glenelg. When Donald McDuff became postmaster in 1864 he changed the name to Cornabus after his hometown in Scotland. In 1873 Mark Armstrong sold land to the Toronto, Grey and Bruce Railway on condition the town be renamed; it was called Markdale, after him.

MARKHAM
Pop. 129,501. In the Reg. Mun. of York, on the Rouge River and Hwys. 7 & 48, 35 km NE of Toronto. The area's first settlers arrived in 1790 before the area had been surveyed. Four years later, 64 German families from Genessee, N.Y. arrived, led by William Berczy. They cut a wagon track through the forest from York (now Toronto), which eventually became Yonge St. Berczy built a mill and the place was known as German Mills. English immigrants and then French followed, and in 1826 Joseph Reesor from Pennsylvania bought land and laid out a townsite he called Reesorville. The name was not popular, and the Germans began calling the place Mannheim. When the post office opened in 1828 it took the name Markham after the township, which was named in honour of The Right Reverend William Markham, archbishop of York until his death in 1803.

MARKSTAY
Pop. 436. In Hagar T., Sudbury Dist., on Hwy. 17, 30 km E of Sudbury. The community supposedly got its name from a message sent to a telegraph operator of the Canadian Pacific Railway. The employee, named Mark, had applied for a transfer to another CPR point. He received a message stating: "Mark stay where you are." The post office of Markstay opened in 1892.

MARLBANK
Pop. 206. In Hungerford T., Hastings C., on C. Rds. 13 & 32, 23 km NW of Napanee. The settlement was first called Allan Mills. When the post office was established in 1860 it was named Marlbank for the large deposits of marl (a fine clay) in the area.

MARMORA

Pop. 1,386. In Marmora T., Hastings C., on the Crowe River and Hwys. 7 & 14 and C. Rd. 3, 53 km NE of Peterborough. The community grew up in the 1820s around iron works started by Irish immigrant Charles Hayes in 1823. From 1873 to 1880 gold was mined by the Gatling Gold and Silver Mining Company, and cobalt was mined in the area until 1915. In the 1950s, the Marmoratown Mining Company (Bethlehem Steel Corporation) operated a strip mine for iron ore. Twenty million tons (18,140,000 tonnes) of limestone were first stripped from above the extensive magnetite beds. Concentrate was sent by rail to Picton for shipment by boat to mills in New York State. The operation closed in the 1970s, but the enormous open pit still draws sightseers. Marmora derives its name from *marmor*, the Latin word for marble, which is still quarried in the area.

MARTINTOWN

Pop. 437. In Charlottenburgh T., Stormont, Dundas, and Glengarry C., on the Raisin River and C. Rds. 18 & 20, 20 km N of Cornwall. The community is named after enterprising settler Malcolm McMartin. Between 1801 and 1803 he built a sawmill, planing mill, carding mill, and an ashery on the west side of the river. On the east side of the river he built a flour and grist mill and later a store.

MARYHILL

Pop. 377. In the Reg. Mun. of Waterloo, on C. Rds. 26 & 30, 14 km NW of Kitchener. First known as New Germany because many settlers were from Germany, and then named Rottenburg, the settlement changed its name to Friburg when the post office opened in 1851. The spelling was later modified to Freiburg. In 1941 the name was changed yet again, to Maryhill, after a popular woman in the community, Mary Kloepfner.

MARYSVILLE

Pop. 380. In Frontenac C., on Wolfe Island on Hwys. 95 & 96, 5 km SE by ferry boat from Kingston. The post office was established in 1845 and named after the first postmaster, Mary Hitchcock.

MASSEY

Pop. 1,138. In Salter T., Sudbury Dist., on the Spanish River and Hwys. 17 & 553, 96 km SW of Sudbury. The post office opened as Massey in 1889, named after the Massey family of Toronto.

MATACHEWAN

Pop. 479. In Cairo T., Timiskaming Dist. on a tributary of the Montreal River, 2 km from its confluence and Hwys. 66 and 566, 56 km SW of Kirkland Lake. First called Dokis Trading Post, the post office was established as Matachewan in 1935. The Indian word means "the current (of the river) is heard."

MATHESON

Pop. 605. In Matheson T., Cochrane Dist., on the Black River and Hwys. 11 & 101, 60 km NW of Kirkland Lake. First named McDougall Chute after an early trapper when the post office opened in 1907. In 1911 the name was changed to Matheson Station to honour provincial treasurer Arthur J. Matheson. In 1916 a massive forest fire destroyed 500,000 acres (202,500 ha) of timber and the communities of Matheson, Porquis Junction, Iroquois Falls, Kelso, Nushla, and Raymore—with a loss of more than 200 lives.

MATTAWA

Pop. 2,491. In Papineau T., Nipissing Dist. at the junction of the Mattawa and Ottawa Rivers and Hwys. 17 & 553, 62 km E of North Bay. The Indian name means "meeting of the waters." In 1837 Mattawa House became an important Hudson's Bay Company post and a centre of the fur trading and lumbering businesses. Today the Otto Holden hydro project is a major employer.

MATTICE

Pop. 750. In Eilber T., Cochrane Dist. on the Missinabi River and Hwy. 11, 64 km W of Kapuskasing. Residents first named their community Missinaibi. The post office was established as Mattice in 1915. The origin of the name is not known.

MAXVILLE

Pop. 794. In Kenyon T., Stormont, Dundas, and Glengarry C., on C. Rds. 20 & 22, 63 km E of Ottawa. Many of the settlers came from Perthshire, Scotland, where from 1810 to 1815 there were almost continuous crop failures. Duncan P. MacDougall built the first home and a mill in 1869. So many settlers were "Macs" that the place was first named Mac's Corners and then Macsville. One story is that the four corners of the settlement were each farmed by a Mac, each of whom donated 160 acres (64.75 ha) for a townsite. In early days the Campbells of Athol were the mail carriers, bringing the mail on horseback three times a week. The rider reached Macsville after midnight and since he often fell asleep and passed through the town without stopping, residents took turns watching for him. They soon grew fed up with this and demanded their own post office. When it opened in 1880, it was called Maxville. Just north of the community on County Rd. 20 is Glengarry Congregational Church. The log church is the oldest remaining chapel in Ontario built by Congregationalists.

MAYNARD

Pop. 244. In Augusta T., Leeds and Grenville C., on C. Rd. 26, 24 km NE of Brockville. The post office was established as Maynard in 1866, named after Moses Maynard Jr., an early Brockville merchant.

McGREGOR

Pop. 277. In Anderton T., Essex C., on C. Rds. 10 & 11, 18 km SE of Windsor. First known as Colchester Station, the community was named McGregor when the post office was established in 1881. The origin of the name is not known.

McKELLAR

Pop. 240. In McKellar T., Parry Sound Dist., on Hwy. 124, 20 km NE of Parry Sound. The township was surveyed into farm lots in 1869 by J. W. Fitzgerald, and the first settler was trapper Peter Leach, who had arrived the previous year. McKellar Village, as it was first called, was the second stop on the pioneer route from Parry Sound to the northern townships of the district. Early travellers and incoming settlers stayed at the McKellar House, run by William Thompson. The community took its name from the township, which had been named after the Hon. Archibald McKellar (1816-1894), MPP for Bothwell from 1867 to 1875.

McKERROW

Pop. 312. In Baldwin T., Algoma Dist., on Hwy. 17, 2 km E of its junction with Hwy. 6, 69 km SW of Sudbury. A post office was established as Espanola Station in 1908. In 1932 the name was changed to McKerrow to honour J. O. (Jack) McKerrow, traffic manager of Abitibi Pulp and Paper Company.

MEAFORD

Pop. 4,283. In St. Vincent T., Grey C., at the mouth of Big Head River and Nottawasaga Bay (an inlet of Georgian Bay) and Hwy. 26 and C. Rds. 7 & 12, 28 km E of Owen Sound. Settled by David Miller after whose wife Peggy the place was first named Pegg's Landing. A sister settlement was called Stephenson's Landing after an innkeeper named Stephenson, and there was much rivalry between the two places. In 1840 the post office was established as St. Vincent after Admiral Sir John Jervis, earl St. Vincent, after whom the township was also named. In 1858 the town was named Meaford after Meaford Hall, the Staffordshire estate of Lord St. Vincent. The Rt. Hon. Sir Lyman Poore Duff (1865-1955) was a native of Meaford. He was an expert in constitutional law and held many appointments, including that of chief justice of Canada from 1933 to 1944. The hero of a popular dog story is buried in Beautiful Joe Park on Victoria Crescent. During a visit to Meaford in the 1890s, Margaret Marshall Saunders heard from William Moore how he had rescued an abused dog from its cruel owner. She told the story in the novel *Beautiful Joe*, which by 1939 had been translated into 10 languages and sold seven million copies. Miss Saunders was awarded the C.B.E. for her contribution to securing humane treatment for animals.

MEADOWVALE VILLAGE

Pop. 240. In the City of Mississauga, Reg. Mun. of Peel, on the Credit River, 37 km W of Toronto. The community was settled and named by John Crawford in 1831. "Village" was recently added to the name to differentiate historic Meadowvale from an urban development of the same name, also within the City of Mississauga.

MELBOURNE

Pop. 311. In Ekfrid T., Middlesex C., on Hwy. 2 and C. Rd. 9, 41 km SW of London. A post office named Ekfried was established in 1832. The name was later corrected to Ekfrid, the township's name, which was taken from Ekfrid, king of Northumbria, a kingdom of ancient Britain. In 1857 the community's name was changed to Longwood; in 1882 the name was changed to Wendigo, and in 1887 the current name was adopted. The origin of the name is not known.

MERLIN

Pop. 755. In Raleigh & Tilbury East ts., Kent C., and C. Rds. 7 & 8, 20 km S of Chatham. There were scattered farms in the area in the 1820s, but the townsite wasn't settled until 1830 when a Mr. Smith and his five sons and John Powell arrived. In the 1840s Rev. William King founded a settlement nearby of former U.S. slaves. The place was first called Smith's Corners, but there was another place by that name in Ontario, so when the post office opened in 1868 it was called Merlin—either after Merlin in Scotland, or a small European falcon.

MERRICKVILLE

Pop. 968. In Montague T., Lanark C., and Wolford T., Leeds and Grenville C., on the Rideau River and Hwy. 43 and C. Rds. 15 & 16, 66 km S of Ottawa. The first settler was William Merrick, a United Empire Loyalist of Welsh descent from Massachusetts, who arrived in 1794. Wood from his mill built the first frame structure in what is now Ottawa. The house in which Col. John By lived while supervising construction of the Rideau Canal between 1826 and 1832 still stands in the village, as does the 1832 blockhouse erected beside the canal. The first transportation in and out of Merrickville was manpower. Settler John McCrae would carry up to 200 pounds (90.7 kg) of goods on his back on a two-day, 45-km hike to Brockville. The place was known as Mirrick's Mills, Mirickville, Merricksville, and Meyrick Ville before the post office opened in 1829 as Merrickville. The first nursery and seed farm in Ontario was located just east of the village. In 1908, the Rev. Ernest Thomas, after returning from a visit with Gen. Baden-Powell in England, organized one of Canada's first Boy Scout troops.

METCALFE
Pop. 1,272. In Osgoode T., Carleton C., on C. Rds. 6 & 113, 30 km SE of Ottawa. The community was named after Sir Charles Metcalfe.

METROPOLITAN TORONTO
Pop. 2,133,559. Legal description for a metropolitan corporation combining the five cities of Toronto, North York, York, Etobicoke, Scarborough, and the Borough of East York, which together cover 400 square kilometres (154 sq mi). (See entry under TORONTO.)

MIDLAND
Pop. 12,171. In Tay T., Simcoe C., on Georgian Bay just N of Hwy. 12, 51 km NW of Barrie or Orillia. French Jesuit missionaries established the mission of Sainte-Marie-Among-the-Hurons (3 km southeast of the present site of Midland) in 1639 and opened the first hospital and church in Ontario. The mission was a fortified place of refuge for Huron Indian converts. When the Iroquois destroyed the Huron nation the outpost was burned by the missionaries and abandoned in 1649. Fathers Gabriel Lalemant and Jean de Brebeuf were captured by the Iroquois and tortured to death. The mission was reconstructed in 1964 and today is a major tourist attraction. On a hill overlooking the reconstructed Sainte Marie is a twin-spired stone cathedral built in 1926, which honours the eight missionaries martyred in Huronia. In 1830, five of the priests were canonized by the Roman Catholic Church. The bay off Severn Sound which is off Georgian Bay and on which Midland is located, was called successively Christendom, Gloucester, and Munday's; the latter for the first settlers, Israel and Asher Munday, who arrived in 1872 along with the Midland Railway, which had been pushed through from Port Hope via Beaverton. John Smith named the place Midland for its location midway between Penetanguishene and Victoria Harbour.

MILDMAY
Pop. 981. In Carrick T., Bruce C., on Otter Creek on Hwy. 9, 9 km S of Walkerton. The first settler, Samuel Merner, had the area surveyed in 1867, and the village was known briefly as Mernersville. The following year, when the post office was established, the place was named Mildmay after Mildmay Park in Scotland.

MILFORD BAY
Pop. 258. In Monck T., Muskoka Dist., on Lake Muskoka and Hwy. 118, 17 km NW of Bracebridge. The post office was established as Milford Bay in 1889. The origin of the name is not known.

MILLBANK

Pop. 327. In Mornington T., Perth C., on C. Rds. 6, 7, & 11, 28 km NE of Stratford. The first settler was John Freeborn, who arrived in 1847 and built a mill. When the post office opened in 1852, he named it Millbank because his mill was built on the edge of a bank.

MILLBROOK

Pop. 1,098. In Cavan T., Peterborough C., on Baxter Creek, a tributary of the Otonabee River and C. Rds. 10 & 28, 21 km SW of Peterborough. First settler John Dyell came from Ireland in 1816, cleared a farm and built a mill by the brook, giving Millbrook its name. A fire in 1876 destroyed all the buildings on the north side of King St.; the school burned down in 1887, and the town and township hall suffered the same fate a year or two later. The first mounted band in Canada was formed in Millbrook in 1875. The Light Cavalry Band was connected with the Prince of Wales Dragoons.

MILLIKEN

Pop. 509. Part of the Town of Markham in the Reg. Mun. of York, 16 km NE of Toronto. The post office was established in 1858 and named Milliken after early settler Norman Milliken.

MILTON

Pop. 30,529. In the Reg. Mun. of Halton, on Sixteen Mile Creek and Hwy. 401, 53 km SW of Toronto. In 1821, Sarah and Jasper Martin were the first settlers. Jasper built a mill, and the farmers who brought their grain called the tiny settlement Martin's Mills. At a meeting in 1837, it was decided to rename the community. Jasper Martin had died, but his four sons maintained the business and were prominent in the community. They were partial to the English poet Milton, and on their suggestion Martin's Mills was renamed Milton. In the 1870s the Joseph brothers invented a threshing machine, which reduced the time required to separate grain from chaff. The P. L. Robertson Manufacturing Company was the world's first producer of socket-head screws, which proved invaluable to boat builders, electricians, furniture makers, and the manufacturers of the Model T Ford. The company was established in 1907 and at one time employed 20 percent of Milton's work force.

MILVERTON

Pop. 1,501. In Mornington T., Perth C., on Hwy. 19, 24 km N of Stratford. The first settler, Andrew West, a shoemaker from New York State, arrived in 1848 and, according to local lore, exchanged a pair of boots for land. He opened a shoe store and tavern and the settlement was named West's Corners when the post office was established in 1854. In 1871, at the suggestion of local Presbyterian minister Rev. Peter Musgrave, the community was renamed Milverton after the village in Somersetshire, England, where Musgrave had been born.

MINAKI

Pop. 350. In Kenora Dist. on Sand Lake (a widening of the Winnipeg River) and Hwy. 596, 51 km NW of Kenora. The community dates from the Wolsley Expedition of 1870 when the place was called Winnipeg River Crossing. A post office was established in 1912 as Minaki, an Indian word meaning "beautiful country." The Canadian National Railway put the community on the map when it opened a luxury summer lodge in 1914. To provide a nine-hole golf course, the railroad bought a Manitoba farm and hauled 30 rail cars of topsoil to Minaki. Minaki Lodge was destroyed by fire in 1925 but by 1927 Scottish stone masons and Swedish loggers had rebuilt it. The Ontario government took over the lodge in 1974 and poured $40 million into it before selling it at a tremendous loss to the Radisson Hotel Corp. of Minneapolis. Radisson turned the place around and sold it in 1987 to the Four Seasons hotel group, which operates the lodge from May to October.

MINDEMOYA

Pop. 388. In Carnarvon T., Manitoulin Dist., on Manitoulin Island in Lake Huron and on Hwys. 542 & 551, 199 km SW of Sudbury. The post office was established as Mindemoya in 1880. Mindemoya is an Indian word meaning "old woman."

MINDEN

Pop. 1,004. In Minden T., Haliburton C., on Gull River and C. Rd. 2, just W of Hwy. 35, 35 km SW of Haliburton, 94 km SE of Huntsville. The township was surveyed in 1858 by J. W. Fitzgerald and named after the town of Minden in Westphalia, Germany. The Gull River watershed was a traditional camping ground for Indian bands hunting in the Lake Simcoe region. The Clergy House, built about 1870 and believed to be the oldest remaining log structure in Haliburton, served as headquarters for itinerant Anglican missionaries at the turn of the century.

MINESING

Pop. 350. In Vespra T., Simcoe C., on Hwy. 26 and C. Rd. 28, 16 km NW of Barrie. The post office was established as Minesing in 1867. Minesing is an Indian word for "island." Eight kilometres south of Minesing, an historic plaque marks the former site of the Willow Creek Depot. During the War of 1812, "Fort Willow" was an important storage depot for supplies. It was near the end of the Nine Mile Portage, which connected the landing place at the headwaters of Kempenfelt Bay (today the site of Barrie), to Willow Creek.

MISSANABIE

Pop. 227. In West T., Algoma Dist., on Dog Lake and the N terminus of Hwy. 651, 54 km N of Hwy. 101, 68 km E of Wawa. The post office was established in 1893. Missanabie is an Indian word meaning "pictures in the water."

MISSISSAUGA

Pop. 385,156. In Reg. Mun. of Peel, on Lake Ontario immediately W of Toronto. The land originally belonged to the Mississauga Indians, and in 1805 four chieftains met with Hon. William Claus, deputy superintendent of Indian Affairs, at Government House at the mouth of the Credit River. The Indians sold the southerly portion of their lands, 70,784 acres (28,667.5 ha), for £1,000. The new township was surveyed the following year, and settlers began moving in. The first was Philip Cody, who opened an inn in Sydenham, later known as Fonthill and then Dixie. By 1974 the City of Mississauga had incorporated the communities of Cooksville, Clarkson, Lake View, Erindale, Meadowvale, Churchville, Lorne Park, Dixie, Burnhamthorpe, Malton, Sheridan, Park Royal, Cloverleaf, Applewood, Derry West, Port Credit, Streetsville, and part of Oakville. Mississauga is an Indian word for "river in the north of many mouths."

Between 1826 and 1847, a band of Mississauga Indians who had converted to Christianity formed a settlement on the Credit River and with government assistance built log houses, a sawmill, school, and chapel. By 1840, 500 acres (202.5 ha) were under cultivation and there were 50 houses. The first aerodrome and flying school in Canada was established at Long Branch, now a part of Mississauga, in 1915, and for a time the first flying units of the Royal Flying Corps, Canada, were based there. The muddy terrain proved unsuitable for a flying school, and after 1917 the facility provided only ground training for cadets. The Hon. Thomas Laird Kennedy (1878-1959) represented the riding of Peel in the Ontario legislature for all but one term over a 40-year period. He was nicknamed "Old Man Ontario" and served as minister of agriculture in three administrations and as premier from 1948 to 1949. In 1979 a train carrying dangerous chemicals derailed inside the city limits. More than 250,000 people were safely evacuated.

MITCHELL

Pop. 3,078. In Fullarton and Logan ts., Perth C., on the North Thames River and Hwys. 8 & 23, 21 km NW of Stratford. The founders of the town were William Hicks and his son John, who opened a tavern on the Huron Road in 1837. The community was named Mitchell after a black settler. One of Canada's most popular hockey players was born in Mitchell in 1902. Howie Morenz played 14 seasons in the National Hockey League,

12 of them for the *Montreal Canadiens*. He was a three-time winner of the Hart Trophy for the league's most valuable player.

MITCHELL'S BAY

Pop. 220. In Dover T., Kent C., on Mitchell Bay of Lake St. Clair and C. Rds. 34 and 42, 23 km NW of Chatham. The post office was established in 1872 and named after an early settler.

MITCHELL'S CORNERS

Pop. 457. Part of the Town of Newcastle, Reg. Mun. of Durham on C. Rds. 4 & 34, 10 km NE of Oshawa. The community took its name from Mitchell's School built in 1861 by R. B. Mitchell, a descendant of early settler Mr. B. Mitchell.

MONKTON

Pop. 521. In Logan and Elma T., Perth C., on Hwy. 23 and C. Rd. 9, 37 km N of Stratford. The first building, T. M. Daly's blacksmith shop, was erected in 1857. The origin of the name is unknown.

MONO MILLS

Pop. 400. In Mono T., Dufferin C., on the Humber River and C. Rd. 7, 1 km S of Hwy. 9, 9 km E of Orangeville. The township's first settler was George McManus, who came in 1823. At one time Mono Mills rivalled nearby Orangeville as the township's fastest-growing community, but the opening of the Prince of Wales and Victoria roads gave Orangeville the edge as the main stage stop between Brampton and Owen Sound. The origin of the community's name is not clear. Residents prefer the version that the name derives from Mona, daughter of Chief Tecumseth, but there is some doubt that he even had a daughter. The name may have been chosen by Sir Peregrine Maitland, lieutenant-governor of Upper Canada from 1818 to 1828. He favoured Spanish names and named the townships of Oso, Zorra, and Lobo—bear, she-fox, and wolf. Mona is Spanish for monkey.

MONTEITH

Pop. 247. Part of the Town of Iroquois Falls, Cochrane Dist., on a tributary of the Black River and Hwy. 577, 1 km N of Hwy. 11, 14 km S of Iroquois Falls. The place was first known as Driftwood City and later named Monteith after a minister of agriculture, who in 1908 chose the site for a provincial experimental and demonstration farm. In 1920 the farm, with added buildings, became Monteith Academy, a boarding school that supplied secondary education to Northern Ontario at a time when there were few high schools. It later became an industrial farm for young offenders and in 1940 served as an internment camp for 5,000 war prisoners. In 1947 the institution reverted to being a reform institution.

MOONBEAM

Pop. 859. In Fauquier T., Cochrane Dist., on Moonbeam Creek, and Hwys. 11 & 581, 21 km SE of Kapuskasing. First settled in 1913. Flashing lights falling from the sky like moonbeams into a little creek gave Moonbeam Creek its name, according to area oldtimers. The community took its name from the creek.

MOOREFIELD

Pop. 375. In Maryborough T., Wellington C., on Mallet River and C. Rd. 10, 45 km NW of Guelph. In 1852 Richard Moore and his family of 10 settled in what is now Moorefield. In 1872 the post office was established and named Moorefield after the Moore family.

MOORETOWN

Pop. 410. In Moore T., Lambton C., on the St. Clair River and C. Rd. 33 (St. Clair Parkway), 20 km S of Sarnia. When surveyor Mahlon Burwell interviewed the inhabitants of the township in 1826 to establish land claims they had negotiated with the Indians, he found 15 French-speaking and five English-speaking families located along the St. Clair River. John Courtney, one of the English residents, claimed to have been on his land since 1804. The Indians gave up their claim to Moore in 1827, and a reserve was set up for them along the Sombra border, which was purchased by the Crown in 1843. The Township of Moore was named by Sir John Colborne in 1829 in honour of Sir John Moore, the British general killed in Spain in 1809 at the Battle of Corunna. The survey of the township was completed in 1829 by Roswell Mount, who squeezed as many lots along the St. Clair River as possible, many of which were given to veterans of the Napoleonic Wars. Mooretown was the oldest settlement along the river and headquarters for the Mooretown Mounted Infantry, which saw action along the river during the Fenian Raids, from 1866 to 1870.

MOOSE CREEK

Pop. 420. In Roxborough T., Stormont, Dundas, and Glengarry C., on Moose Creek and C. Rd. 15, 35 km NW of Cornwall. A small waterfall nearby that rarely freezes was used by moose as a winter drinking hole. The creek was named Moose Creek, and the community took the same name.

MOOSE FACTORY

Pop. 1,452. In Cochrane Dist., on the Moose River, 24 km from its mouth at James Bay and 298 km by rail N of Cochrane. The second Hudson's Bay Company fort was built by Charles Bayly on what was then called Hayes Island in 1672. It was captured by the French in 1686 and renamed Fort St. Louis. It was returned to the company in 1730 and has been in continual operation since. A stone forge inside the blacksmith shop is one of the oldest "structures" in Ontario. The original shop was built in the late 1600s, but was moved back from the riverbank in 1820. Because the forge had to be transported a long distance, it was dis-assembled and rebuilt, stone by stone, at the present location. In summer when the Ontario Northland Railway runs excursion trains from Cochrane six times a week, an apprentice smithy runs the forge and explains its operation to visitors. A plaque in front of the Hudson's Bay Staff House recalls the fate of Arctic explorer Henry Hudson. In 1610 Hudson navigated the treacherous Hudson Strait and explored the inland waters of Hudson Bay. After a bleak winter in James Bay the navigator was cast adrift in an open boat by his mutinous crew on the journey back to England.

MOOSONEE
Pop. 216. In Cochrane Dist., on the W bank of the Moose River, 20 km from its mouth in James Bay and the N terminus of the Ontario Northland Railway, 300 km N of Cochrane. Moosonee is Ontario's only tidal port. In 1631-1632 Thomas James explored the waters of Hudson and James bays and successfully wintered his crew on nearby Charlton Island. His vivid account of the winter of hardships discouraged further exploration of the area for almost a century. The community was founded in 1903 when the Revillon Frères Trading Company of France established a post to compete with the Hudson's Bay Company, which has had a post at nearby Moose Factory on Moose (or Factory) Island since 1672. The rail line was completed to Moosonee in 1932, and the post office was established in the same year as Moosonee, which the French called "home of the moose."

MOREWOOD
Pop. 326. In Winchester T., Dundas C., on C. Rds. 7 & 13, 33 km NW of Morrisburg. The post office was established as Morewood in 1862. The history of the community and the origin of its name are not known.

MORPETH
Pop. 270, in Howard T., Kent C., on Hwys. 3 & 21 and C. Rd. 17, 40 km SE of Chatham. Although Morpeth is about 3 km from Lake Erie, it was first called Antrim Port because it was the point through which passed both the Michigan Central Railway and the Lake Erie & Detroit Railway. The post office was established in 1832 as Howard. In 1851 the name was changed following a whiskey-inspired brawl over whether the place should be renamed Morpeth or Jamestown. The Morpeth side stole the whiskey of the Jamestown side, so the story goes, and also won the argument.

MORRISBURG

Pop. 2,237. In Williamsburgh T., Dundas C., on the St. Lawrence River and Hwys. 2 & 31, 43 km SW of Cornwall. Morrisburg was a tiny frontier settlement in 1813 when an American force of more than 4,000 men marched down the shores of the St. Lawrence River towards John Crysler's farm near the site of the present village. The Americans were met and defeated by 800 Canadian militia, British regulars, and Indian supporters. The actual battle site was flooded in 1958 by the St. Lawrence Deep Waterway Project, but the battle is commemorated at Upper Canada Village a few kilometres east of Morrisburg. The community was first called West Williamsburg but renamed in 1851 after the Hon. James Morris, postmaster general for Canada from 1851 to 1853. Sir James Pliny Whitney (1843-1914) was born in the township and first elected to the Ontario legislature in 1888 where he served as leader of the opposition for nine years. With the Liberal defeat in 1905 he became Ontario's sixth premier, a post he held until his death.

MOUNT ALBERT

Pop. 1,894. In the Reg. Mun. of York, on C. Rd. 13, 2 km E of Hwy. 48, 39 km N of Toronto. First known as Birchardtown, the community was called Newland when the post office was established in 1852. The name was changed to Mount Albert in 1864. The origin of the name is not known.

MOUNT BRYDGES

Pop. 1,557. In Caradoc T., Middlesex C., on Hwy. 81 and C. Rd. 14, 24 km SW of London. The community arrived with the Great Western Railway (now the Canadian National Railway) in 1854. The place was first known as Hartford and then Caradoc after the township. It was later named Mount Brydges. The Mount is because it stands on the highest point of land in the area and Brydges was to honour C. J. Brydges, general manager of the Grand Trunk Railway from 1861 to 1874.

MOUNT ELGIN

Pop. 288. In Oxford T., Oxford C., on Hwy. 19 and C. Rd. 18, 25 km SW of Woodstock. The post office was established as Mount Elgin in 1851. The history of the community and the origin of its name are not known.

MOUNT FOREST

Pop. 3,713. In Arthur T., Wellington C., on the S branch of the Saugeen River and Hwys. 6 & 89, 69 km S of Owen Sound. Settlement followed shortly after the original survey of the Garafraxa Road made by Charles Rankin between Fergus and Owen Sound. The survey was started in 1837, interrupted by the Mackenzie Rebellion and completed in 1841. When the post office was established in 1851 it was named Maitland

River, as the South Saugeen River was then called. The place was also called Maitland Bush, Maitland Hills, and Maitland Woods. In 1853 the post office was renamed Mount Forest.

MOUNT HOPE

Pop. 557. In Glanbrooke T., Reg. Mun. of Hamilton-Wentworth on Hwy. 6, 13 km S of Hamilton. The community was first called Briggs Corner after the first settler, Alma Briggs. The post office was established as Glanford in 1847, and in 1872 the name was changed to Mount Hope after a church built on a hill. A plaque at Hamilton Civic Airport in Mount Hope commemorates Canadian women aviators. In 1928, after training in Hamilton, Eileen Vollick became the first woman in Canada to hold a private pilot's licence.

MOUNT PLEASANT

Pop. 700. In Brantford T., Brant C., on C. Rds. 24 & 26, 5 km S of Brantford. First settled in 1799 by Henry Ellis who named the place after his home in Wales. In 1840, well-heeled Scottish shoemaker Richard Tennant built a unique octagonal home, which had a number of owners, including The Royal Canadian Legion, before becoming a restaurant in 1974. There are half a dozen or more octagonal buildings across Ontario, but no others with eight roof gables. Mount Pleasant native Augusta Stowe Gullen (1857-1943) was the first woman to graduate in medicine from a Canadian university. With her mother, Dr. Emily Stowe, she was a forceful leader in the struggle for female suffrage.

MOUNT SALEM

Pop. 230. In Malahide T., Elgin C., on C. Rds. 40 & 45, 26 km SE of St. Thomas. The place was first called Hamburg, but when the post office opened in 1853 it was named Salem. In 1868 the name was modified to Mount Salem.

MUNSTER

Pop. 1,544. In the Reg. Mun. of Ottawa-Carleton, on C. Rd. 45, 37 km SW of Ottawa. When the post office was established in 1864, some residents wanted to call their community Tibbins Corners after an early settler. There were many settlers of Irish origin, so the name eventually chosen was Munster after a city in Ireland.

MURILLO

Pop. 271. In Oliver T., Thunder Bay Dist., 32 km W of Thunder Bay. The post office was established as Murillo Station in 1880, but "station" was soon dropped and the name now is officially Murillo. The origin of the name is not known.

NAIRN

Pop. 249. In East Williams T., Middlesex C., on the Ausable River and C. Rd. 19, 36 km NW of London. Donald McIntosh, an agent of the Canada Land Company, established the village and built mills. He named the settlement after Nairn in Scotland. The post office opened as Nairn in 1857, and closed in 1914. Sir George W. Ross (1841-1914), born in Nairn, was a teacher and school inspector before he entered politics in 1872. Following the retirement of A. S. Hardy, Ross became the fifth premier of Ontario, from 1899 to 1905.

NAIRN CENTRE

Pop. 459. In Nairn T., Sudbury Dist., on the Spanish River and Hwy. 17, 51 km SW of Sudbury. When the Canadian Pacific Railway's Algoma Branch from Sudbury to Sault Ste. Marie was completed in 1886, the only buildings on the site of what is now Nairn Centre were the station, the section house, and the shanties of itinerant trappers and lumberjacks. The station then was known as Nelson. The new village took the name of Nairn at the suggestion of an engineer from Nairn, Invernesshire, Scotland. In 1897 the post office, previously called Nelsonville, also took the name Nairn Centre.

NAKINA

Pop. 900. In Nakina T., Thunder Bay Dist., on Hwy. 584, 66 km N of Geraldton. In 1913 Nakina was a construction base for workers on the National Transcontinental Railway. In 1923, when Canadian National Railways took over the line, the divisional point was transferred from Grant (west of Cochrane) to Nakina. A post office was established in 1923. Nakina is an Indian word meaning "land covered with moss."

NANTICOKE

Pop. 20,441. City in Reg. Mun. of Haldimand-Norfolk formed through amalgamation of the towns of Port Dover and Waterford and the village of Jarvis and the annexation of parts of Rainham, Townsend, Walpole, and Woodhouse townships. Nanticoke is a Delaware Indian name meaning "crooked creek." The original community of Nanticoke is 2 km north of the mouth of Nanticoke Creek and Lake Erie, 12 km southeast of Simcoe.

NAPANEE

Pop. 4,604. In Richmond and North Fredericksburgh ts., Lennox and Addington C., on the Napanee River, 11 km from its mouth at the Bay of Quinte off Lake Ontario on Hwys. 2 & 41 and C. Rds. 8, 9, and 24, just

S of Hwy. 401, 38 km W of Kingston. In 1785 the government commissioned a United Empire Loyalist from New York, Robert Clark, to build a mill at Appanea Falls on the Napanee River—then known as the Appanea River. The mill was operated by government agent James Clark, and the place became known as Clarkville. In 1799 the mill was purchased by Kingston businessman Richard Cartwright, and the settlement was called Cartwrightville. By 1812 the river and community were known as Napanee, an Indian word for "flour." The post office was established in 1820 as Napanee Mills but the "Mills" was soon dropped. The Macpherson House, built prior to 1830 by Allan Macpherson, Napanee's first postmaster, is a fine example of late Georgian architecture and now home of the Lennox and Addington Historical Society.

NAUGHTON

Pop. 1,028. In Graham T., Nipissing Dist., on C. Rd. 55, 18 km SW of Sudbury. In 1824 the Hudson's Bay Company built a trading post at Whitefish Lake to discourage independent traders from working the area north of the French River. In 1887 the post was moved to Naughton to facilitate rail shipments. The post office was opened in 1902 as Naughton. Naughton was first named McNaughtonville after Andrew McNaughton from Sudbury. McNaughton went for a walk in the woods and got lost in fog, touching off a successful manhunt.

NAVAN

Pop. 1,392. In Reg. Mun. of Ottawa-Carleton, on C. Rd. 28, 24 km E of Ottawa. The post office was established as Navan in 1861. The origin of the name is not known.

NEPEAN

Pop. 97,883. City in the Reg. Mun. of Ottawa-Carleton adjoining Ottawa to the W. The city was incorporated in 1978, but the settlement had its beginnings in 1809. In that year, Ira Honeywell started clearing land on 1,000 acres (405 ha) given to him by his father, a United Empire Loyalist, who had been granted the land after it was surveyed in 1798. The township and city were named after Sir Evan York Nepean, an English nobleman, who served as under-secretary in the Colonial Department until 1795.

NESTOR FALLS

Pop. 315. In Godson T., Kenora Dist., on Hwy. 71, 87 km NW of Fort Frances. A summer post office was established in 1935; it became a year round post office in 1937. The origin of the name is not known.

NEUSTADT

Pop. 519. In Normanby T., Grey C., on the S fork of the Saugeen River and

C. Rds. 10 & 16, 64 km S of Owen Sound. The first settler, in 1855, was David Winkler, a native of Germany. He laid out a village, which was soon peopled by German immigrants. The post office opened in 1856 as Newstead and the following year the name was changed to Neustadt, German for "new town." In the early 1900s several fires destroyed a number of village businesses, and in 1908 a flood washed away many village streets and most of the wooden sidewalks. The village is the birthplace of John George Diefenbaker, 13th prime minister of Canada, from 1957 to 1963.

NEWBORO
Pop. 268. In North Crosby and South Crosby ts., Leeds and Grenville C., on the N shore of Newboro Lake and Hwy. 42, 62 km NE of Kingston. The site of the community was a portage point on the Ottawa-Kingston route. It was first known as The Isthmus, or Isthmus. Settlement dates to 1827 when two companies of the British army's construction corps, the Royal Sappers and Miners, worked on building the Rideau Canal. The area surrounding The Isthmus had long been settled by United Empire Loyalists but lack of waterpower had left the isthmus virtually unoccupied. In 1824, the home of William Buck Stevens was the only one at the site. When the Rideau Canal was completed, steamboats began plying the waterway, and a stagecoach service was started from Newboro. The first sod for the Brockville to Westport Railway was turned at Newboro in 1886, and the line was completed in 1888. Over the years there were many fires; the worst, called the Kennedy Fire, in 1874, destroyed 26 buildings. The growing community called itself New Borough, and the post office opened in 1836 as Newboro.

NEWBURGH
Pop. 640. In Camden East T., Lennox and Addington C., on the Napanee River, 11 km N of Napanee and C. Rds. 2, 11, & 17, 30 km NW of Kingston. Newburgh was once the largest incorporated village in Ontario. The first of a number of sawmills was built in 1824, and the place was known as The Hollow. When three Americans with shady business practices moved in, the name was changed to Rogue's Hollow. One of the Americans was influential, and when the post office opened in 1846, he had it named Newburg after his hometown on the Hudson River in New York. The "H" was added in 1862. In 1887 a fire destroyed all of Newburgh's stores and numerous homes, a total of 84 buildings; within the year, 66 structures had been rebuilt. In 1872, brothers John and James Thomson from New Jersey, established the Newburgh Paper Mills, using their revolutionary process for producing paper from wood pulp.

NEWBURY

Pop. 398. In Mosa T., Middlesex C., on C. Rd. 1, 47 km NE of Chatham. The community had its beginnings with the arrival of the Great Western Railway in 1851 and was first called Wardsville Station. In the same year, Robert Thompson built the first house. When the post office opened in 1854, Thompson became the postmaster. The name chosen was Newbury; somehow, the post office opened as Newburg, but the error was soon corrected. The origin of the name is not known.

NEWCASTLE

Pop. 37,769. Town in Reg. Mun. of Durham, on Lake Ontario 80 km E of Toronto. The town was formed in 1974 by the amalgamation of the Village of Newcastle, the Town of Bowmanville, the townships of Clarke and Darlington, and the police village of Orono. Newcastle was the name of a port south of Brighton, named after the county seat of Northumberland in England. It was to have been the capital of the newly created Newcastle District, but the idea was dropped after the sinking of the schooner *Speedy* off Presqu'ile. The *Speedy* was en route to the new capital for a murder trial. The defendant, judge, jury, and many influential people of the time were lost in the shipwreck.

In 1868, Samuel Wilmot established one of the earliest full-scale fish hatcheries in North America on the banks of nearby Wilmot Creek. Joseph E. Atkinson (1865-1948) began his publishing career as a teenager collecting outstanding debts here for the *Port Hope Times*. In 1899 he became editor and manager of the *Toronto Evening Star*, which he built into Canada's largest daily newspaper. Massey-Ferguson, one of the world's largest manufacturers of farm machinery, started here as a modest family business in 1848. Under three generations of enterprising Masseys the company prospered and in 1879 was relocated from Newcastle to larger premises in Toronto.

NEWCASTLE VILLAGE

Pop. 2,065. In Reg. Mun. of Durham, just N of Lake Ontario and Hwys. 2, 35, 115, and 401, 80 km E of Toronto. The present-day Newcastle Village was first known as Ragg Corner, after a Major Ragg, until 1838 when a company was formed to build Bond Head Harbour, named after Sir Francis Bond Head, lieutenant-governor of Upper Canada at the time. The community was called Bond Head from 1838 to 1853 when the name was changed to Port Newcastle. The post office was established in 1845 as Newcastle. Newcastle was incorporated as a village in 1857 and is now called Newcastle Village to distinguish it from the Town of Newcastle formed in 1974 by regional government.

NEW DUNDEE
Pop. 1,358. In Wilmont T., Waterloo C., on Alder Creek, and C. Rd. 12, 16 km SW of Kitchener. John Miller settled in 1830 and called the place Bonnie New Dundee after the city on the Firth of Tay in Scotland. When the post office was established in 1852, the name chosen was New Dundee.

NEW HAMBURG
Pop. 3,923. In Wilmot T., Reg. Mun. of Waterloo, on the Nith River and Hwys. 7 & 8, 19 km SW of Kitchener. Settlement began in the early 1830s with a group of about 50 English and German immigrants. A grist mill built by Josiah Cushman formed the nucleus of the community. Many died in a cholera epidemic that swept the area in 1834. The post office was established in 1851 as New Hamburg after Hamburg in Germany. The town possesses a charter issued by Queen Victoria to the Wilmot Agricultural Society granting the privilege of setting up a market and carrying on business.

NEWINGTON
Pop. 207. In Osnabruck T., Stormont, Dundas, and Glengarry C., on C. Rds. 12 & 14, 37 km NW of Cornwall. Jacob Baker was the first settler. When the post office was established in 1862, he became the postmaster and named the place Newington after his hometown of Newington-on-Stoke in England.

NEW LISKEARD
Pop. 5,159. In Dymond T., Timiskaming Dist. at the N end of Lake Timiskaming at the mouth of the Wabi River, on Hwy. 11, 8 km N of Haileybury and 160 km N of North Bay. The first settler was William Murray who built a house in the early 1890s. A short time later the Ontario government opened up four townships at the head of Lake Timiskaming and Crown Land Agent John Armstrong persuaded Murray to subdivide some of his land for a townsite. There was limited development until 1896 when Thomas McCamus and Angus McKelvie built a sawmill at the mouth of the river. In that year a post office was established as Thornloe, after a bishop. Armstrong managed to have the name changed to Liskeard, after his hometown in Cornwall, England. When there was confusion with the southern Ontario town of Leskard, the name was changed to New Liskeard. In 1903, when railway workers discovered one of the world's largest deposits of silver at nearby Cobalt, the population soared.

NEW LOWELL
Pop. 244. In Sunnidale T., Simcoe C., on Coates Creek and C. Rd. 9, 27 km SW of Barrie. The site was first settled by the Paton family in 1853.

Two years later the Northern Railway built a line through the area. Among those attracted to the area was the American firm of Jacques and Hay from Lowell, Mass. In 1860 the company established lumber mills and a wood products factory, which produced spindles and curled hair for furniture upholstery. When the post office opened in 1856, the settlement was named Sunnidale Station. In the 1860s the community was renamed New Lowell by the furniture company after its head office in Massachusetts.

NEWMARKET

Pop. 37,277. In Reg. Mun. of York on the Holland River and Hwy. 9, just E of Hwy. 11, 48 km N of Toronto. The place was settled around 1801 when Timothy Rogers and Samuel Lundy, Quakers from Pennsylvania, secured land grants for a number of Quaker "friends." In 1810 the Religious Society of Friends built a frame meeting house that was the first permanent place of worship in this part of the province and which still stands. After 1806, when Elisha Beman came from New York State and erected mills and a distillery, the place was called Beman's Corners. The settlement soon became an important trading centre for people who previously had to travel to Toronto to do their marketing. The Indians, too, found a new market when William Roe opened a fur-trading depot in 1816. When the post office was established in 1823, settlers asked that the place be called Newmarket. The author of the *Jalna* novels, Mazo de la Roche (1879-1961), was born in Newmarket. She wrote numerous plays, poems, short stories, and articles, but it was her chronicles of the Whiteoak family that gained her an international reputation.

NEWTONVILLE

Pop. 478. In the Town of Newcastle, Reg. Mun. of Durham on Hwy. 2, 18 km SW of Port Hope. The community was laid out in 1834 and was first known as Clarke Village after the township in which it was then located. In 1835 the post office was established as Clarke. In 1946 the name was changed to Newtonville. The origin of the name is not known.

NIAGARA FALLS

Pop. 70,540. City in the Reg. Mun. of Niagara, on the Niagara River and Hwys. 20, QEW and the Niagara Parkway, 20 km SE of St. Catharines. The city is connected to Niagara Falls, N.Y. by three bridges—the Rainbow, Whirlpool Rapids, and Cantilever bridges. Father Louis Hennepin was the first white man to see Niagara Falls, and he told the world about it in grossly exaggerated reports published in Europe. (The Falls are 176 feet [53.64 m] high; Hennepin described their height as 600 feet [182.8 m.]) By the 1790s the region was fairly well populated but settlement was scattered. The first village in the area was Drummondville, formed in 1831 and named for Gen. Sir Gordon Drummond. The Village of Clifton was started by Capt. Ogden Creighton in 1832. Samuel Zimmerman built the first bridge across the Niagara Gorge in 1848 and founded the Village of Elgin in 1855. The post office, established in 1852, was called Suspension Bridge. In 1881 the post office name was changed to Niagara Falls. Niagara, the name assigned to the area, derives from an Indian word Onghiara or Oniawgarah meaning "thundering waters."

The thundering falls and cliff-lined Niagara Gorge have drawn daredevils to the place since 1828. That's when Sam Patch, Niagara's first stuntman, set up a 100-foot (30.4-m) tower near Goat Island above the Falls and made two jumps without injury. The crowds weren't generous when Patch passed the hat, so he took his act to the Genessee River in New York State and died on his first jump. In the late 1850s, Frenchman Jean Francois Gravelet, billing himself as The Great Blondin, walked a tightrope across the gorge. When a mere walk no longer satisfied spectators, Blondin expanded his act to include somersaults, walking blindfolded, and riding a bicycle. He made the trip with his hands and feet manacled, cooked an omelette on his tightrope, and once lowered a rope to the *Maid of the Mist*, hauled up a bottle of champagne, and drank it. In 1901 Annie Taylor became the first person to go over the Falls in a barrel. She was unhurt. A decade later, Englishman Bobby Leach made the trip in an all-steel barrel. He was badly injured but after six months in hospital began wandering the world, capitalizing on his exploit. Fifteen years later, in New Zealand, he slipped on an orange peel and died of complications from a leg fracture. Eight people have survived plunging over the Falls in a variety of contraptions; the list of those who have perished is much longer.

NIAGARA-ON-THE-LAKE

Pop. 12,050. In Reg. Mun. of Niagara, on Lake Ontario at the mouth of the Niagara River, 24 km N of Niagara Falls. The region was settled in the late 1700s by United Empire Loyalists, who had been forced to leave their homes after the American Revolutionary War. The settlers were led into the area by Butler's Rangers, a renowned corps stationed at Fort Niagara under the command of Lieut-Col. John Butler. The community had been called Lenox, West Niagara, and British Niagara by the time Lt.-Gov. John Graves Simcoe arrived in 1792, proclaiming the town the capital of Upper Canada. He renamed it Newark, as the place had provided an "ark" of safety for the Loyalists. The first five sessions of the legislature of Upper Canada were held at Newark, but in 1796 the capital was moved further away from the American border, to York, (now Toronto). In 1798 the name Newark was changed to Niagara. (Niagara derives from an Indian word Onghiara or Oniawgarah meaning "thundering waters.") In 1813 Niagara was burned to the ground by retreating American forces. In 1903 the name was changed to Niagara-on-the-Lake to avoid confusion with Niagara Falls.

The Niagara Agricultural Society, founded in 1792, was the first organization in Ontario devoted to the advancement of agriculture. In addition to distributing information on breeding and planting technologies, the society introduced several varieties of fruit into the Niagara Peninsula. The first newspaper to be published in Ontario, the *Upper Canada Gazette*, was produced at Newark for five years before moving to Toronto. It was a semi-official and then official organ of the government and continued publishing under various names until 1845. The first independent newspaper in Upper Canada was the *Canada Constellation*, published at Newark by brothers Gideon and Sylvester Tiffany from 1799 to 1800. The enterprise died in its first year from lack of government aid and insufficient subscribers.

The Law Society of Upper Canada was founded in Newark in 1797 to regulate the activities and responsibilities of the legal profession. In 1832 it moved to new quarters in Osgoode Hall in Toronto. The Niagara Library, established in 1800 with a collection of 80 books, was the first circulating library in Upper Canada. St. Mark's Anglican Church was built between 1804 and 1810 and during the War of 1812 was used as a hospital by the British and as a barracks by the Americans. St. Andrew's Church, an outstanding example of Greek Revival ecclesiastical architecture, was built in 1831 to replace an earlier Presbyterian church burned by American forces in 1813. It still contains its original high pulpit and box pews, typical of the 1830s, but rarely found in Ontario today.

NICKEL CENTRE

Pop. 11,063. Part of the Town of Coniston in the Reg. Mun. of Sudbury, 20 km NE of Sudbury. Nickel Centre was created by regional government in 1973.

NIPIGON

Pop. 2,377. In Nipigon T., Thunder Bay Dist., on Nipigon Bay of Lake Superior at the mouth of the Nipigon River and Hwys. 11 & 17, 107 km NE of Thunder Bay. Six to seven thousand years ago, the first known surface mining of copper in the Americas was being conducted throughout this region of the Lake Superior basin. The copper was traded extensively and used for tool-making by native people in the area until the introduction of iron by European traders. The town grew up on the site of a trading post established in 1678 by Daniel Greysolon, Sieur Dulhut (or DuLuth), and replaced in 1820 by a Hudson's Bay Company post called Red Rock House. (Dulhut was a French soldier who, in 1678,

NNN

explored the Sioux country around Lake Superior, claiming what is now Minnesota, for France. The city of Duluth, Minn. was named in his honour.) The post office was established in 1872 as Red Rocks. The name refers to the Palisades of the Pijitawabik—pillar-like cliffs that rise along the Lake Nipigon shoreline about 38 km north of Nipigon. In 1889 the post office was renamed Nipigon, an Indian word meaning "deep, clear water," or "water full of fish" or "the lake you cannot see the end of."

NIPISSING

Pop. 718. In Nipissing T., Parry Sound Dist., on South River, 6 km S of Lake Nipissing and Hwy. 654, 30 km S of North Bay. Settlement started with completion of the Rosseau-Nipissing Road, authorized by the government in 1864 and open for winter traffic by 1873. A post office was established in 1870 as Nipissingan and changed in 1881 to Nipissing, an Indian name meaning "little water." The same name was given to Lake Nipissing, relating its size to nearby Georgian Bay.

NOBEL

Pop. 766. In McDougall T., Parry Sound Dist., on Hwy. 69, 11 km NW of Parry Sound. The post office was established as Ambo in 1910. The community is a company town centred around Canadian Industries Ltd. (CIL), which operates an explosives plant. In 1913 CIL changed the name of the community to Nobel to honour Alfred Bernhard Nobel (1833-1896), the chemist and inventor who patented gunpowder in 1863 and dynamite in 1866 and who was the founder of the Nobel Prize for Peace.

NOBLETON

Pop. 2,200. In Reg. Mun. of York, on Hwy. 27 and C. Rd. 11, 45 km NW of Toronto. Settlement began in 1812, and the place is named after Joseph Noble, an early storekeeper. In 1857 William Munsie changed the name of the post office to Lammer Moor. The villagers objected and the name was changed back to Nobleton.

NOELVILLE

Pop. 460. In Cosby, Mason, and Martland United T., Nipissing Dist. on Hwys. 64 and 535, 68 km SW of Sturgeon Falls. The place was first called Cosby, after the township, when the post office opened in 1904. In 1911 the name was changed to Noelville after former lumberman and store owner, Noel Desmarais.

NORLAND

Pop. 368. In Laxton and Somerville ts., Victoria C., on the Gull River near its mouth on the W shore of Shadow Lake and Hwys. 35 & 503, 46 km N of Lindsay. By 1860 the community was known as McLaughlin's Mills after a sawmill and grist mill built by early settler Alexander A.

McLaughlin on the Gull River. When the post office was being named in 1862, Rev. Bayard Taylor, a guest at the time of Mr. McLaughlin, suggested the name Nordland after a village in Africa where he had been working. It was decided to omit the "d" and make the name Norland, indicating the small community was at the end of civilization in Victoria County.

NORTH AUGUSTA

Pop. 289. In Augusta T., Leeds and Grenville C., on Kemptville Creek and C. Rds. 15 & 28, 24 km NW of Brockville. The place was first known as Bellamy's Mills after brothers Edward, Samuel, Chauncey, and Hiram Bellamy who came to the area in the 1820s and took over a sawmill owned by the original Loyalist settler, Daniel Dunham. The brothers added a grist mill, distillery, potashery, and general store. Another early settler was tanner Aaron B. Pardee, who was a prominent figure in the Sons of Temperance movement and to whose memory an imposing monument stands in the local Presbyterian cemetery. Ironically, he was a cousin of the Bellamy brothers whose enterprises included a distillery. The divisions within the Methodist Church before Church Union in 1884 were clearly visible within the small community. In 1871, when the population totalled 400, there were three Methodist churches: the Wesleyan Methodist, the Episcopal Methodist, and the New Connection Methodist. The origin of the community's name is not known.

NORTH BAY

Pop. 51,313. In Nipissing Dist. at the NE end of Lake Nipissing and Hwys. 11, 17, & 63, 125 km E of Sudbury. The city's site is on the old Nipissing passageway part of the northern route travelled by fur traders. Etienne Brûlé visited in 1610 and Samuel de Champlain in 1615, and trading posts were established. Permanent settlement didn't start until the Canadian Pacific Railway arrived in 1882 and then it carried on with a vengeance; within 43 years North Bay was incorporated as a city. Early settler John Ferguson is credited with unwittingly giving the place its name when he ordered building materials from Pembroke and asked that they be shipped to him at the north bay (of Lake Nipissing.) North Bay calls itself "Gateway to the North."

NORTHBROOK

Pop. 378. In Kaladar T., Lennox and Addington C., on Beaver Creek and Hwy. 41, 62 km NW of Napanee. The place was first called Flint's Mills and the post office opened in 1856 as Flint. The following year the name was changed to Kaladar, after the township. In 1890 the community was renamed Northbrook.

NORTH COBALT

Pop. 1,133. In Timiskaming Dist., on Hwy. 11B, 3 km NE of Cobalt, 10 km S of New Liskeard. The settlement was first known as Port Cobalt and then Argentile Station. The name was changed to North Cobalt in 1908. After the discovery of a major silver vein 3 km southwest of here in 1903, Ontario's first provincial geologist, Dr. Willet G. Miller, christened that place Cobalt after an element of the iron group associated with native silver.

NORTH GOWER

Pop. 1,253. In North Gower T., Carleton C., on Steven Creek, and C. Rds. 5, 6, & 73, 29 km S of Ottawa. The first settler, in 1820, was Stephen Blanchard after whom the creek was named Stephen Creek, and the community was named Stephensville. The post office opened in 1847 as North Gower after the township. Gower Township was named after Admiral John Levenson Gower, second son of the first earl of Gower.

NORTH PELHAM

Pop. 400. Part of the Town of Pelham in the Reg. Mun. of Niagara, 16 km NW of Welland. The first settlers in North Pelham were John Crowe in 1784 and Jacob Reece in 1786. The community was first known as Cook's Corners. When the post office was established in 1853, the village took its name from the township. Pelham derives from the family name of the duke of Newcastle.

NORTH SPIRIT LAKE

Pop. 203. In Kenora Dist., on the S. shore of North Spirit Lake, 298 km N of Dryden. The post office was established in 1972. The name is a translation of Memequish which is a Saulteaux Indian name for "butterfly," or "spirit of the woods."

NORTH WOODSLEE

Pop. 220. In Rochester T., Essex C., on Belle River and C. Rds. 27 & 46, 25 km SE of Windsor. The history of the community and the origin of its name are not known.

NORTH YORK

Pop. 544,560. A city within Metropolitan Toronto, formerly a borough of Metropolitan Toronto. The City of North York is bounded on the N by the Ts. of Vaughan and Markham; on the E by the City of Scarborough; on the S by the Borough of E York and on the W by the Humber River. Lester Bowles Pearson (1897-1972) was born in North York. He was the first Canadian to win the Nobel Prize, which was awarded for his peace-making role in the Suez Crisis of 1956. He was prime minister of Canada from 1963 to 1968. The Hon. George Stewart Henry (1871-1958) was also born in North York and began his political career as a councillor for York Township. He was premier of Ontario from 1930 to 1934.

NORVAL

Pop. 490. Part of the Town of Halton Hills, Reg. Mun. of Halton on the Credit River and Hwy. 7 and C. Rds. 10 & 19, 10 km SW of Brampton. The community was founded by James McNabb, a veteran of the Battle of Queenston Heights in the War of 1812. In 1820 McNabb built a dam across the Credit River and established flour, flax, and sawmills. His leg was crushed by a millstone in 1830, and had to be amputated above the knee, after which he leased his mills to John Barnhart. The place was first called McNabbville, but when a post office was opened in the mid-1800s it was named Norval, possibly for Norval Creek in Vermont from which area a number of settlers had come.

NORWICH

Pop. 2,117. In Norwich T., Oxford C., on Hwy. 59 and C. Rd. 18, 23 km S of Woodstock. In 1810, brothers-in-law Peter Lossing and Peter De Long purchased 15,000 acres (6,075 ha) in Norwich Township. The following year nine families from Dutchess County, New York joined them to form the nucleus of one of the most successful Quaker settlements in Upper Canada. The place was first named Norwichville and was also known as Quaker's Village because the Society of Friends (Quakers) had established two meeting houses. When the post office opened in 1830, the settlement was called Norwich after Norwich in Norfolk, England. Emily Howard Jennings Stowe (1831-1903) was born in Norwich Township to Quaker parents. She became the first female physician to practise in Canada and was a passionate advocate for social reform.

NORWOOD

Pop. 1,225. In Asphodel T., Peterborough C., on the River Ouse and Hwys. 7 & 45 and C. Rd. 40, 26 km NE of Peterborough. In 1824, Joseph A Keeler, from Colborne, began operating a mill he had built on land granted him for his services in the War of 1812. The community was known as Keeler's Mills until the post office opened in 1841 as Norwood. Keeler's daughter suggested the name, having found it in a book describing a suburb of London, England.

OOO

OAK RIDGES

Pop. 2,500. Part of the Town of Richmond Hill in the Reg. Mun. of York, on Hwy. 11 and C. Rd. 11, 32 km N of Toronto. Windham was the name of the dePuisaye Huguenot settlement on Yonge St. in 1799. It later became the distinct communities of Oak Ridges and Jefferson. The post office opened as Oak Ridges in 1851. Oak Ridges was named for large oak trees on a high ridge.

OAKVILLE

Pop. 98,404. In the Reg. Mun. of Halton, on Lake Ontario at the mouth of Sixteen Mile Creek and on Hwy. 2 and the QEW, 35 km SW of Toronto and 35 km NE of Hamilton. The town was founded by Col. William Chisholm who had moved with his United Empire Loyalist parents to the nearby Burlington Beach area in 1793. In 1827 Chisholm bought land at the mouth of Sixteen Mile Creek, built mills, laid out a town plot, and opened the harbour to shipping. The settlement was first called Sixteen Mile Creek. Robert Baldwin Sullivan, a friend of Chisholm's, suggested the place be called Oakville for the white oak that grew there and were being used for barrel staves and later ship building. In 1855 the Great Western Railroad passed through Oakville, and in 1939 the Queen Elizabeth Way was opened, linking Oakville with Toronto and Niagara Falls. In 1953 the Ford Motor Company built an assembly plant in Oakville.

OAKWOOD

Pop. 601. In Mariposa T., Victoria C., on Hwy. 7 and C. Rd. 8, 11 km W of Lindsay. One of the first settlers was James Tift who arrived in 1833. The community was named for the forest of white oak that originally covered the area.

ODESSA

Pop. 902. In Ernestown T., Lennox and Addington C., on Millhaven Creek, and Hwy. 2, just S of Hwy. 401, 23 km W of Kingston. Joshua Booth, a United Empire Loyalist, was the first recorded landowner. He arrived with Jessup's Rangers in 1784. The Rangers were a Loyalist force raised in 1776 in the neighbourhood of Albany by Edward Jessup (1735-1816). John Link built a grist mill in 1830, and the post office opened as Mill Creek in 1838. The name was changed to Odessa in 1855 to commemorate the 1854 siege by the British during the Crimean War of the Russian city Odessa.

OIL CITY

Pop. 278. In Enniskillen T., Lambton C., on Hwy. 21, 40 km SE of Sarnia. The post office was established in 1874, and the community was named after the oil boom in the area.

OIL SPRINGS

Pop. 645. In Enniskillen T., Lambton C., on Black Creek, and Hwy. 21, 48 km SE of Sarnia. The first commercial oil well in North America started production in 1857 when J. M. Williams of Hamilton struck free oil in an excavated well. Later that year Williams built Canada's first oil refinery. The community, surveyed for settlement by W. H. Donnelly in 1832, was first called Black Creek because of a black, oily substance floating on the creek's water. The early settlers, who arrived in 1842, used the black gummy substance for medicinal purposes. The first gushing oil well began producing in 1861, and the oil stampede was on. The village was brightly lighted by fluid lamps; there were nine hotels, several saloons, and 12 general stores. A toll plank road connected Black Creek to Sarnia, and stage coaches ran four times daily. In 1859 Black Creek was renamed Oil Springs. The Oil Museum of Canada, with a working oil well on the property, is a tourist attraction.

OMEMEE

Pop. 872. In Emily T., Victoria C., on the Pigeon River at the foot of Pigeon Lake and Hwy. 7 and C. Rds. 7 & 38, 24 km W of Peterborough. In 1825 William Cottingham built a mill on the Pigeon River and a community began to form, largely made up of Irish Catholic immigrants from County Cork. The place was called Williamstown, after William Cottingham, until the post office opened in 1832 and was named Emily after the township. In 1857 the name was changed to Omemee after the Omemee (Pigeon) Indians, a sub-tribe of the Mississaugas, who had once hunted in the area.

OMPAH

Pop. 223. In Palmerston and North and South Canonto ts., Frontenac C., on the SE shore of Palmerston Lake and on Hwy. 509, 110 km N of Kingston. The post office opened as Ompah in 1865. Ompah is an Indian word meaning "long step" or long portage."

ONAPING

Pop. 974. In the Reg. Mun. of Sudbury, on C. Rd. 8, just N of Hwy. 144, 38 km NW of Sudbury. The post office was established as Onaping in 1956. Onaping is a Cree word meaning "red paint" or "vermillion."

ONAPING FALLS

Pop. 5,153. In the Reg. Mun. of Sudbury, formed in 1973 by the amalgamation of the Town of Levack and the Improvement Dist. of Onaping. First named Town of Dowling and changed to Town of Onaping Falls.

OPASATIKA

Pop. 450. In Cochrane Dist., on the Opasatika River and Hwy. 11, 30 km NW of Kapuskasing. Founded in 1923 by settlers from northern Quebec. The name is an Indian word for "drying place," in this case the drying of lumber cut at the sawmill.

ORANGEVILLE

Pop. 15,293. In Mono T. and East Garafraxa T., Dufferin C., on the Credit River and Hwys. 9, 10, 24, & 136, 70 km NW of Toronto. The first land patent was issued to land surveyor Ezekiel Benson in 1820. James Greggs built a saw- and flour mill in 1832, and Orange Lawrence built another sawmill in 1844. The community was called The Mills until the post office opened in 1851 as Orangeville after Orange Lawrence, the first postmaster.

ORILLIA

Pop. 23,893. In Orillia T., Simcoe C., at the S end of Lake Couchiching and Hwys. 11 & 12, 38 km NE of Barrie. Samuel de Champlain spent the winter of 1615 at the Huron capital of Cahiague, 14 km west of Orillia. Settlers didn't begin arriving until 1832, after the British government had built a reserve for the Chippewa Indians at the Narrows. The place was known by early settlers as Invermara, but when the post office was established in 1835 the settlement was called Orillia, believed to be taken from the Spanish word *orilla*, meaning riverbank. For a time the settlers and Chippewa villagers shared the site, but in 1838 the settlers petitioned the government to relocate the Indians at Rama on the other side of Lake Couchiching, and a village was built for them there in 1839. Canadian historian and humourist Stephen Butler Leacock, head of McGill University's faculty of political science, spent his summers at nearby Old Brewery Bay. In his best-known comic novel, *Sunshine Sketches of a Little Town*, he parodied many of Orillia's leading citizens, some of whose descendants still have not forgiven him. In 1957, Leacock's house and library were bought by the town and turned into a museum, the Stephen Leacock Memorial Home.

In 1906 the Tudhope factory was producing high-wheeled automobiles called the Tudhope-McIntyre. These were followed by the Everett and the Fisher. During the First World War the factory turned to the manufacture of war supplies and did not resume automobile manufacturing after the war. Leslie Frost, premier of Ontario from 1949 to 1961 was a native of Orillia. Writer Mazo de la Roche attended school there and songwriter/singer Gordon Lightfoot was born there as was one of the world's greatest rowers, Jake Gaudaur. Franklin Carmichael (1890-1945), a founding member of the Group of Seven, was a native of Orillia. Historian and writer Goldwin Smith, (who died in 1910 and donated his Toronto home, The Grange, for the first Art Gallery of Ontario), gave land to Orillia for an unusual opera house, which was built in 1895. Smith stipulated the opera house must be combined with a farmers' market; both are still in operation.

ORLEANS

Pop. 17,226. In Reg. Mun. of Ottawa-Carleton, on the Ottawa River 1 km S of Hwy. 17, 14 km NE of Ottawa. The first settler was Joseph Viseneau. The post office was established in 1860 and named Orleans by Monsignor Ebrard for the French city. It was incorporated as a police village in 1922 under the name St. Joseph d'Orléans. The presently accepted name is Orleans.

ORONO

Pop. 1,931. In Clarke T., Durham C., on Orono Creek and Hwys. 35 & 115, 18 km N of Bowmanville. The post office was established in 1852. During a meeting in the blacksmith shop to select a name for the post office, a visitor from Maine is reported to have suggested Orono after a famous Indian chief.

ORWELL

Pop. 251. In Malahide T., Elgin C., on Hwy. 3, 8 km E of St. Thomas. The community was first called Catfish Corners. The post office opened as Temperanceville in 1849, and in 1856 the name was changed to Orwell. The origin of the name is not known.

OSGOODE

Pop. 1,300. In the Reg. Mun. of Ottawa-Carleton, on the Castor River and C. Rd. 114, 48 km S of Ottawa. One of the first settlers was Archibald McDonnell of Cornwall, who had been an officer in the Glengarry Militia before the War of 1812. During the war he was promoted to the post of deputy assistant adjutant-general on the staff of the general commanding the forces along the St. Lawrence frontier. He was often required to carry urgent military dispatches and on occasion stayed in the saddle for two days and two nights, sometimes literally riding his horse to death. For his services he was granted 800 acres (324 ha) of land in Osgoode Township, established in 1798 and named after then chief justice of Upper Canada, William Osgoode. The post office was established as Osgoode Station in 1881, and in 1962 the name was shortened to Osgoode.

OSHAWA

Pop. 120,904. City in the Reg. Mun. of Durham, on Lake Ontario at the mouth of Oshawa Creek and Hwys. 2 & 401, 51 km E of Toronto. The first settler arrived in 1791. After Edward Skea opened a store in 1835, the place became known as Skea's Corners. The first dock was built in 1840. When the post office was established in 1842 a meeting was held to determine a name. Several Indians from Lake Scugog were in town trading their furs and attended the meeting. They suggested the name Oshawa, which means "where the canoe is exchanged for the trail." As the community grew it gradually absorbed surrounding settlements including Gibbs Mills, Skea's Corners, Kedron, Cedarvale, Oshawa Port, Port Oshawa, Oshawa Junction, and Cedar Brae.

In 1878, Robert McLaughlin and his two sons moved their carriage company from nearby Enniskillen to Oshawa, expanding it into the largest carriage works in the British Empire. When the factory burned in 1899, the Town of Oshawa gave the company an interest-free loan of $50,000 because more than 600 residents were employed by the carriage works. As the motor car became popular, the McLaughlins moved with the times, producing their first McLaughlin-Buick motor car in 1907. The company evolved as General Motors of Canada Ltd. and Oshawa acquired the nickname "The Motor City." Visitors come to Oshawa today to see Parkwood (the estate of the late Colonel McLaughlin), the Canadian Automotive Museum, and Winfields Farm, one of Canada's premier stud farms. Oshawa native Gordon D. Conant (1885-1953) was Ontario's 12th premier, serving from 1942 to 1943.

OSNABURGH HOUSE

Pop. 600. On the N shore of Osnaburgh Lake (an extension of Lake St. Joseph and widening of the Albany River), on Hwy. 599, 262 km N of Ignace. A trading post of the Hudson's Bay Company was built in 1786 to counter inroads being made in the territory by the North West Company. The post was rebuilt in 1794 and closed from 1810 to 1815. Since 1815 it has been in continuous use. The post is sometimes called Albany House. The origin of the name Osnaburgh is not known.

OTTAWA

Pop. 303,747. Capital of the Dominion of Canada and city in Reg. Mun. of Ottawa-Carleton on the Ottawa and Rideau Rivers, and Hwys. 16, 17, 31, & 417, 110 km N of Brockville and 200 km W of Montreal. Ottawa is linked with Hull, Quebec, across the Ottawa River by five automobile bridges and one railway bridge. There were only a few settlers in the area when Col. John By and his Royal Engineers arrived in 1826 to construct the Rideau Canal, which would eventually link Ottawa with Kingston at Lake Ontario. The first settler on the site of what is now Ottawa was

Jehiel Collins, a United Empire Loyalist from Vermont. He settled at a canoe landing below Chaudiere Falls, and the place was known as Collins' Landing until he sold out to Caleb Bellows and returned to Vermont. The settlement was called Bellow's Landing and later, Richmond Landing. Colonel By laid out a townsite at the northern terminus of the 208-km-long canal project; by 1827 the settlement was known as Bytown. In 1855 the name was changed to Ottawa, after an Indian band that occupied an important position on the route between the Ottawa River and Georgian Bay.

The Canadian government dithered from 1841 to 1857 on selecting a site for the national capital. In 1857 it passed the buck—and the short list of five sites—to Queen Victoria. She chose Ottawa for five reasons, all of which were valid at the time: the site was politically acceptable to both Canada East and Canada West; it was centrally located; it was remote from the hostile United States; it was industrially prosperous, and it had a naturally beautiful setting at the confluence of two major rivers. The Parliament Buildings were in use by 1866, and Ottawa was confirmed in its status the following year by the British North America Act, which established the Dominion of Canada.

Thanks to the efforts of the National Capital Commission (NCC), Ottawa has remained beautiful. The NCC works with all municipalities within the 3,000-square-kilometre (1,158-sq-mi.) National Capital Region, (which includes neighbouring Hull and a big chunk of Quebec), to coordinate development in the best interests of the entire region. The result is a profusion of beautiful parks, bicycle paths, jogging trails, and the world's longest skating rink—a 6.4-km-long stretch of the Rideau Canal kept cleared and smooth and provided with heated huts, food concessions, and skate-sharpening and rental services. The city also contains a very long list of beautiful and/or historically important buildings and is the scene annually of hundreds of festivals, expositions, celebrations, presentations, and other special events.

OTTERVILLE
Pop. 665. In Norwich T., Oxford C., on Big Otter Creek and C. Rd. 19, 29 km SE of Woodstock. John Earls and Paul Avery settled the site in 1807 and built grist and sawmills. The post office was established in 1837, taking its name from the creek, along whose banks otter made their homes. The otter, a large member of the weasel family, is harvested in Canada for its valuable pelt.

OWEN SOUND
Pop. 19,913. In Grey C., on Owen Sound off Georgian Bay at the mouths of the Sydenham and Pottawattomi Rivers, and Hwys. 6, 10, 21, & 26 and C. Rds. 1 & 15, 63 km W of Collingwood. In 1616 Samuel de Champlain

visited an Indian encampment called Wadineednon, translated as "beautiful valley." By the early 1840s the site was the northern terminus of the Garafraxa Colonization Road and free land grants were offered along its length, subject to settlement duties. John Telfer, government-appointed land agent for the new town, was one of the first settlers, in 1842. The settlement was first known as Sydenham or Sydenham Bay after Lord Sydenham, governor-in-chief of Canada from 1838 to 1841. Sailors landing here called it Owen's Sound because the bay beside which it was located was named for Capt. William Fitzwilliam Owen who charted it in 1815. The post office opened in 1846, as Owens Sound; in 1857 Owens lost its "s." Owen Sound was the hometown of First World War flying ace William Avery "Billy" Bishop, credited with destroying 72 enemy aircraft and forming the Royal Canadian Air Force after the war. His boyhood home is a museum. Another popular tourist attraction is Tom Thomson Memorial Art Gallery. Thomson was a local artist, who inspired the formation of the Group of Seven Canadian painters.

OXDRIFT

Pop. 248. In Eton T., Kenora Dist., on Hwys. 17 & 605, 16 km NW of Dryden. The post office was established as Oxdrift in 1898. The place got its name from Swedish labourers watching some oxen cross a stream where the Canadian Pacific Railway line was under construction.

PAISLEY

Pop. 945. In Elderslie T., Bruce C., on the Saugeen River at the confluence of the Teeswater and Lockerby rivers and Willow Creek and C. Rds. 1, 3, & 11, 23 km NW of Walkertown. In the spring of 1851, Simon Orchard built a cedar raft at Walkerton, loaded his family and personal effects on to it, and floated down the Saugeen River in search of a new homestead. The first night they stopped at what is now Paisley and decided to settle there. Three weeks later he was joined by his brother-in-law, Samuel Rowe, who built the first tavern. The place was first called Mud River, but when the post office was established in 1872 it was named Paisley after the city in Renfrewshire, Scotland, an area from which many of the settlers had emigrated. Because there are six bridges inside its boundaries and three more nearby, Paisley is nicknamed the "Village of Bridges."

PAKENHAM

Pop. 351. In Pakenham T., Lanark C., on the Mississippi River and Hwy. 15 and C. Rd. 20, 15 km SE of Arnprior. John Powell and Robert Harvey settled in 1823. They built a log cabin and a grist mill on the riverbank, calling the site Little Falls. Because of the mill, the place was soon called Harvey's Mills. The post office was established in 1832 and took its name from the township. Packenham Township honours Sir Edward M. Pakenham, brother-in-law of the duke of Wellington, who was killed in 1815 at the Battle of New Orleans. A limestone bridge across a series of rapids in the Mississippi River, built at the turn of the century, is believed to be the only five-span stone bridge in North America.

PALERMO

Pop. 269. Part of the Town of Oakville, Reg. Mun. of Halton, on Hwys. 5 & 25, 15 km NE of Burlington. The place was settled in 1805 by Lawrence Hagar, a United Empire Loyalist from Maryland. The settlement was first called Hagartown. When the post office opened in 1837, a public meeting was held to select a new name for the community. Dr. William Cobban proposed the name Palermo to honour Lord Nelson, duke of Palermo.

PALGRAVE

Pop. 600. In the Reg. Mun. of Peel, on the Humber River and Hwy. 50, 43 km N of Brampton. The settlement was first known as Buck's Town after Barney "Buck" Dolan, an early hunter and tavern keeper. When the post office was established in 1869 the name Palgrave was "imposed" on the predominantly Irish population of Buckstown, according to the Ontario

Geographic Names Board. The community was so named to honour Englishman Sir Francis Turner Palgrave—poet, critic, and editor—who published the *Golden Treasury of English Songs and Lyrics.*

PALMER RAPIDS
Pop. 295. In Raglan T., Renfrew C., on the Madawaska River and Hwy. 515, 30 km SE of Barry's Bay. The post office was named Palmer Rapids in 1872 after a farmer who settled in the area in 1848.

PALMERSTON
Pop. 2,085. In Minto T., Wellington C., and Wallace T., Perth C., on the Maitland River and Hwy. 9 and C. Rds. 2 & 5, 70 km NW of Guelph. The first settler was Thomas McDowell, a native of Ireland, who arrived in 1854. The place was called Dryden when the post office opened in 1866. In 1872, at the suggestion of Township Reeve John McDermott, the community was renamed Palmerston to honour Lord Palmerston, prime minister of Great Britain. In 1855 the Ontario Vaccine Farm was established by local physician Dr. Alexander Stewart and was the first institution in Ontario to produce smallpox vaccine. In 1916 the operation was transferred to the University of Toronto.

PARIS
Pop. 7,907. In South Dumfries T., Brant C., at the confluence of the Grand and Nith rivers, and Hwys., 2, 5, & 24A, 29 km E of Woodstock. The first settler was William Holme, who arrived in 1821 and built a mill in which he ground plaster to sell as fertilizer to local farmers. The settlement then was called The Forks of the Grand River. In 1828, Vermont native Hiram Capron arrived, laid out a townsite and in 1832 built the first grist mill. Shortly after building the mill, Capron named the settlement Paris for the large plaster-of-Paris beds that he and partners bought in 1842 and developed into a profitable enterprise. His leadership in the community earned him the nickname "King." Capron built a mansion, later owned by textile magnate John Penman and called Penmarvian, which remains a local landmark. Penman left the house to the Presbyterian Church of Canada for use as a home by retired ministers. A plaque on a main street store commemorates the world's first long distance telephone call. Alexander Graham Bell received the call from nearby Brantford on Aug. 10, 1876. Nine cobblestone buildings in town and four in adjacent South Dumfries Township were erected by Levi Boughton between 1825 and 1865. Cobblestones six to nine inches long were set in horizontal rows in a bed of mortar.

PARKHILL
Pop. 1,471. In West Williams T., Middlesex C., on Parkhill Creek and Hwy. 81 just N of Hwy. 7, 50 km NW of London. Parkhill was established

in 1860 after the Grand Trunk Railway came through the area. The settlement was first known as Westwood, the name of the railway station, (so called because the place was in the west and in a deep woods of maple, beech, and oak). There was already a post office in Ontario by that name so the name was changed to Swainby for the hometown in Yorkshire, England, of postmaster James Plews. In 1864 the name was changed again to Park Hill, this time for Park Hill, Rosshire, Scotland, the hometown of prominent resident Simon McLeod. The community was plagued by fires and in one of them in 1882, the town's early records were lost.

PARRY ISLAND

Pop. 232. In Cowper T., Parry Sound Dist., on Parry Island in Parry Sound off Georgian Bay, 13 km SW of Parry Sound. The community takes its name from that of the district, named after Arctic explorer Sir Edward Parry. On Parry Island at Depot Harbour is the largest of Ontario's 300 ghost towns. Depot Harbour was founded over 100 years ago by timber baron John Rudolphus Booth, who built a rail line from Ottawa through Algonquin Park to Georgian Bay. When the railway reached Parry Sound, Booth refused to pay the inflated property prices residents asked for, so he built his own town on the island just south of Parry Sound. The population reached 3,000 before Booth sold his railway to Canadian National Railways, which moved the railhead to Parry Sound in 1928. (See entry under Parry Sound).

PARRY SOUND

Pop. 5,895. In Dist. of Parry Sound, on Parry Sound off Georgian Bay at the mouth of the Seguin River just off Hwy. 69, 85 km W of Huntsville. The Ojibway name for the place was Wausakausing, meaning "shining waters." The area was surveyed between 1822 and 1825 by Capt. Henry Wolsey Bayfield, who called the place Parry Sound for Sir William Edward Parry, the Arctic explorer. In 1857 the timber rights were owned by James and William Gibson of Willowdale and there was a small community. In 1863, William Beatty of Thorold came to Parry Sound with his father and brother in search of timber rights. They bought out the Gibsons and also entered the steamship business, becoming pioneers in the Canadian shipping industry. Their first vessel, the 200-ton (198 tonne) wooden sidewheeler *Waubuno*, was built for them in 1865 at Port Robinson in the Niagara Peninsula, and made weekly trips between Parry Sound and Collingwood. In 1879, bound for Parry Sound, it sank in a gale in Georgian Bay with a loss of 24 lives.

"William the Younger," as he became known. bought out his father's and older brother's interests in Parry Sound and laid out a townsite. He was a member of the Reform Party and a Wesleyan Methodist. To protect his community from the evils of alcohol he created the "Beatty Covenant," requiring purchasers of lots to sign an agreement prohibiting alcohol on their land. Violations meant forfeiture of the land. The agreement was held binding during the lives of Queen Victoria's children and for 20 years and 10 months after the deaths of all parties involved. The restrictions remained effective until a plebiscite was held in 1950! When John Rudolphus Booth was constructing his Ottawa, Arnprior, and Parry Sound Railway across the province, Beatty inflated land prices in the Parry Sound area. Booth bought nearby Parry Island and turned it into a booming railway terminus and Great Lakes port with a population of 3,000. When Canadian National Railways bought Booth's assets in 1928, it moved the railhead to Parry Sound and Parry Island became Ontario's largest ghost town. (See entry under Parry Island.) Canada's largest sightseeing cruise ship operates out of Parry Sound. The 550-passenger *Island Queen* offers daily cruises through the 30,000 Islands of Georgian Bay from June through Thanksgiving.

PAUDASH
Pop. 386. In Cardiff T., Haliburton C., on Hwys. 28 & 121, immediately NE of the NE tip of Paudash Lake, 13 km SW of Bancroft. The post office was established in 1888 as Paudash, the name being taken from the Indian chief, Captain Paudash.

PEFFERLAW
Pop. 1,491. In Reg. Mun. of York, on Pefferlaw Brook and C. Rd. 12, 85 km NE of Toronto, 4 km S of Lake Simcoe. The place was first called Johnson's Mills after its founder, a Lieutenant Johnson of the British Navy. In 1851, when the post office opened, it was named Pefferlaw, a Gaelic word meaning "beautiful hills."

PELEE ISLAND
Pop. 644. Part of Essex C., 13 km SW of Point Pelee in Lake Erie. Except for tiny Middle Island, Pelee Island is the southernmost point of Canada. The island was leased from the Indians in 1788 by Thomas McKee and purchased in 1823 by William McCormick for $500. In 1838 a combined force of infantry, militia, and Indians crossed the ice and routed some 300 American supporters of Mackenzie's Rebellion from Pelee Island. In 1865 three Kentuckians discovered the island's moderate climate was conducive to growing grapes. They founded a winery named Vin Villa which flourished until prohibition. In 1979 the Pelee Island Winery started business. Its grapes are processed on the mainland. The island's name is derived from the French word *pelee*, meaning "bare," or "bald." Each autumn 700 hunters arrive to fill 18,000 pheasants with buckshot. The island municipality has raised pheasants since 1932 and profits from the hunts help to reduce taxes.

PPP

PELHAM

Pop. 12,430. Town in the Reg. Mun. of Niagara. The town was formed by regional government in 1970 from the former T. of Pelham, which contained the communities of Fonthill, Ridgeville, Fenwick, and North Pelham. Pelham derives from the family name of the duke of Newcastle.

PEMBROKE

Pop. 13,595. City in Renfrew C., on the Ottawa River at the mouths of the Indian and Muskrat rivers opposite Allumette Island, Que., and Hwys. 41, 62, & 148, 4 km NE of Hwy. 17, 68 km NW of Arnprior. Peter White founded the settlement, arriving in 1828 after service with Nelson in the Baltic and Sir James Yeo's squadron on Lake Ontario during the War of 1812. The community developed in two sections—Lower Town, which became Campbelltown and then Moffatt, and Upper Town, which became Mirimichi and then Sydenham. In 1839 the communities joined and became Pembroke after the Hon. Sidney Herbert, a son of the earl of Pembroke and secretary of the British Admiralty. In 1884 Pembroke became the first Canadian community to pioneer commercial electric lighting.

PENETANGUISHENE

Pop. 5,533. In Tiny and Tay ts., Simcoe C., on Penetang Harbour off Georgian Bay and Hwy. 93, 53 km NW of Barrie. In the 1600s the place was the site of an Ojibway encampment named Wenrio and later another Indian settlement named Ihonatiria. In 1793 Lieutenant-Governor Simcoe chose the place as a naval headquarters and military post, which was active during the War of 1812. The fort garrisoned that year was Fort Penetanguishene, an Indian name meaning "white rolling sand." The first civilian home was built by Dedin Revolte in 1828. The property once occupied by the fort is now a provincial jail for the criminally insane. St. James-on-the-Lines Anglican Church, built to serve the military personnel stationed at the fort is still in use today. Its name derives from the line, or communications road, from Toronto to Penetanguishene. The church has a very wide central aisle to permit soldiers to march in, four abreast. The pews are all different from each other, their construction having been assigned to different men of the garrison.

PERKINSFIELD

Pop. 266. In Tiny T., Simcoe C., on C. Rds. 6 & 25, 10 km SW of Midland. The place was first known as Perkins for lumberman N. A. Perkins but the post office was established in 1880 as St. Patrick. In 1909 the name was changed to Perkinsfield.

PERTH

Pop. 5,463. In Drummond T., Lanark C., on the Tay River and Canal and Hwys. 7, 43, & 509, 83 km SW of Ottawa. In 1815, 700 Scottish immigrants landed at Quebec City and a number of them found their way to this area where they established a community on the River Tay, naming it Perth, after Perthshire in Scotland. A short time later, 2,000 veterans of the Peninsular War and the War of 1812 arrived, and Perth became a bustling centre for the territory, (now the counties of Renfrew, Lanark, and Carleton). The town connected itself to the Rideau Canal in 1833 by digging the 11-km-long Tay Canal, which was only used for a few years before railroads overtook shipping. In 1892 the world's largest cheese was manufactured at Perth for exhibition by the dominion government at the Chicago World's Fair. It measured six feet (1.8 m) in height and 28 feet (8.5 m) in circumference and weighed 22,000 pounds (9,979 kg). A cement replica stands on the grounds of the CPR station. The last fatal duel in Canada was fought in 1833 between law students John Wilson and Robert Lyon in what is now a park called Last Duel Park. The duelling pistols are in the Perth Museum.

PETAWAWA

Pop. 5,189. In Petawawa T., Renfrew C., on Allumette Lake (a widening of the Ottawa River), and near the mouth of the Petawawa River on Hwy. 17, 19 km NW of Pembroke. The village owes its large population to a nearby military camp, which opened as a summer camp in 1905 and became a permanent camp in 1916. The village and camp take their name from a corruption of the Indian name for the river, Pitwewe, meaning "where one hears the noise of the waters."

PETERBOROUGH

Pop. 62,005. City in Peterborough C., on both banks of the Otonabee River, part of the Trent Canal System, and Hwys. 7, 7A, 7B, 28, & 115, 122 km NE of Toronto. When the first settler, Adam Scott, arrived in 1821 to build a mill, the place was known by the Indians as Nogojiwanong, "the place at the end of the rapids." For a time the settlement was called Indian Plain, and then was known as Scott's Plains, Scott's Mills, and Scott's Landing. In 1825, in an effort to alleviate poverty and starvation in Ireland, the British government sponsored a settlement of Irish families in the area. Under the supervision of Peter Robinson, about 2,000 people from County Cork were established in the region in what became known as the Robinson Settlement. In 1829 the post office opened as Peterborough, in honour of Peter Robinson.

In 1870 Jonathan Stephenson built the first basswood canoe, now known as the Peterborough canoe and still in production. The incandescent lamp, invented by Thomas Edison, led to formation of the Edison

Electric Co., in Peterborough in 1890. Two years later the company changed its name to Canadian General Electric Co. A plaque in Fleming Park recalls Sir Sandford Fleming (1827-1915), who came from Scotland in 1845 and settled in Peterborough. Of his many achievements he is likely best known as the inventor of Standard Time, the universal system for reckoning time, which was adopted in 1884. The city's trademark is the world's highest Lift Lock on the Trent Canal, which lifts vessels—and the water in which they're floating—65 feet (19.8 m). The Hunter Street Bridge spanning the Otonabee River is the longest unreinforced concrete bridge in the world, and Centennial Fountain in Little Lake is the highest jet fountain in Canada, shooting water 250 feet (76 m) into the air.

PETERSBURG

Pop. 420. In Reg. Mun. of Waterloo, on C. Rds. 6 & 12, 10 km W of Kitchener. John Ernst was the first settler in 1832. The post office was established as Petersburg in 1842, named after Peter Wilker, a farmer and blacksmith and one of the early settlers, who died in 1889 at the age of 82.

PETROLIA

Pop. 4,168. In Enniskillen T., Lambton C., on Bear Creek, a tributary of the Sydenham River and C. Rd. 4, 1 km W of Hwy. 21, 26 km SE of Sarnia. Samuel Eveland was the first settler, in 1861. In that year oil was discovered both at Petrolia and Oil Springs, but developers were drawn first to Oil Springs. When production slowed at Oil Springs by about 1866, developers came to Petrolia and the community boomed. Fifteen wells were pumping and 100 drilling rigs were operating, burning 50,000 cords of wood a year. In the 1880s Imperial Oil was organized and it built the largest oil refinery in Canada. The place was first called Enniskillen after the township and then Durance after the first postmaster, in 1858, Daniel Durance. The following year the name was changed to Petrolea, derived from petroleum. The spelling Petrolia, by which the community is now known, was an early clerical error, which remained uncorrected.

PICKERING

Pop. 56,132. Town in Reg. Mun. of Durham created by regional government in 1974. The town was formed with parts of Pickering Township, excluding a portion annexed to the Town of Ajax and a portion annexed to the Borough of Scarborough, now the City of Scarborough.

PICKERING VILLAGE

Pop. 3,350. In the Town of Pickering, Reg. Mun. of Durham, on Duffin's Creek, 5 km from Pickering Harbour and Hwy. 2, 35 km E of Toronto. Augustus Jones surveyed the area in 1791 and found it abundant in game and fish. He named the creek after Duffin, an early Irish pioneer who disappeared in mysterious circumstances. Bloodstained boards in Duffin's cabin suggested that he had been murdered, but no evidence of that was ever found. The first settler was William Peak in about 1799, and others followed in 1801 and 1802; most had army connections and were therefore entitled to land grants. The place was called Canton until the post office was opened in 1829 as Pickering after Pickering in Yorkshire, England. In 1900 the word "Village" was added.

PICKLE LAKE

Pop. 527. In Ponsford T., Patricia Dist., on Pickle Lake and Kawinogans River and Hwy. 599, 292 km N of Ignace. The post office was established in 1976. The origin of the name is not known.

PIC RIVER I.R.

Pop. 266. In Pic T., Thunder Bay Dist., on Lake Superior at the mouth of the Pic River on Hwy. 627, 24 km SE of Marathon. There was a Hudson's Bay trading post on the site in the early 1800s. The origin of the name is not known.

PICTON

Pop. 4,049. In Hallowell T., Prince Edward C., on Picton Bay, an arm of the Bay of Quinte on Lake Ontario and Hwys. 33 & 49 and C. Rd. 17, 37 km SE of Belleville. Twin settlements of United Empire Loyalists developed at the head of Picton Bay, starting with Hallowell in 1786. Rev. William Macaulay founded a community on 500 acres (202.5 ha) of land granted to his United Empire Loyalist father. He named the place after Gen. Sir Thomas Picton, a major-general in the Napoleonic Wars. Macaulay built St. Mary Magdalene Church in 1825 and acted as its first rector. When Hallowell and Picton united in 1837, the influential Macaulay succeeded in retaining the name Picton.

The town has strong associations with Sir John A. Macdonald, Canada's first prime minister. Macdonald's father operated a flour mill here and young John practised law at the Greek Revival-style county courthouse while managing a law office for an ailing cousin. That courthouse, completed in 1834, is still in use, as is Macaulay's church. Just outside Picton is a small white frame church known as The White Chapel or Conger Chapel. It was the first meeting house, built by the Methodists in 1809, and has been maintained as a place of worship longer than any other Methodist church in Ontario. An historic plaque at Glenwood Cemetery recalls Letitia Youmans (1827-1896). She was a school teacher and mother who became publicly active in temperance reform in 1874 by organizing a Women's Christian Temperance Union in Picton. Later she served as first president of the W.C.T.U. of Ontario and of the federal organization. Sir Rodmond P. Roblin (1853-1937), a native of Prince Edward County, moved to Winnipeg at the age of 24 and entered provincial politics. During his influential years as premier of Manitoba (1900-1915) he ardently promoted western grain trade and railway expansion.

PIKANGIKUM I.R.

Pop. 1,091. In Kenora Dist., on the E shore of Pikangikum Lake, 75 air km N of Red Lake. The reserve belongs to the Pikangikum Band. The post office was established in 1953. Pikangikum is an Indian word for "dirty water narrows."

PINEWOOD

Pop. 289. In Dilke T., Rainy River Dist., on Rainy River and Hwys. 11 & 619, 72 km NW of Fort Frances. In 1877 the post office was established as Pine River; in 1895 the name was changed to Pinewood.

PLANTAGENET

Pop. 823. In North Plantagenet T., Prescott and Russell C., on the Nation River and Hwy. 17 and C. Rd. 9, 64 km NE of Ottawa. In 1811, Montreal merchants Abner Hagar and his brother Jonathan bought property in the area and built a dam to operate a sawmill. Jonathan returned to the United States during the War of 1812, and Abner formed a partnership with John Chesser. The village took its name from the township, which had been named for the line of English kings starting with Henry II.

PLATTSVILLE

Pop. 571. In Bradford-Blenheim T., Oxford C., on the Nith River and C. Rds. 8 & 42, 32 km NE of Woodstock. The community was named for its founder, Edward Platt, who settled in 1811.

PLEASANT POINT

Pop. 350. In Fenelon T., Victoria C., on the E shore of Sturgeon Lake and C. Rd. 11, 15 km N of Lindsay. The first settler, in 1855, was a man named Bell. In the mid-1890s John Hay bought land, divided it into lots and sold them as cottage sites. In 1913 a Pleasant Point Cottagers' Association was formed. Over the years the place was known as Burnell, Byrnell, Hayes Point, and Hay's Point, but when it was incorporated as a police village in 1927, it was named Pleasant Point.

POINTE AU BARIL

Pop. 237. In Harrison T., Parry Sound Dist. at the tip of a point on the E shore of Georgian Bay, 50 km by boat NW of Parry Sound. The post office was established as Pointe au Baril in 1892. The place was named by fur traders, who placed a light in a barrel on shore to guide them back to land after they had finished their evening's fishing.

POINT EDWARD

Pop. 2,216. In Sarnia T., Lambton C., on Lake Huron at the head of the St. Clair River, Canadian terminus of the International Blue Water Bridge to Port Huron, Mich. and Hwys. 7, 40, and 402, 100 km W of London. The place was settled in 1838 by J. P. Slocum from New York State, who arrived seeking fishing privileges. Point Edward was chosen for the western terminus of the Grand Trunk Railway from Riviere du Loup, Que., because the swift current in the narrowest part of the river at that point kept the waters ice-free for the operation of train ferries to Port Huron. The place was first called Huron, but was renamed Point Edward in 1860 to commemorate a visit that year by the Prince of Wales, later Edward VII.

PONTYPOOL

Pop. 712. In Manvers T., Victoria C., 1 km E of Hwy. 35, on C. Rd. 12, 31 km SE of Lindsay. James Leigh, John Jennings, and William Ridge Sr. were among the first settlers, in 1853. They named the place after Pontypool in Wales, a name meaning "a place of pools."

PORCUPINE

Pop. 2,498. Part of the City of Timmins in Cochrane Dist. at the N end of Porcupine Lake, on Hwy. 101, 13 km E of Timmins. The river, lake, district, and community are named after an island shaped like a porcupine in a nearby river. The first gold claim was staked in 1905 about 16 km south of where Hwy. 101 crosses the Frederick House River. The first gold mine went into production in 1907 on Gold Island in Nighthawk Lake. In the 50 years following Benny Hollinger's discovery of gold quartz in the Porcupine area, more than 45,000 claims were staked. Porcupine is often called "The Golden City."

PORT ALBERT

Pop. 255. In Ashfield T., Huron C., on Lake Huron at the mouth of Nine Mile River, 1 km E of Hwy. 21, 15 km N of Goderich. The place was laid out in 1842 by the Land Department as a townsite, but the community, despite its pretty location, never developed much beyond its present population. It was sometimes called Albert, but in 1851 the post office was established as Port Albert. The origin of the name is not known.

PORT BOLSTER

Pop. 453. In the Reg. Mun. of York, on the SW shore of Lake Simcoe and C. Rd. 23, 65 km NE of Toronto. The community is named after early settler T. Bolster, who arrived around 1860.

PORT BURWELL

Pop. 648. In Bayham T. Elgin C., on Lake Erie at the mouth of Otter Creek and Hwy. 19 and C. Rd. 42, 25 km S of Tillsonburg. Joseph DeFields and James Gibbons are believed to have been the first settlers, each building a log cabin at this point along the Talbot Road in 1812. There was little growth until deputy-surveyor Col. Mahlon Burwell and Col. Thomas Talbot surveyed the townsite in 1830, and Burwell offered free land to settlers willing to build there. Burwell also gave land for construction of Trinity Anglican Church. It was built in 1836 and is a fine example of early Gothic Revival architecture. The settlement was named after Mahlon Burwell in 1830.

PORT CARLING

Pop. 682. Part of Muskoka Lakes T., Dist. Mun. of Muskoka, on the Indian River, which connects lakes Muskoka and Rosseau and Hwy. 118, 28 km NW of Bracebridge. Michael and Alexander Bailey settled in 1865, after the Free Grant Colonization Road was opened from Washago, through Muskoka, to Parry Sound in 1858. The settlement was first known as Indian Village. Benjamin Hardcastle Johnston was appointed postmaster in 1868. When he was asked to name the settlement he honoured Sir John Carling, MP for London and Ontario's first minister of public works, who was visiting at the time on a fishing trip.

PORT COLBORNE

Pop. 17,893. City in the Reg. Mun. of Niagara, on Lake Erie at the S end of the Welland Canal and Hwys. 3, 58, & 140, 10 km S of Welland. Permanent settlement did not start until the construction of the Welland Canal in 1832. The place was first known as Gravelly Bay but was named after Sir John Colborne, governor of Canada, by Hon. William Hamilton Merritt.

PORT CREDIT

Pop. 14,540. Part of the City of Mississauga in the Reg. Mun. of Peel, on Lake Ontario at the mouth of the Credit River and Hwys. 2 & 10, 6 km W of Toronto. The place was established in 1791 by Col. John Graves Simcoe who suggested the erection of an inn, which was built in 1798. Little settlement followed until the 1817-22 period. The name, first given to the river, harks back to early fur-trading days when British traders, meeting with Indians at the mouth of the river each spring, extended credit for supplies until the following spring if the Indians did not have sufficient furs to pay in full. The place was first known as Mouth of the Credit. The post office was established as Port Credit in 1842.

PORT DOVER

Pop. 4,530. Part of the City of Nanticoke, Reg. Mun. of Haldimand-Norfolk, on Lake Erie at the mouth of the Lynn River and Hwy. 6 and C. Rd. 5, 13 km SE of Simcoe. French Sulpician missionaries wintered on the site in 1669-1670, but no settlers came for more than a century. In the early 1800s United Empire Loyalists began to arrive. Daniel McQueen built a dam and a mill near a ford across the River Lynn, and the site became known as Dover Mills or Dover, after the English port of Dover. In 1814 Port Dover and nearby Ryerse's Mills, Now Port Ryerse, were destroyed in a raid by 800 American soldiers led by Lt.-Col. John Campbell. The raid was subsequently condemned by a U.S. Army court of inquiry, and the settlers gradually began to rebuild. The post office was established as Port Dover in 1832. Port Dover has the world's largest fresh water fishing fleet and because of its sandy beaches is a popular summer vacation area.

PORT ELGIN

Pop. 5,909. In Saugeen T., Bruce C., on Lake Huron and Mill Creek and Hwy. 21 and C. Rd. 17, 47 km SW of Owen Sound. The town is built on the site of a 14th-century Iroquois village. Archaeological excavations at the "Nodwell" Indian village site have yielded many stone tools, hunting weapons, and pottery vessels. Lachlan McLean, the first settler, built a tavern in 1849. He was followed by a number of settlers of German origin. The post office was established as Normanton in 1854. In 1874 the name was changed to Port Elgin to honour James Bruce, eighth earl of Elgin who was governor general of Canada from 1847 to 1854. Port Elgin is Ontario's official weigh-in centre for the World Pumpkin Federation, a non-profit worldwide organization dedicated to the growing of giant pumpkins.

PORT FRANKS

Pop. 700. In Bosanquet T., Lambton C., on Lake Huron at the original mouth of the Ausable River, 2.5 km N of Hwy. 21, 64 km NE of Sarnia. The first post office opened in 1854 as Goldcreek and closed in 1870. When the post office reopened in 1874, it was renamed Port Franks after Charles Franks, vice-president of the Canada Company, which in 1835 owned the land along the shore of Lake Huron.

PORT HOPE

Pop. 10,243. In Hope T., Northumberland C., on Lake Ontario at the mouth of the Ganaraska River and Hwys. 2 & 28, 102 km NE of Toronto. In 1670 a Cayuga Indian village called Ganaraski was on the site and, in a survey in 1791, the village was referred to as Pemetaccutiang. By 1778 Peter Smith was operating a trading post, and the place was called Smith's Creek. The first permanent settler was Myndert Harris, a United Empire Loyalist, who arrived in 1793. By 1817 the place was called Toronto, but to avoid confusion with the former town of York, the name was changed to Port Hope after Col. Henry Hope, lieutenant-governor of Quebec from 1785 to 1789.

PORT LAMBTON

Pop. 926. In Sombra T., Lambton C., on the St. Clair River and C. Rd. 33, 15 km NW of Wallaceburg and connected by ferry service to Roberts Landing, Michigan. The first settler in the area was Francis Baby from Detroit, who settled at Baby's Point, 1.5 km south. Duncan McDonald from Ohio was the first settler on the site of the present community, arriving in 1820. The place was first known as Lambton Village, and was named Port Lambton when the post office opened in 1871. The community took its name from the county, which was named after John George Lambton, earl of Durham and governor-in-chief of British North America and lord high commissioner in 1838.

PORTLAND

Pop. 337. In Bastard and South Burgess T., Leeds and Grenville C., on the E shore of Big Rideau Lake and Hwy. 15, 28 km SW of Smiths Falls. The place was first called Old Landing, but when the post office opened in 1833 the name chosen was Portland after William Henry Cavendish Bentinch, duke of Portland, a prominent Briton of the day. The post office opened as "Potland," but the error was soon corrected.

PORT McNICOLL

Pop. 1,818. In Tay T., Simcoe C., on Hog Bay, an arm of Georgian Bay 2 km N of Hwy. 12, 45 km NW of Orillia. The community owes its existence to a decision by Canadian Pacific Railway to locate its main terminal for upper Great Lakes steamships there in 1909. The railway previously had used Owen Sound, but made the change because of adverse grades on the Toronto-Owen Sound route. The new port facility was named after David McNicoll, vice-president and general manager of the CPR at that time.

PORT PERRY

Pop. 4,712. Part of Scugog T., Reg. Mun. of Durham, on Lake Scugog and C. Rd. 2, just N of Hwy. 7A, 28 km N of Whitby. In 1848, on the former site of an Indian village called Scugog Village, Peter Perry laid out a townsite, which was named Port Perry after him in 1852. Perry, the son of a United Empire Loyalist, lacked formal education, but through force of character became an outstanding member of the Reform Party of Upper Canada and one of the founders of the Clear Grit Party.

PORT ROBINSON

Pop. 867. Part of the City of Thorold, Reg. Mun. of Niagara, on the Welland Canal, 6 km N of Welland. The settlement began at the southern terminus of the Welland Canal in 1824, when construction of the canal started. When the canal opened in 1829, the settlement became a port of entry. It was first called Port Beverley to honour Chief Justice

John Beverley Robinson, a member of the canal company. When the post office was established in 1835, the name was changed to Port Robinson, also to honour Chief Justice Robinson. In its heyday, when teams of horses on shore towed ships through the canal, Port Robinson had four large hotels, several smaller ones, six saloons, many stores and businesses, a shipyard, and two drydocks. Steamers operated between Port Robinson and Buffalo. Then steam tugs replaced the teamsters and the government expropriated the shipyard, which had employed 300 men, in order to enlarge the canal.

PORT ROWAN

Pop. 780. In the Reg. Mun. of Haldimand-Norfolk, on Inner Bay off Long Point Bay of Lake Erie and C. Rd. 42, 27 km SW of Simcoe. The first settlers, the Backhouse family (later changed to Bachus), were operating a grist mill in the area in 1798. The family operated the mill until 1955, when it became an integral part of the Backus Heritage Conservation Area. The mill, (made of hand-hewn timbers and wooden pegs), the Backus home, and a number of other pioneer buildings moved to the site from the region, are open to the public. The hamlet was founded in 1819 by John Dutcher and first called Dutcher's Corners. It was renamed Port Rowan when the post office was established in 1845. The name honours Capt. William Rowan, secretary to Gov. Sir John Colborne in 1839. In November of 1854, Abigail Becker single-handedly rescued eight sailors from the icy waters of Lake Erie when their schooner was wrecked in a fierce storm near Long Point. She received several awards and a personal letter from Queen Victoria for her action, which she maintained was just her "duty."

PORT SEVERN

Pop. 565. In Tay T., Simcoe C., on the Severn River 1 km E of Hwy. 69, 50 km NW of Orillia. The post office was established in 1868, taking the community's name from the Severn River.

PORT STANLEY

Pop. 1,826, in Yarmouth T., Elgin C., on Lake Erie at the mouth of Kettle Creek and Hwy. 4 and C. Rds. 20 & 24, 14 km S of St. Thomas. French explorer Louis Jolliet visited in 1669, when the place was known by the Iroquois as Kanagio and by the Ojibway as Akiksibi. The French named it Riviere de la Chaudiere. Col. Thomas Talbot stayed in the area briefly in the very early 1800s and granted two shoreline lots to his friend Col. John Bostwick, who settled there with his family in 1804. Another early settler was Squire Samuel Price, who alternated serving customers in his store with dispensing justice in a courtroom attached to the store. In 1822 a road was completed between Port Stanley and London, and the following year the settlement was named Port Stanley after Governor General Lord Stanley, who had visited the harbour while staying with Colonel Talbot. The London and Port Stanley Railway, opened in 1856 and closed for a number of decades, now operates excursions year round between Port Stanley, Union, and St. Thomas.

PORT STANTON
Pop. 500. In Orillia T., Simcoe C., on the SW shore of Sparrow Lake (a widening of the Severn River), 2 km NW of C. Rds. 38 & 49, 22 km N of Orillia. The settlement was first known as Sparrow Lake. A summer post office was opened in 1907, and the place was named after the first postmaster, Frank Stanton.

PORT SYDNEY
Pop. 259. Part of the Town of Huntsville, Muskoka Dist., on the S shore of Mary Lake and C. Rds. 10 & 44, 21 km N of Bracebridge. The post office was established as Mary Lake in 1871. In 1874 the name was changed to Port Sydney after Sydney Smith, who settled in 1869, took an active interest in the community, and was its chief employer for 50 years.

POTTAGEVILLE
Pop. 831. In the Reg. Mun. of York, on C. Rd. 16, 58 km N of Toronto. The post office was opened in 1876. The community was named after Edward Pottage, a bailiff and leading citizen, who lived in the village from 1844 to 1879.

POWASSAN
Pop. 1,093. In South Himsworth T., Parry Sound Dist., on Genesee Creek (a branch of the South River) and Hwys. 11 & 534, 30 km S of North Bay. The first houses were built on a bend in the river known as Bingham Chute because a firm called Bingham and Dey operated a lumber planing mill there. In 1891, when the post office was established, the community was called Powassan, an Indian word meaning "bend in the river."

PRESCOTT
Pop. 4,413. In Augusta T., Leeds and Grenville C., on the St. Lawrence River and Hwy. 2, 26 km NE of Brockville and 5 km SW of Johnstown where Hwy. 16 from Ottawa joins Hwy. 2. The first settler was Col. Edward Jessup, a landowner from Albany, N.Y. When hostilities broke out between Britain and the American colonies, Jessup recruited and led a regiment for the British cause, which became known as Jessup's Rangers. Jessup's loyalty was rewarded with a large grant of land, which he surveyed as a townsite and named Prescott after Gen. Robert Prescott, governor-in-chief of Canada from 1797 to 1807. Until then the place had been known variously as Augusta, New Oswegatchie, Johnstown, Royal Township # 6, and Fort Wellington.

Its location, at the head of rapids on the St. Lawrence River, quickly made Prescott a major "forwarding" or trans-shipment point between small boats to negotiate the rapids and larger boats above and below them to more economically carry cargoes longer distances. Because of the site's importance in the nation's transportation system, Fort Wellington was built in 1812, garrisoned until 1826, and enlarged in 1838. It saw action in the War of 1812, the Rebellion of 1837, and the Fenian Raids, but because it was never attacked and is fully restored, it remains today one of the best preserved forts in Canada. In 1838, a misguided Polish expatriate, Nicholas von Schultz, raised a band of 200 Americans and crossed the St. Lawrence River to free Canada from British rule. The force landed near Prescott and occupied a stone windmill just east of Fort Wellington. They were soon ousted by troops in what came to be known as the Battle of the Windmill. Another historic site, just west of Prescott, is the Little Blue Church, built in 1809 and rebuilt in 1845. Barbara Heck, founder of Methodism in North America, is buried there. Sir Richard W. Scott, author of Canada's Temperance Act of 1878, was born in Prescott in 1825 as was Canada's first military flyer, William F. Sharpe, in 1893.

PRESTON
Pop. 19,030. Part of the City of Cambridge, Reg. Mun. of Waterloo on the Speed River near its confluence with the Grand River, and Hwys. 8 & 401, 10 km SE of Kitchener. Preston was once called Cambridge after the duke of Cambridge, son of George III, and has passed that name on to the city of which it is now a part. Preston's first settler was John Erb, a Swiss-German Mennonite from Pennsylvania and a brother of Abraham Erb, founder of Waterloo. John Erb built a mill and the place became known as Erb's Mills. The name was later changed to Cambridge, and in 1830, at the suggestion of Squire Scollick, an early settler, it was named Preston after the city in Lancashire, England. That year warm mineral springs were discovered, and Preston enjoyed a brief international reputation as a health spa. The North American Hotel, later the Kress Hotel, is said to have been Ontario's first hotel to provide a bath with running water. The City of Cambridge was formed in 1973 by the amalgamation of the city of Galt in North Dumfries Township and the towns of Hespeler and Preston in Waterloo Township. (See entry under Cambridge.)

PRICES CORNERS
Pop. 500. In Oro and Orillia T., Simcoe C., N of Bass Lake, on Hwy. 12 and C. Rd. 22, 8 km W of Orillia. The post office, opened in 1874, was named for early settler Thomas Price Sr.

PRINCE ALBERT

Pop. 329. In the Reg. Mun. of Durham, on the SW shore of Lake Scugog and C. Rds. 2 & 21, 27 km N of Whitby. The post office was established in 1840 as Reach. In 1863 it was renamed Prince Albert.

PRINCETON

Pop. 502. In Blandford-Blenheim T., Oxford C., on Horner's Creek, and C. Rd. 3, 1 km N of Hwy. 2, 22 km E of Woodstock. The place was first known as Governor's Road Settlement, and a post office was opened there in 1793 during the clearing of the Dundas Road, also known as Governor's Road. The place was renamed for Princeton, New Jersey by early settler Col. Thomas Hornor (1767-1834) a native of New Jersey, who settled there in 1795 and built the first sawmill in Oxford County. Princeton was the site of a famous murder in 1890, though it isn't known why the case inspired so much interest, since there was never any doubt as to the guilt of the murderer. Reginald Birchall was found guilty of the murder of a young man named Benwell, whom he had lured to Canada as a prospective settler. Benwell is buried in Princeton Cemetery.

PUCE

Pop. 1,611. In Maidstone T., Essex C., on Lake St. Clair and Hwy. 2 and C. Rd. 25, 25 km E of Windsor. In 1874 the place name was spelled Patello. The post office opened in 1875 and the name was spelled Patillo. In 1893 the post office name was changed to Puce, derived from Riviere-aux-Puces. *Puce* is French for "flea."

QUEENSTON

Pop. 500. Part of the Town of Niagara-on-the-Lake, Reg. Mun. of Niagara, on the W bank of the Niagara River at its mouth at Lake Ontario, S terminus of the Bruce Trail and Hwy. 55, C. Rd. 87 and the Niagara Parkway, 10 km N of Niagara Falls. Robert Hamilton is considered to be the founder of Queenston. He emigrated to Canada from Scotland during the American Revolution and in 1789 secured land near the portage point. He built wharves and storehouses and a mansion, and ran a thriving trans-shipping business hauling freight between Queenston and Chippewa. In those days the place was known as The Landing, West Landing, or Lower Landing. The name Queenston is believed to have originated from Lt.-Gov. John Graves Simcoe's regiment, the Queen's Rangers, which was stationed at the place in 1792.

In 1812, Queenston was the scene of the famous Battle of Queenston Heights in which Gen. Sir Isaac Brock was killed. Today a 185-foot-high (56.3-m) shaft with interior stone stairs to a lookout, built in 1854, marks his grave. In 1813, Laura Secord hiked 30 km from her home in Queenston to warn British soldiers of a surprise attack being planned by the Americans. Two days later the British and their Native allies intercepted the Americans' attack and forced their surrender at the Battle of Beaver Dams. Today's visitor can tour Laura's house, which has been faithfully reproduced by the Laura Secord Candy Shops and contains one of the country's finest collections of period furnishings. William Lyon Mackenzie, who lived in Queenston from 1823 to 1824, is credited with having brought responsible government to Canada. The Niagara Parks Commission opened Mackenzie's house to the general public in 1990, and artifacts relating to him and his crusade are gradually being collected and put on display.

QUEENSVILLE

Pop. 1,099. In the Reg. Mun. of York on C. Rd. 13, 2 km E of Hwy. 20, 49 km N of Toronto. The place was first known as The Four Corners. The post office was established in 1851 as Queensville. The history of the community and the origin of its name are not known.

RAINY RIVER

Pop. 893. In Atwood T., Rainy River Dist., on Rainy River and Hwys. 11 & 600, at the N end of a bridge across the Rainy River from Baudette, Minnesota, 88 km W of Fort Frances. The place was first settled by trappers and called Beaver Mills. By the 1870s lumbering had become the main industry in the area. The post office opened as Rainy River in 1886. Rainy River was incorporated as a town in 1904 and destroyed by fire the following year. The town was immediately rebuilt.

RANGER LAKE

Pop. 400. In Algoma Dist. on the S shore of Ranger Lake and Hwy. 556, 94 km NE of Sault Ste. Marie. The history of the community and the origin of its name are unknown.

RAYSIDE-BALFOUR

Pop. 13,702. A town in the Reg. Mun. of Sudbury created by regional government in 1973 by the amalgamation of the former Township of Rayside and part of the former Township of Balfour, including the communities of Azilda and Chelmsford.

REDBRIDGE

Pop. 215. In Widdifield T., Nipissing Dist., on Hwy. 63, 18 km E of North Bay. The post office was established as Redbridge in 1925. The origin of the name is not known.

RED LAKE

Pop. 2,065. In Red Lake T., Kenora Dist., on the S shore of Red Lake at the N terminus of Hwy. 105, 169 km N of Vermilion Bay, 94 km E of Kenora. The townsite was a canoe route stop in 1786. The Northwest Company established a post in 1821. Rich gold deposits were discovered on the shore of 71-square-mile (184-sq-km) Red Lake in 1925 by two brothers named Howey and George McNeeley along with W. F. Morgan. News of the discovery brought hundreds of gold seekers with dog teams, and 10,000 claims were staked. Between 1930 and 1968, more than $300 million worth of gold was mined. The community was named after the lake which, according to Indian legend, got its name when a giant moose, shot dead by a hunter's arrow, fell into the water, where it bled for many days, colouring the lake red.

RED ROCK

Pop. 1,260. In Red Rock T., Thunder Bay Dist., on Nipigon Bay of Lake Superior at the E terminus of Hwy. 628, 8 km E of Hwy. 17, 108 km NE of Thunder Bay. The first homesteaders were Mr. and Mrs. Arve Adolph

Arola who came from Port Arthur (now Thunder Bay) in 1915. The first settlers were involved in logging, and the town now has a large pulp and paper mill. The town took its name from massive, dark red rock outcroppings near the Trans-Canada Highway. The rock formations were created 2.5 billion years ago during the Precambrian era and have been exposed by millions of years of erosion and probable gouging by Pleistocene glaciers.

RENFREW

Pop. 7,914. In Horton T., Renfrew C., on the second chute of the Bonnechere River, 14 km from the Ottawa River and Hwys. 60 & 132, 34 km W of Arnprior. A squatter named Coyle spent a season at the site in 1820, but Renfrew's founder was a Dutch French-Canadian named Joseph Brunette, who arrived in 1823. The settlement was originally known as Second Chute, as it was one of four sets of chutes into the river used for lumbering. By 1840, retired fur trader John McDougall had established the first store. When the community needed a bridge and hesitated to raise the tax rate, McDougall, as magistrate, sentenced a band of rivermen, who had been convicted of raiding homesteads, to hard labour building a bridge. When the post office opened in 1848 the settlers named their community Renfrew after the town and shire in Scotland, one of the ancestral seats of the Royal Stuarts.

RICHARDS LANDING

Pop. 413. In Algoma Dist. on the NW side of St. Joseph Island and Hwy. 548, 45 km SE of Sault Ste. Marie. The post office was established as St. Joseph in 1846. In 1882 the name was changed to Richard's Landing. The origin of the name is not known.

RICHMOND

Pop. 2,667. In the Reg. Mun. of Ottawa-Carleton, on the Jock River (a tributary of the Rideau River) and C. Rds. 5 & 10, 32 km SW of Ottawa. Richmond was one of four settlements of military veterans intended to form a chain of potential defence across eastern Upper Canada. The other communities were Perth, Lanark, and March. Richmond Military Settlement was settled around 1818 and named after Charles Lennox, fourth duke of Richmond who was governor-in-chief of Canada from 1818 to 1819. He was a career soldier and fought at least two duels, one with the duke of York. Lennox was in Canada only a short time before he was bitten by a pet fox and died of hydrophobia.

RICHMOND HILL

Pop. 57,082. Town in Reg. Mun. of York, on Hwys. 7, 11, & 404, 16 km N of Toronto. Balser Munshaw was the first settler, in 1794, but did not stay; neither did the next two settlers, John and Edward Stooks. In 1797,

William B. Peters came into possession of the Munshaw lands, and settled. In 1799, about 40 exiled French royalists led by Joseph Geneviéve, Comte de Puisaye, attempted to form a settlement in uncleared townships along Yonge St. The noblemen and their servants could not adapt to the rigours of pioneer life, and by 1806 most had returned to Europe. Abner Miles arrived between 1798 and 1802 and built a mill, after which the community was named Miles' Mills. The place was later known as Mount Pleasant.

In 1819 the settlement was named after Charles Lennox, fourth duke of Richmond, who was governor-in-chief of Canada from 1818 to 1819. He was a career soldier and fought at least two duels, one with the duke of York. Lennox died in office after a short time in Canada, of hydrophobia, after being bitten by a pet fox. In 1931 the widow and son of David Alexander Dunlap built the David Dunlap Observatory in Richmond Hill and presented it to the University of Toronto. Dunlap was a financier and philanthropist, who bankrolled the Timmins brothers in the LaRose silver mine at Cobalt and the giant gold strike in Timmins.

RICHVALE
Pop. 3,392. Part of the Town of Richmond Hill in the Reg. Mun. of York on Hwy. 11 and C. Rd. 73, 16 km N of Toronto. A post office was established as Richvale in 1931. The village was annexed by the Town of Richmond Hill in 1971. The origin of the name is not known.

RIDGETOWN
Pop. 3,152. In Howard T., Kent C., on Hwy. 21 and C. Rd. 19, 37 km E of Chatham. The first settlers were United Empire Loyalists, who arrived in 1823. By 1828 they had built a log schoolhouse. The Western Ontario Experimental Farm was established at Ridgetown in 1922 and developed into Ridgetown College of Agricultural Technology. The community was named for the high ridge on which it is located.

RIDGEWAY
Pop. 1,793. Part of the Town of Fort Erie, 1 km S of Hwy. 3, 14 km W of Fort Erie. Settlement began in the mid-1850s upon completion of the Buffalo and Lake Huron Railway between Fort Erie and Goderich on Lake Huron. The Battle of Ridgeway was fought nearby in 1860 during the Fenian Raids. Ridgeway was named for its location on Ridge Road.

RIPLEY
Pop. 574. In Huron T., Bruce C., on C. Rds. 6 & 7, 53 km N of Goderich. The place was settled in 1852 by 100 Scottish immigrant families from the Island of Lewis, the most northerly island of the Outer Hebrides. The community was named Ripley when the post office was established in 1856, after a town in Derbyshire, England. In 1874 the post office name

was changed to Dingwall after a Scottish town. The railroad retained the name Ripley, so to avoid confusion the community was renamed Ripley in 1880.

RIVER VALLEY

Pop. 222. In Gibbons T., Nipissing Dist., on the Temagami River and Hwys. 539 and A539, 37 km NW of Sturgeon Falls. The community started as a lumber camp in 1890, and the first permanent settler was F. X. Cataford, who arrived in 1896 from Butte, Montana. The post office was established as River Valley in 1900.

RIVERVIEW HEIGHTS

Pop. 237. In Augusta T., Leeds and Grenville C., on the St. Lawrence River and Hwy. 2, 3 km SW of Prescott. The residential suburb of Prescott was established in 1967.

ROCKCLIFFE PARK

Pop. 2,295. In the Reg. Mun. of Ottawa-Carleton. A residential suburb of Ottawa on a height of land overlooking the Ottawa River north of the City of Vanier. The area was first known as McKay's Bush and was part of an extensive land grant made in 1832 to Rideau Canal contractor Thomas McKay. In 1838 McKay built a mansion he called Rideau Hall, which since 1865 has been the residence of the governor general of Canada. In 1925 the community was incorporated as a village and named Rockliffe Park after the local landscape. It is one of the most exclusive residential areas in Canada; there are only 24 km (15 mi) of roads, no industry, no commerce, no churches, and no apartments.

ROCKLAND

Pop. 5,119. In Clarence T., Prescott and Russell C., on the Ottawa River and Hwy. 17 and C. Rd. 21, 32 km NE of Ottawa. William C., Edwards was the founder of the town, building two sawmills, the first in 1868. Edwards was also the first postmaster, in 1867, and gave the community a name descriptive of its surroundings.

ROCKWOOD

Pop. 1,068. In Eramosa T., Wellington C., on Hwy. 24 and C. Rd. 29, 11 km NE of Guelph. The community, settled in the early 1800s, was first known as Brotherstown. In 1848, early settler William Wetherald changed the name to Rockwood for the rocky, wooded area in which it is located. In 1850, Wetherald, a Quaker and native of England, opened a boarding school for boys. The school remained in operation for 32 years and was noted for its high academic standards. Some of its pupils included A. S. Hardy, Ontario's fourth premier; Sir Adam Beck, founder of Ontario Hydro, and James J. Hill, pioneer railway promoter and builder. In nearby

Rockwood Park, on the Speed River, there are some interesting pot-holes—holes worn into solid rock at the foot of a waterfall by the revolutions of a stone.

RODNEY

Pop. 992. In Aldborough T., Elgin C., on C. Rds. 3 & 4, 56 km SW of St. Thomas. The first settler and founder was William Hoskins, a weaver from England who came to the township in 1854. Hoskins built a home, by mistake, on the wrong lot (the 7th Concession, rather than the 6th); so he had to build another house for his family. The community was first known as Centreville, but when the post office was established in 1865 it was named Rodney after Admiral Rodney of the British Navy who had distinguished himself in the Seven Years' War.

ROSSEAU

Pop. 221. In Humphrey T., Parry Sound Dist., on the N shore of Lake Rosseau and Hwys. 141 & 632 and C. Rd. 3, 37 km SE of Parry Sound. In 1861 a survey party for the proposed Parry Sound Road set up a camp and stores at the site of what is now the community of Rosseau. When the road was completed in 1867 it passed through the camp. A settlement began to develop, particularly after locks were built between Lake Rosseau and Lake Muskoka in 1871, making Rosseau the northwest terminus of the steamship route from Gravenhurst on Lake Muskoka. In the 1860s the Muskoka lakes began to draw tourists from the south and American entrepreneur W. H. Pratt built a large and well-appointed hunting and fishing lodge on the shore at Rosseau. Named Rosseau House, but known as Pratt's, it was regarded as the finest hotel in the Muskokas. It burned down in 1883. The lake, river, and community all take their name from early fur trader Jean Baptiste Rousseau. When the post office was established in 1866, the first "u" was dropped from the name.

ROSSLYN VILLAGE

Pop. 700. In Paipoonge T., Thunder Bay Dist., 16 km W of Thunder Bay. A post ofice was established as Rosslyn Village in 1912. The origin of the name is not known.

ROSSMORE

Pop. 350. In Ameliasburg T., Prince Edward C., on the Bay of Quinte and Hwy. 62, 3 km S of Belleville. In 1881 the post office was established as Ross More. In 1908 the name contracted to Rossmore. The origin of the name is not known.

ROUND LAKE CENTRE

Pop. 226. In Hagarty T., Renfrew C., on the S shore of Round Lake and

Hwy. 82, 55 km SW of Pembroke. The post office was established as Round Lake Centre in 1931.

RUSSELL

Pop. 1,255. In Russell T., Prescott and Russell C., on the Castor River and C. Rds. 3 & 6, 33 km SE of Ottawa. The first settlers were John Mattice from Cornwall, who built a sawmill, and William Duncan from Baie des Chaleurs, Que., who built an oatmeal mill. The place was first known as Castor (French for "beaver") and then Russell, after the county, when the post office was established in 1848. The first postmaster was John Duncan, and in 1852 he managed to have the community's name officially changed to Duncanville. The post office name did not change however, and in 1900 the community's name was officially changed back to Russell. Russell took its name from the county, named in 1792 to honour Peter Russell, administrator of the government of Upper Canada in the absence of Lt.-Gov. John Graves Simcoe.

RUTHVEN

Pop. 699. In Gosfield South T, Essex C., on Hwy. 3, 7 km W of Leamington. The community was first known as Inkermanville. When the post office opened in 1860, the place was named Ruthven after the first postmaster, Hugh Ruthven.

SSS

SACHIGO LAKE I.R.
Pop. 450. In Kenora Dist. on the N shore of Sachigo Lake at the mouth of the Sachigo River, 620 km NW of Thunder Bay. The post office opened in 1969. The origin of the name is unknown.

ST. AGATHA
Pop. 213. In the Reg. Mun. of Waterloo on C. Rds. 9 & 12, 11 km NW of Kitchener. The post office was established as St. Agatha in 1852. The origin of the name is unknown.

ST. ALBERT
Pop. 450. In Cambridge T., Prescott and Russell C., on the Castor River and C. Rd. 7, 45 km SE of Ottawa. The post office was established as St. Albert in 1880. The origin of the name is unknown.

ST. ANDREWS
Pop. 592. In Cornwall T., Stormont, Dundas, and Glengarry C., on the Raisin River and Hwy. 138 and C. Rd. 18, 10 km NW of Cornwall. Most of the early settlers were from Scotland, and they named their community after Scotland's patron saint. One of the first Roman Catholic churches in Upper Canada was built at St. Andrews in 1801. St. Andrew's Church is the oldest remaining stone structure in the province erected as a church. In the War of 1812 it was used as a hospital. In the graveyard are the tombstones of Hon. John Sandfield Macdonald, a prime minister of Canada and the first premier of Ontario, and Simon Fraser, a fur trader and explorer who died in 1862. Fraser joined the North West Company in 1792 and for 12 years was in charge of all operations west of the Rocky Mountains. A memorial to Fraser was erected by the Hudson's Bay Company in 1921.

ST. CATHARINES
Pop. 120,567. In the Reg. Mun. of Niagara on Lake Ontario and the Welland Canal and the Queen Elizabeth Way, 64 km E of Hamilton. The city is nicknamed "the Garden City" or "the Best Blooming Town in Ontario" because the soil and climate of a strip of the south shore of Lake Ontario is ideal for growing grapes and plants such as wisteria, magnolia, and forsythia, which are abundant. The city had its beginnings on the site of a crudely built Indian bridge across Twelve Mile Creek. The site is believed to have been one of the most heavily populated Indian encampments in North America prior to the arrival of the first settlers. The burial grounds alone covered an area of five or six acres (2-2.4 ha). The first settlers are believed to have been United Empire Loyalists John

Hainer and Jacob Dittrick, who arrived in 1790, and other Loyalists, predominantly former members of Butler's Rangers, soon arrived.

The community was called St. Catharines after the first wife of the Hon. Robert Hamilton. Hamilton was superintendent of the Western District, a member of the first executive council of Upper Canada, and owner of much land in the area. The name was interchangeable for a time with The Twelve, after the creek, or Shipman's Corners after a tavern owned by Paul Shipman. The first wooden canal, started in 1824 by the Welland Canal Company, was completed by 1833 between Port Dalhousie (now part of St. Catharines) on Lake Ontario, and Port Colborne on Lake Erie. Competitive rowing became popular in Canada in the 1860s, and in 1880 the first Royal Canadian Henley Regatta for international rowers was held in Toronto. In 1903 a section of the old Welland Canal at Port Dalhousie was chosen as the permanent site for this popular competition. In 1931 the course was changed slightly and a reinforced concrete stand to seat 3,000 people was built. In 1874 Dr. Theophilus Mack established the St. Catharines Training School for Nurses. The school endorsed the Florence Nightingale system of training based on a sound knowledge of hygiene and medicine, and was the first school of its kind in Canada. St. Catharines is also the home of Ridley College, established by the Anglican Church in 1889, and Brock University, chartered by provincial act in 1964.

ST. CHARLES
Pop. 400. In Casimir, Jennings, and Appleby ts., Sudbury Dist., on Hwy. 535, 12 km S of Hwy. 17, 38 km W of Sturgeon Falls. The post office was established in 1902. The origin of the name is unknown.

ST. CLAIR BEACH
Pop. 3,367. In Maidstone T., Essex C., on the S shore of Lake St. Clair, 14 km E of Windsor. The residential community, immediately east of Tecumseh, was incorporated as a village in 1914.

ST. CLEMENTS
Pop. 461. In the Reg. Mun. of Waterloo on C. Rds. 10 & 15, 18 km NW of Kitchener. The post office, named for the first church built in the area, was established in 1853.

ST. EUGENE
Pop. 458, in East Hawkesbury T., Prescott and Russell C., on C. Rds. 10 & 14, 20 km SE of Hawkesbury. The post office was established as St. Eugene in 1861. The origin of the name is not known.

ST. GEORGE
Pop. 994. In South Dumfries T., Brant C., on Hwy. 5 and C. Rd. 13, 16 km

N of Brantford. Obed Wilson built the community's first house in 1814, although Peter Bauslaugh is credited with being the founder. The first postmaster was Col. George Stanton, after whom the village was named St. George Brant in 1835. The community was also known as St. George West, St. George Halton, and St. George Canada West. Just west of town is the birthplace and childhood home of Adelaide Hunter-Hoodless, who established domestic science courses in the public school system and founded the Women's Institute movement, the YWCA, and the Victorian Order of Nurses. The homestead is now a museum, which contains furnishings and personal belongings of the Hunter and Hoodless families that reflect the period when Adelaide lived there (1850-1880). The Hon. Harry C., Nixon (1891-1961) served the Ontario legislature for 42 years in a variety of posts. In 1943 he served briefly as premier of Ontario.

ST. ISIDORE-DE-PRESCOTT
Pop. 723. In South Plantagenet T., Prescott and Russell C., on the Scotch River and C. Rds. 3 & 9, 65 km E of Ottawa. Lumbermen cleared the site in 1824 as they cut timber in the area and floated it down the Scotch River to the Nation River and from there to the Ottawa River. French-Canadian settlers began moving into the area in the 1850s. The first settler was Peter McLaurin of Quebec, who built a house in 1845. Several years later his brother, Magloire, built the community's second house. The place was called Scotch River Mills, but the Scottish lumbermen had called it Kerry and when a post office opened in 1863 it was named Kerry. In 1883 the post office name was changed to St. Isidore de Prescott. The origin of the name is not known.

ST. JACOBS
Pop. 1,525. In Woolwich T., Reg. Mun. of Waterloo, on the Conestogo River and C. Rd. 17, just W of Hwy. 86, 12 km N of Kitchener. John E. Bowman settled in the area in the 1820s, but the community didn't begin to develop until the late 1840s, when Solomon Bauman built a sawmill on the river. The place was first called Jacobstettel by the German and Pennsylvania Dutch settlers, but the name had changed to St. Jacobs by the time a post office opened in 1852. The name honours Jacob Snider and Jacob Eby, early millers. In 1875 Elias Weaver Bingman Snider revolutionized Canadian flour milling by installing German-built flour milling rollers in his mill.

ST. JOACHIM
Pop. 539. In Rochester T., Essex C., on Hwy. 2 and C. Rd. 31, 39 km E of Windsor. The post office, established in 1883, was called St. Joachim River Ruscom. In 1943 the post office name was changed to St. Joachim. The origin of the name is not known.

ST. MARYS

Pop. 4,923. Town in Perth C., at the confluence of the North Thames River and Trout Creek and C. Rds. 19 & 28, 35 km NE of London. The town was founded in 1841 by United Empire Loyalist Thomas Ingersoll, a brother of Laura Secord, heroine of the War of 1812. The town was planned by the Canada Company, which chose the location because of falls over rocky ledges in the river, which provided a potential power source. The place was first called Little Falls and was so named when the post office opened in 1845. As the community prospered and grew, Little Falls was no longer considered an appropriate name. When Thomas Mercer Jones, commissioner of the Canada Company, and his wife, Mary, visited the town, Mrs. Jones was asked to suggest a new name. She christened the place St. Marys after herself and subscribed the sum of £10 towards construction of a new stone school. Today the town's nickname is "Stonetown" because of the many limestone buildings built between 1850 and the early 1900s—and there are some beauties: the 1880 neo-Gothic opera house, the 1891 Romanesque town hall, and the 1899 water tower.

The two rivers caused surveyors of the Grand Trunk Railway some problems as they were pushing the rail line west from Toronto. They couldn't bypass the town, because, in the late 1880s, more wheat was being shipped from St. Marys than from any other market in the country, including London and Toronto. The solution was to build two stone viaducts that remain in use today. The 11 stone pillars used in their construction required 20 double teams of horses, 100 labourers, 50 quarrymen, and 20 masons to put them in place. The pillars carry the rails across a span of more than 700 feet (213 m), 70 feet (21.3 m) above the rivers. Automobiles cross the rivers at a lower level, on two of the last stone bridges remaining in Ontario.

St. Marys has produced a prime minister, and Canada's most successful retail businessman, and Thomas Edison worked nearby—until he had to leave town in a hurry. The prime minister was Sir Arthur Meighen, who headed the Conservative government in 1920 and 1921 and briefly in 1926. The retailer was Northern Irish immigrant Timothy Eaton, who joined his brothers James and Robert in a business in St. Marys. Timothy and James handled dry goods, and Robert looked after the groceries. The operation was successful, but in 1869 Timothy opened a store in Toronto that used a cash system instead of barter and credit. The rest is North American merchandising history.

When Thomas Alva Edison was 16 or 17, he was a night operator at St. Marys first railway station, located a couple of kilometres outside town. To ensure operators didn't sleep on the job, they were required to tap out the code word for "six" every half-hour. Edison invented a device that automatically sent the code when a crank was turned, and he had the watchman turn the crank every half-hour, while he slept. The scam worked well—until the night a message came to hold a train in the passing track. Edison failed to relay the message to the train crew. Fortunately, the engineers saw each other's train in time to stop. During the subsequent investigation, Edison quietly slipped away—to invent the phonograph and electric light bulb and to take out patents on 1,029 other inventions.

ST. PASCAL

Pop. 206. In Clarence T., Prescott and Russell C., on C. Rd. 1, 36 km NE of Ottawa. In 1886 the post office was established as The Lake. In 1909 the name was changed to St. Paschal Babylon, and in the same year the spelling error was corrected to St. Pascal Babylon. In current usage Babylon has been dropped. The origin of the name is not known.

ST. THOMAS

Pop. 28,405. City in Elgin C., on Kettle Creek and Hwys. 3 & 4, 29 km S of London. The settlement was founded in 1810 by Capt. Daniel Rapelje from New York State, a veteran of several battles in the War of 1812. He built a grist mill and laid out his farm in lots, which he sold to settlers. He donated one of the lots for St. Thomas Anglican Church, which was built in 1824 and is still standing. Also in 1824, Dr. Charles Duncombe and Dr. John Rolph opened Upper Canada's first medical school which they called The Talbot Dispensatory. Dr. Duncombe was an ardent supporter of William Lyon Mackenzie's Reform Party, played an active role in the Rebellion of 1837, and was forced to flee to the United States after Mackenzie's defeat at Montgomery's Tavern.

On Christmas morning, 1870, fire wiped out half of St. Thomas' business section. The water supply was low, the hoses were in poor condition, and the only way the volunteer fire department could bring the fire under control was to tear down wooden structures in the fire's path. In the 1870s both the Canada Southern and the Great Western Railways built their lines through St. Thomas. In 1885, the largest elephant ever in captivity was accidentally killed by a train at St. Thomas after performing with the Barnum and Bailey Circus. In 1985 a statue of Jumbo 10 percent larger than life size was erected at the western entrance to the city despite considerable opposition. The monument has drawn up to 101,500 visitors in a single year. St. Thomas was the home of Mitchell F. Hepburn, premier of Ontario from 1934 to 1942. The community was first called Kettle Creek Village and then Stirling, but when the post office was opened in 1825 it was called St. Thomas to honour Col. Thomas Talbot, the colonizer of southern Ontario, who established thousands of settlers along the Talbot Road. (The *St.* was added for assonance).

ST. WILLIAMS

Pop. 418. In Walsingham T., Norfolk C., on C. Rds. 16 & 42, 45 km SE of Tillsonburg. The first settlers, in the early 1800s, were the Cope family, after which the settlement was first known as Cope's Landing. In 1831 the post office was established as Walsingham. In 1869 the name was changed to St. Williams after William Gillaspey, an early settler. The first provincial forest nursery in Canada was established in 1908 on 100 acres (40.5 ha) of wind-eroded, sandy soil, largely through the efforts of conservationist Edmund Zavitz. The nursery now covers more than 4,000 acres (1,620 ha) and produces millions of seedlings annually for reforestation projects across the province.

SALEM

Pop. 465. In Nichol T., Wellington C., on the Irvine River and C. Rds. 7 & 18, 25 km NW of Guelph. The first settler was Sem Wissler, whose ancestors had immigrated to Pennsylvania from Switzerland about 1730. Wissler settled on the present site of Salem in 1845. Wissler called the place Salem and sometimes "City of Peace." When the post office was established in 1863, the place was called Wynford. Wissler was the first postmaster. By 1867 the name of the post office had been changed by Scots and United Empire Loyalists to Salem, after the Salem in Cumberland County, Nova Scotia.

SANDFORD

Pop. 201. In Uxbridge T., Reg. Mun. of Durham, on C. Rd. 11, 43 km NW of Whitby. The post office was established as Sandford in 1862. The history of the community and the origin of its name are not known.

SANDY COVE

Pop. 1,550. In Innisfil T., Simcoe C., on the W side of Lake Simcoe, 12 km SE of Barrie. The site was historically a favourite camping ground of Indians. Summer cottages were built in the area in the 1890s. A post office was established as Sandy Cove in 1966.

SANDY LAKE I.R.

Pop. 1,323. In Kenora Dist. on the N shore of 270-square-mile (699-sq-km) Sandy Lake, (an expansion of the Severn River.) There is a trading post on the lake. The reserve is the home of the Deer Lake Indian band.

SARNIA

Pop. 70,877. In Lambton C., at the foot of Lake Huron and head of the St. Clair River and Hwys. 7, 40, 40B, & 402, connected by the Bluewater Bridge and a railway tunnel to Port Huron, Michigan, 96 km W of London. In 1679, Sieur de René Robert Cavelier LaSalle berthed *Griffon* at the site on its maiden voyage from Niagara to Green Bay, a voyage from which it never returned. (The ship was presumed to have sunk in the Mississagi Strait off Manitoulin Island in Lake Huron.) The place was known as Les Chutes (The Rapids) when the first settler, Ignace Cazelet (who later anglicized his name to Causley) arrived in 1807. Lt. Richard E. Vidal was one of the first English-speaking settlers who arrived in 1832 to establish a trade route from The Rapids to Detroit. On one of Vidal's periodic visits to England, his home was taken over by eight members of the Ferguson family, who turned it into the area's first tavern—until Vidal returned and evicted them.

The French settlers wanted to retain the name Les Chutes; the English settlers wanted to call the place Buenos Aires, and Scottish settlers preferred the name New Glasgow. At a meeting in 1836 attended by Sir John Colborne, the governor of Canada, his suggestion of Port Sarnia as a name broke the deadlock. Colborne had earlier served as governor of Guernsey, one of the Channel Islands, the Roman name of which had been Sarnia. Sarnia is at the northern end of the St. Clair Parkway, a parks development system administered by a commission of representatives of the Ontario government, the counties of Lambton and Kent, and the cities of Chatham and Sarnia. The greatest concentration of Canada's petrochemical industries is just south of Sarnia, in an area called Chemical Valley. The Bluewater Bridge, built in 1938 to link Sarnia with Port Huron, is believed to be the only bridge in the world owned by two countries.

SARSFIELD
Pop. 344. In the Reg. Mun. of Ottawa-Carleton on C. Rd. 28, 23 km E of Ottawa. The post office was established as Sarsfield in 1874. The origin of the name is not known.

SAUBLE BEACH
Pop. 517. In Amabel T., Bruce C., on Lake Huron and C. Rds. 8 & 21, 26 km NW of Owen Sound. A sandy beach 11 km long attracted the first cottagers in the early 1900s and earned the nickname "Canada's Daytona Beach." Today there are more than 3,000 cottages along the beach. The name derives from a corruption of the French word *sable* (sand).

SAULT STE. MARIE
Pop. 78,568. In Algoma Dist. on the St. Marys River, which connects Lake Superior and Lake Huron and Hwy. 17 and the S terminus of the Algoma Central Railway, linked to Sault Ste. Marie, Mich., by a railway bridge and highway bridge. The Sault, as it's known, has always been a natural meeting place. Long before Etienne Brûlé "discovered" the rapids in 1622, Ojibway tribes gathered near them because, in winter, the fast waters of the rapids were often the only open water for miles around, and

whitefish could always be easily caught. The Indians called the place Pawating, meaning "bounding or turbulent waters." Brûlé named the place Saut de Gaston to honour Baptiste Gagnon, duc d'Orléans, brother of Louis XIII and, at that time, heir to the throne of France. In 1668 Père Jacques Marquette established a mission at the site and named it Sainte Marie du Sault. The first of a series of locks to help boats past the rapids was built by the North West Company from 1797 to 1798. The post office opened as Sault Ste. Marie in 1846. In 1870 the United States refused to permit the steamer *Chicora*, carrying Colonel Wolseley's Red River expedition, to pass through the locks at Sault Ste. Marie. The incident, known as "the *Chicora* Incident," led to the construction of a Canadian canal, which was completed in 1895. In 1814, Swiss-born Montreal fur trader Charles Ermatinger built a fine stone residence, which today is a museum and the oldest stone residence in Canada west of Toronto.

SAVANT LAKE

Pop. 350. In Thunder Bay Dist. on Hwy. 599, 121 km NE of Ignace. The place was first known as Asylum # 2. When the post office was established in 1920 it was named Bucke. In 1927 the name was changed to Savant Lake. The origin of all three names is unknown.

SCARBOROUGH

Pop. 470,406. On Lake Ontario, one of the five cities and one borough that comprise the Municipality of Metropolitan Toronto, which covers 400 square kilometres (154.4 sq mi). The area was surveyed by Augustus Jones in 1791. Because of the majesty of the 90-metre-high clay bluffs, Jones called the area The High Lands of Toronto and named the township Glasgow. Two years later, the wife of Lt.-Gov. John Graves Simcoe saw the 9-km-long cliffs from a surveyor's boat. She talked of building a summer residence there and calling it Scarborough after the town with great grey cliffs in Yorkshire, England. Scottish stone mason David Thomson from Dumfriesshire is believed to have been the first resident of Scarborough. He built a log cabin on the banks of Highland Creek near the site of what is now Scarborough General Hospital. Thomson's job was in York, now Toronto, but he made the long treks home because he wanted a healthy place to raise his family, away from the marshy lands of Toronto.

SCHREIBER

Pop. 1,968. In Thunder Bay Dist. on the N shore of Lake Superior and Hwy. 17, 94 km SE of Nipigon. The place was first called Isbester's Landing, after a Colonel Isbester, who landed troops there in 1869, during the first Riel Rebellion. The Canadian Pacific Railway tracks reached the place by 1885, and a settlement began about 2 miles (3 km) inland, on the site of the railway construction camp. The place was named Schreiber after Sir Collingwood Schreiber, then engineer-in-chief of the CPR and later deputy minister of the federal Department of Railways and Canals. A town hall was built in 1885, which provided a public library, auditorium, barber shop—and the first bathtubs in Schreiber, which could be rented for 25 cents a night.

SCHUMACHER

Pop. 2,421. In Cochrane Dist. on Hwy. 101, 2 km E of Timmins. The place was named after a Mr. Schumacher who started the McIntyre Mine, later part of the Hollinger holdings.

SCOTLAND

Pop. 622. In Oakland T., Brant C., on Malcolm's Creek and Hwy. 24 and C. Rds. 3, 4, & 15, 19 km SW of Brantford. The place was founded by the Malcolm families, Scottish pioneers, and was first known as Malcolm's Mills. The post office opened in 1852 as Scotland. The origin of the name is not known.

SCUDDER

Pop. 200. In Pelee T., Essex C., on the N shore of Pelee Island in Lake Erie. The post office was established as Pelee Island North in 1896. In 1903 the name of the post office was changed to Scudder after a Dutchman who devised drainage canals on the island in 1888, vastly increasing the amount of arable land.

SEACLIFFE

Pop. 450. In Mersea T., Essex C., on Pigeon Bay of Lake Erie and Hwy. 18, 2 km SW of Leamington. Incorporated as a police village in 1924. The name describes the physical location of the village on the shore of Pigeon Bay.

SEAFORTH

Pop. 2,100. In Tuckersmith and McKillop ts., Huron C., on Hwy. 8 and C. Rd. 12, 34 km SE of Goderich. The townsite was once a swamp where two roads intersected and was known as Four Corners or Steene's Corners for Andrew Steene, the first settler. The intersection was marked with a fingerboard pointing the direction and distances to Egmondville, Ainleyville, and Goderich and as a result was also called Guide Board Swamp. In 1855, James Patton (later a law partner of Sir John A. Macdonald) and Barrie lawyers Lefroy and Bernard, purchased land expecting that the Buffalo and Lake Huron Railway would cross their property. They laid out a townsite, called it Seaforth after a town in Scotland, and launched a successful campaign to lure the railroad to their future town and away from the already established communities of

Egmondville and Harpurhey. When the railroad line came through the townsite, businessmen moved there from Egmondville and Harpurhey, and the three lawyers were able to sell their swampland at a substantial profit. In 1877 fire destroyed 12 acres (4.8 ha) of the business section. The Hon. William Aberhart, founder of the Social Credit Party and premier of Alberta from 1935 to 1943, was a native of Seaforth. The town was also the home of the Beaver lacrosse team, which at one time was world champion.

SEAGRAVE
Pop. 372. Part of Scugog T. in the Reg. Mun. of Durham, on C. Rd. 2, 37 km N of Whitby. The post office was established as Seagrave in 1973. The origin of the name is not known.

SEARCHMONT
Pop. 312. In Hodgins T., Algoma Dist., on Hwy. 532, 49 km NE of Sault Ste. Marie. The place was first known as Goulais. When the post office was established in 1903, the community was named after hotel owner Peter Searchmont.

SEBRINGVILLE
Pop. 201. In Ellice T., Perth C., on Black Creek and Hwy. 8 and C. Rd. 12, 8 km NW of Stratford. The place was first called Black Creek. In 1852, when the post office opened, the community was named Sebringville after P. A. Sebring, who had built the first sawmill and who was also the first postmaster.

SEELEY'S BAY
Pop. 234. In Rear of Leeds and Lansdowne T., Leeds and Grenville C., on the Rideau Canal and Hwy. 15, 21 km NW of Gananoque. The community had its start in 1825, when John Seeley bought 200 acres (81 ha) of land around the bay. When the post office was established in 1851, the place was named Seeley's Bay. The Seeley family lived out their lives at the site and were buried in an early cemetery, which has disappeared.

SEINE RIVER VILLAGE
Pop. 393. In Rainy River Dist. at the E end of Wild Potato Lake, 2 km S of Hwy. 11, 105 km E of Fort Frances. The post office was established as Seine River in 1895. The place is also known as Seine River Village. The origin of the name is unknown.

SELBY
Pop. 208. In Richmond T., Lennox and Addington C., on Sucker Creek and C. Rd. 11, 1 km E of Hwy. 41, 43 km W of Kingston. The community was first called Gallagher's Corners after a Mr. Gallagher who operated

a tavern a short distance east on what is now Hwy. 41. The village was laid out by John McKim. The post office was established in 1853, when early settler Edward Storr gave it the name Selby after his hometown in Yorkshire, England.

SELKIRK

Pop. 421. Part of the City of Nanticoke in the Reg. Mun. of Haldimand-Norfolk, on C. Rds. 3 & 53, 2 km N of the N shore of Lake Erie and 56 km S of Hamilton. The place was first named Williamsville after the first settler, William Steel. It was subsequently known as The Corners, Stoney Creek, and Enterprise. In 1836 the post office was established as Walpole after the township in which it was then located. In 1855 the name was changed to Selkirk. The origin of the name is unknown.

SEVERN BRIDGE

Pop. 300. In Morrison T., Muskoka Dist., on the Severn River and Hwy. 11, 22 km NE of Orillia. The post office was established as Severn Bridge in 1861.

SHAKESPEARE

Pop. 649. In South Easthope T., Perth C., on Hwys. 7, 8, & 59 and C. Rd. 14, 12 km E of Stratford. The place was founded in 1832 by David Bell and first known as Bell's Corners. When the post office opened in 1849, it was called Bell's Corners-Wilmot, Wilmot being a settlement 14 kilometres distant. In 1852, hotel owner Alexander Mitchell, who was also postmaster, proposed naming the settlement after his favourite poet-playwright, and his suggestion was adopted.

SHALLOW LAKE

Pop. 456. In Keppel T., Grey C., on Hwy. 70, 15 km NW of Owen Sound. The first settlers were a Mr. and Mrs. Butterworth; John Spencer, Mrs. Butterworth's son from a former marriage, and his bride. The family arrived in 1862 and built a log cabin and barn. The post office was established in 1891, named after nearby Shallow Lake. In 1884 R. J. Doyle opened a cement works, using marl from the bed of Shallow Lake. Marl is a chalky deposit high in calcium carbonate.

SHANNONVILLE

Pop. 270. In Tyendinaga T., Hastings C., on the Salmon River and Hwy. 2 and C. Rd. 7, 13 km NE of Belleville. The community was first known as Mohawkwoods, then as Merchison's Mills, and as Shannonville when the post office was established in 1833. The origin of the name is not known.

SHANTY BAY

Pop. 335. In Oro T., Simcoe C., on the N shore of Kempenfelt Bay off Lake

Simcoe and C. Rd. 20, 13 km NE of Barrie. The community was founded by Col. Edward G. O'Brien, a government land agent commissioned to locate a group of escaped slaves in Oro Township about 1830. In the course of his duties, Colonel O'Brien decided to settle in the township and acquired a grant of 400 acres (162 ha) on Kempenfelt Bay. Other settlers, some of them half-pay British officers, also took up land at the site, living in rude shelters while building more substantial homes. (Half-pay officers received half pay as pensions because they had been wounded or because they remained available for recall to active service). It was the appearance of these shanties against the sparkling waters of Lake Simcoe that led O'Brien to call the place Shanty Bay. St. Thomas' Church was built by local parishioners using a construction technique known as "rammed earth." Wet clay mixed with straw was compacted into wooden moulds and left to harden. When completely dry, the mud walls were reinforced with a coating of plaster to protect them from the elements. The church still stands and is one of the few surviving structures of its kind in Ontario. In 1908 a government dock was built, and passenger service to points around the lake was made available on the steamers *Geneva* and *Islay*.

SHARBOT LAKE

Pop. 381. In Oso T., Frontenac C., on Sharbot Lake and Hwy. 38, 4 km S of Hwy. 7, 72 km N of Kingston. The lake and community take their names from the Sharbot family, which was farming in the area in the 1870s. The post office was established as Sharbot Lake in 1877. A roadside picnic area built beside Hwy. 7 in 1932 has become Sharbot Lake Provincial Park.

SHARON

Pop. 1,646. In Reg. Mun. of East Gwillimbury on C. Rds. 12 & 13, 50 km N of Toronto. The community was founded around 1812 by David Willson, son of an Irish immigrant from New York. Willson was a Quaker minister who broke away to form his own religious sect, which he called the Children of Peace, and which contemporaries called the Davidites. Willson and his followers built a temple called the Temple of Sharon, which has no architectural equal in the world. For a time the community was called Davidtown, but when the post office was opened in 1841 it was called Sharon after the temple, which now is operated as a museum. In July each year since 1980, Music at Sharon features singing groups.

SHEDDEN

Pop. 413. In Southwold T., Elgin C., on Hwy. 3 and C. Rd. 20, 15 km SW of St. Thomas. The community was first called Wilkie's Corners, but when the post office opened in 1875 the place was named Corseley. In 1883 the name was changed to Shedden after John Shedden, a prosperous local stock grower killed in an accident while boarding a train.

SHEFFIELD

Pop. 304. In the Reg. Mun. of Hamilton-Wentworth on Hwy. 8, 10 km SE of Cambridge. The first settler was Rev. John A. Cornell in 1809. In 1837 the post office was established as Sheffield after Sheffield, England.

SHELBURNE

Pop. 3,123. In Melancthon T., Dufferin C., on Hwys. 10 & 89 and C. Rd. 12, 53 km S of Collingwood. In 1864 William Jelly, a native of the Brockville area, built a hotel on the site, which he called the British Canadian Hotel. Travellers, however, called it Jelly's Tavern, and the place became known as Jelly's Corners. Before the post office was established, some residents wanted the place called Tanderagee after a town in Ireland, but members of Parliament named the place Shelburne after the earl of Shelburne, who had been instrumental in ending the War of 1812.

SIMCOE

Pop. 14,197. In the Reg. Mun. of Haldimand-Norfolk on the Lynn River and Hwys. 3 & 24, 31 km S of Brantford. In 1795 Canada's first lieutenant-governor, John Graves Simcoe, camped overnight at the site (then known by the Indian name Shain-e-ong), on his way to establish Fort Norfolk on Lake Erie. Simcoe subsequently granted lands to potential colonizers, including Aaron Culver, who received land on the condition that he build mills. By 1812 Culver had built a sawmill and a grist mill, and a community had formed around them. The mills were burned down during the War of 1812, and U.S. troops looted some homes. In 1815, Culver deeded some of his land to William Bird, who built the first store, and the place became known as Birdtown. By 1829 there were two small communities, known as Birdtown and Culver. Residents wanted to call the place Wellington Village, but since there already was a small community by that name near Picton, a second choice had to be made. That year the post office opened as Simcoe, honouring the late lieutenant-governor.

The area where Simcoe camped is now a large park, including Lake George and a stretch of the Lynn River. Each winter thousands come to see Christmas Panorama—dozens of lighted Christmas displays in the park—which started by accident in 1957. That year Simcoe was to have had a big Santa Claus parade, but it was rained out. Folks had worked hard on their floats and wanted to show them off, so they placed them in town parks under floodlights. So many people turned out to see the display that the format was continued and has been successfully copied by Toronto, Niagara Falls, and Sarnia.

SIOUX LOOKOUT

Pop. 3,027. In Drayton T., Kenora Dist., on Minnitaki Lake and Hwys. 72, 516, & 642, 67 km NE of Dinorwic on Hwy. 17, which is 28 km SE of Dryden. In 1784 Edward Umfreville was commissioned by the North West Company to find an alternative to the traditional canoe route to the west, which passed through American-held territory. Umfreville made his way up the Nipigon River and west through a web of rivers to present-day Manitoba, passing the site of present-day Sioux Lookout en route. Indians knew the place as Na Di Is Si Wag and settlers first called it Knowlton. The post office opened as Graham in 1911, but two years later the name was changed to Sioux Lookout. The place takes its name from a hill just west of the townsite, where the Ojibway Indians watched for the raiding Sioux.

SIOUX NARROWS

Pop. 384. In Kenora Dist. on Longpoint Island in Lake of the Woods and Hwy. 71, 80 km SE of Kenora. The post office of Sioux Narrows was established in 1938. The name recalls a battle between the Sioux and Ojibway Indians. At Sioux Narrows, Highway 71 is carried over the longest single-span wooden bridge in the world. The 32-metre (105-ft) central spans are of Douglas fir from British Columbia whose age predates the European settlement of Canada. When it was built in 1935 the 64-metre-long (210-ft) bridge was designed to last 40 years and carry a maximum load of 18 tons (18.28 tonnes). Tests conducted in 1980 found the timbers to be as sound as when the bridge was built, and capable of carrying loads up to 110 tons (111.76 tonnes).

SKEAD

Pop. 325. Part of the Town of Nickel Centre, Reg. Mun. of Sudbury, on the S shore of Wanapitei Lake and Hwy. 86, 28 km NE of Sudbury. The post office was established as Massey Bay in 1921. In 1924 the name of the community was changed to Skead after Kitty Skead, a daughter of Ottawa lumber baron Senator Skead, who married W. J. Bell of Sudbury.

SMITHS FALLS

Pop. 9,047. In South Elmsley T., Leeds and Grenville C., and North Elmsley T., Lanark C., on the Rideau River at the E end of Rideau Lake and Hwys. 15, 29, & 43 and C. Rds. 4 & 17, 83 km SW of Ottawa. Although the spelling has been changed, the community is named after Maj. Thomas Smythe, a United Empire Loyalist who received a Crown grant of land in 1784 and built a sawmill on a series of falls in the Rideau River. Smythe then mortgaged his holdings and failed to meet his financial obligations, and the land was bought by Abel Ward. Ward is considered to be the founder of the town, which for a time was called Wardsville. The name was later changed to Smythe's Falls and then modified to Smith's Falls. In 1968, by an act of the Ontario legislature, the apostrophe was removed from the name. Smiths Falls was the first town in Ontario to have a government-approved plan for the development and expansion of its boundaries. The town is divided into four district wards—residential, commercial, light manufacturing, and heavy industry areas.

SMITHVILLE

Pop. 1,976. In the Reg. Mun. of Niagara on Twenty Mile Creek and Hwy. 20 and C. Rd. 24, 32 km SE of Hamilton. The place was first called Griffintown after United Empire Loyalist Richard Griffin from Nine Partners, New York, who arrived in 1786. The name was later changed to Smithville by his youngest son, Smith Griffin, in memory of his mother, whose maiden name was Mary Smith.

SMOOTH ROCK FALLS

Pop. 2,052. Town in Cochrane Dist. on the Mattagami River and Hwys. 11 & 634, 41 km SE of Kapuskasing. In 1915 a dam, power house, and pulp mill were built on the river where it flowed over a huge face of rock worn smooth by the water. In 1927 the mill was bought by the Abitibi Power and Paper Co. The town is a one-industry, closed company town, which has resulted in the creation nearby of the small communities of Moorville, Unionville, and Clouthierville.

SNELGROVE

Pop. 500. Part of the City of Brampton in the Reg. Mun. of Peel on Hwy. 10 and C. Rd. 14, 8 km NW of Brampton. The place was settled in 1838 by John Snell and first called Edmonton. In 1859 the name was changed to honour Snell and to prevent mail from going to the new community in Alberta of the same name.

SOLINA

Pop. 500. Part of the Town of Newcastle in the Reg. Mun. of Durham, 15 km NW of Bowmanville. The community was first known as Pilchardton, Pilchardtown, Pelchardtown, and Toole's Corners. In 1869, when the post office was being established, teacher John Hughes, who disliked the name Pilchardtown, invited some young men to meet him at the school one evening. He wrote the consonants L, N, and S and the vowels A, I, and O on the blackboard and invited the young men to make a pronounceable name. A ballot was taken to determine the most popular name, and Solina was the winner. The community apparently went along with the name choice.

SOMBRA

Pop. 407. In Sombra T., Lambton C., on the St. Clair River and C. Rds. 2 & 33, linked to Marine City, Michigan, by ferry service, 32 km S of Sarnia. Abraham Smith and Samuel H. Burnham, who arrived in 1821, were the first settlers. The place was first called Shawanese but was later named Sombra, believed to have derived from a Spanish word meaning "shade," and referring to the shady forests that once covered the area.

SOUTH BAY

Pop. 300. In Kenora Dist., 83 km NE of Ear Falls, 226 km N of Dryden. The community is named after South Bay Mine, which opened in 1969.

SOUTH GLOUCESTER

Pop. 503. In the Reg. Mun. of Ottawa-Carleton on Hwy. 31 and C. Rd. 8, 15 km SE of Ottawa. The post office was established as Barton's Corners in 1847 and renamed South Gloucester in 1852. The community is named after Gloucester Township in which it used to be located.

SOUTH LANCASTER

Pop. 231. In Lancaster T., Stormont, Dundas, and Glengarry C., on Lake St. Francis (a widening of the St. Lawrence River) and Hwy. 2, 30 km NE of Cornwall. The post office was established in 1881 as South Lancaster, taking its name from the township, which was named after George III of England, duke of Lancaster.

SOUTH MOUNTAIN

Pop. 365. In Mountain T., Stormont, Dundas, and Glengarry C., on C. Rd. 3, 40 km N of Prescott. The post office was established as South Mountain in 1851.

SOUTH PORCUPINE

Pop. 4,219. Part of the City of Timmins, Cochrane Dist., on the S shore of Porcupine Lake and Hwy. 101, 9 km E of Timmins. The community of Porcupine is 3 km distant on the north shore of the lake. The first prospectors arrived in 1906, before the gold rush of 1909, which opened up the area. In 1911 South Porcupine and Schumacher were incorporated to form the Township of Tisdale, and in the same year a forest fire destroyed the community. The loss of life was never precisely determined but was officially listed as 73. Hundreds spent the night of the fire in the lake, and many were drowned. In the 50 years following Benny Hollinger's 1909 discovery of gold quartz in the Porcupine area, more than 45,000 claims were staked. In 1958 the Porcupine camp produced more gold than any other mining region in the Western Hemisphere.

SOUTH RIVER

Pop. 1,034. In Parry Sound Dist. on the South River, which flows N into

Lake Nipissing on Hwy. 11, 58 km S of North Bay. The river was an early Indian canoe route and was used by European explorers as a means of access to Lake Nipissing from the Muskokas. The settlement was founded by lumbermen, and, when the post office opened in 1882, took its name from the South River.

SOUTH WOODSLEE
Pop. 642. In Maidstone and Rochester ts., Essex C., on C. Rd. 27, 34 km SE of Windsor. The post office was established as South Woodslee in 1877. The origin of the name is unknown.

SOUTHAMPTON
Pop. 2,695. In Saugeen T., Bruce C., on Lake Huron at the mouth of the Saugeen River and Hwy. 21, 38 km SW of Owen Sound. The town's history dates to 1652, when a peace treaty, later broken, was signed between the Iroquois and Ojibway. Nearby Saugeen Indian Reserve is the home of descendants of the Ojibway and their allies. The town plot was surveyed in 1851, and the same year a post office called Saugeen was opened. The name is Indian for either "beautiful river" or "mouth of the river." The last extensive transfer of Indian lands in southern Ontario took place in 1854, when most of the Bruce Peninsula was surrendered to the Crown by the Saugeen and Newash bands of Ojibway. The Hon. James Harvey Price, commissioner of Crown lands, named the place Southampton, in 1890, after his hometown in England. The first settlers were Capt. John Spence and Capt. William Kennedy, former employees of the Hudson's Bay Company, who engaged in commercial fishing and fur trading with the local Indians. When the fishing venture was unsuccessful, Spence sailed along the lakeshore, trading with the Indians, and Kennedy returned to England, subsequently leading an expedition to the Arctic in search of Sir John Franklin.

SPANISH
Pop. 1,063. In Sheddon T., Algoma Dist., on Hwy. 17, 105 km SW of Sudbury. The post office was established in 1887 as Spanish River Station, with the community taking its name from the nearby Spanish River, so named by Admiralty surveyor H. W. Bayfield because Spanish Indians had at one time lived in the area. Another version of the origin of the name is that a Spaniard fled the hand of justice in the lower Mississippi area in the old fur-trade days, and ended up among the uninquisitive *coureurs de bois* and so gave a name to the place.

SPARTA
Pop. 320. In Yarmouth T., Elgin C., on C. Rds. 27 & 36, 19 km SE of St. Thomas. The community was first known as the Quaker Settlement or Yarmouth Corners. When the post office was established in 1841, the

name became Sparta. Whatever significance this name may have had to its founders has been lost over the years. Johnathan Doan, a Quaker from Pennsylvania, was the first settler on 200 acres (81 ha) of land he acquired in 1815. When he became agent for 3,000 more acres (1,215 ha) he returned to Pennsylvania to convince other Quakers to move north and settle. To encourage settlement, Doan built a saw- and grist mill and a tannery. In 1831 Alvin Jay erected a clay-and-straw blacksmith shop to house the horses of troops involved in the 1837 Rebellion. Joshua Doan was sentenced to hang for his part in the Reform movement; his body was returned to Sparta for burial in the Quaker cemetery. One of Sparta's historic sites today is the Friends' (Quakers') Meeting House, built about 1821.

SPENCERVILLE

Pop. 341. In Edwardsburgh T., Leeds and Grenville C., on the South Nation River and C. Rds. 21 & 44, immediately W of Hwy. 16, 14 km NW of Prescott. Peleg and David Spencer built a sawmill at the site in 1811, and by 1821 they were also operating a grist mill, which served the pioneer settlers of a wide area. When the post office was established in 1841, the place was named after its founder.

SPRINGFIELD

Pop. 561. In South Dorchester and Malahide ts., Elgin C., on C. Rds. 40 & 52, 21 km NE of St. Thomas. The site originally was part of a land grant given to a British officer and his daughter after the American Revolutionary War. When the land was subsequently divided, part of it was purchased by Henry Gilbert, who in turn sold it to Joel Burns. The place was then called Burns' Creek. Archibald Clunas arrived in 1851 and three years later was appointed postmaster of a post office that bore the name Clunas. Meanwhile, Moses Yoder had acquired the Burns property, and his daughter named the place Springfield for the clear, cold springs on her father's farm. The place was known by both names until 1863, when the name was officially changed to Springfield.

STAYNER

Pop. 3,045. In Nottawasaga T., Simcoe C., on Hwys. 26 & 91 and C. Rd. 42, 39 km W of Barrie. The settlement was first known as Warrington, but when the Ontario, Simcoe and Huron Railway (later Northern Railway) came through in 1854, railway officials named the station Nottawasaga after the township, and residents used that name. A few years later the town was renamed Dingwall, but in 1864 the village and the post office took the name Stayner to honour Sutherland Stayner, a local property owner. In the 1880s a rumour circulated that Simcoe County, due to its large size, was planning to set up two county towns.

Stayner, in an ideal position to be chosen the northern town, prevailed upon the Ontario legislature, which in 1888 authorized incorporation of the Town of Stayner. Stayner then became the smallest town in Ontario, a distinction it maintained for some years.

STEVENSVILLE

Pop. 1,257. Part of the Town of Fort Erie, Reg. Mun. of Niagara, on Black Creek and C. Rd. 116, 10 km W of Fort Erie. A post office named Stevensville was established in 1835. The community is said to have been named by a carpenter named Stevens, employed to build McCarthy's Hotel. When the frame was up, Stevens went to the peak and threw a bottle of liquor, naming the place Stevensville.

STEWARTTOWN

Pop. 250. Part of the Town of Halton Hills in the Reg. Mun. of Halton on C. Rds. 3 & 15, 17 km NW of Milton. When the post office was established in 1832, the place was named Esquesing after the township in which the community was located. The township's name was an Indian word meaning "that which lies at the end." The settlement was later named Stewarttown after the original settler, Duncan Stewart, who arrived in the 1820s. Stewarttown is the correct name, although variations have included Stewartstown, Stewarton, Stewart Town, and Stewartown.

STIRLING

Pop. 1,880. In Rawdon T., Hastings C., on Rawdon Creek and Hwys. 14 & 33 and C. Rd. 8, 25 km NW of Belleville. John Bleecker and Caleb Gilbert were allotted a mill site in 1797 on the condition that they build a mill within two years. Bleecker died soon after, but the mill was completed in 1807 by Samuel Rosebush. The community was known as Stirling Mills and Fidlar's Mills for mill owners and Rawdon Mills for the township. Many of the early settlers were Scottish, and since the surrounding countryside reminded them of Stirlingshire in their homeland, they changed the name to Stirling in 1852. Disastrous fires in 1883 and 1909 nearly destroyed the village. After the second fire, a steam fire engine was purchased, and a regular fire brigade was organized. Robert Fletcher's team of horses was said to have been so well trained that the moment the fire bell sounded it galloped on its own to the fire hall. Stirling has one of Ontario's three remaining cobblestone churches, built in the 1850s by local Wesleyan Methodists. Stones 6 to 9 inches (15-22.5 cm) in length were set in horizontal rows in a bed of mortar. Ontario's other two cobblestone churches are in the Paris area.

STITTSVILLE

Pop. 2,652. In the Reg. Mun. of Ottawa-Carleton on C. Rd. 5, 26 km SW of Ottawa. The post office and place name both honour the first settler, Jackson Stitt, who arrived in 1818.

STONEY CREEK

Pop. 45,329. Town in the Reg. Mun. of Hamilton-Wentworth on Lake Ontario at the mouth of Stoney Creek and the Queen Elizabeth Way immediately SE of the City of Hamilton. The first settlers were United Empire Loyalists. The place was a hamlet with one store when the War of 1812 broke out, and it became the site of a famous battle. In the Battle of Stoney Creek in 1813 an attacking force of 2,000 Americans was captured by 700 British troops, under the command of Lt.-Col. John Harvey. The British captured two American brigadier-generals, Chandler and Winder. The battle was considered the turning point that prevented American troops from overrunning Canada. Battlefield House, where Mary Gage tended the wounded of both sides, was the Gage home and is now an historical museum. Stoney Creek was the birthplace of the Women's Institute, formed by Erland Lee, a founder of the Farmer's Institute, assisted by his wife and Mrs. Adelaide Hunter-Hoodless. In 1913 the Battle of Stoney Creek was commemorated by the unveiling of a monument in Battlefield Park. The unveiling was done electronically by Queen Mary from England. She pushed a button on cue, sending an electrical impulse to Canada. The place is believed to have taken its name from Stony Creek, since there was a post office by that name in 1827, the same year the "e" was inserted. Some historians, however, contend that the name came from early settlers Jim Stoney, a trapper, and Edmund Stoney, an Anglican minister.

STONEY POINT

Pop. 1,074. In Tilbury West T., Essex C., on Lake St. Clair and C. Rd. 2, 43 km E of Windsor. The community was first known as Chevalier. When the post office was established in 1865 it was named Stoney Point. In the early 1900s the place was known as Pointe aux Roches. Indians used flint stone from this region for their arrowheads.

STOUFFVILLE

Pop. 12,884. In Markham and Whitchurch ts., Reg. Mun. of York, on Duffin's Creek and Hwy. 47 and C. Rd. 30, 45 km NE of Toronto. The original owner of the land was Abraham Stouffer, who settled in 1806 and after whom the community was named when the post office was established in 1832. Among the early settlers in the area were a number of Quakers who, until 1816, when they established their own organization, had formed part of the Yonge Street Meeting. The Whitchurch Quaker group later split into several factions, but by 1900 it had come together to form Pine Orchard Union Church, which stands today on Vivian Road in Stouffville.

STRAFFORDVILLE

Pop. 644. In Bayham T., Elgin C., on Hwy. 19 and C. Rd. 38, 15 km SW of Tillsonburg. Originally known as Sandytown, the name was changed to Straffordville when the post office was established, in 1851. The origin of the name is unknown.

STRATFORD

Pop. 26,078. In South Easthope T., Perth C., on the Avon River and Hwys 7, 8, & 19 and C. Rd. 21, 36 km W of Kitchener. The attributes of Stratford as a townsite were noted by surveyors as they hacked out the Huron Road from the Waterloo County boundary to Goderich from 1828 to 1829. The place was known as Little Thames, after the river, when William Sargeant and his wife arrived in 1832 and built a hotel, which they called the Shakespeare Inn. A Canada Company official donated a painting of Shakespeare to Sargeant to hang in the hotel. The river had previously been named the Avon by Dr. William "Tiger" Dunlop of the Canada Company, so when the post office was established in 1832 residents agreed the place should be called Stratford after Shakespeare's birthplace in England. In the 1860s, when Stratford was divided into five wards, they were named Shakespeare, Hamlet, Romeo, Avon, and Falstaff.

It wasn't until 1953 that Stratford really capitalized on its Shakespeare connection (thanks to the idea and efforts of newspaper reporter Thomas Patterson.) Patterson set up a committee in 1952 to explore the possibility of holding a theatre festival and sought the advice of leaders in the theatre arts. He arranged through Dora Mavor Moore for Tyrone Guthrie, eminent British producer, to meet the committee in 1952. Patterson held executive posts in the organization that grew out of this committee. The following year, in a massive tent beside the Avon River, Sir Alec Guinness played Richard III. The venture was a huge success, and the 1957 season opened in a permanent home with 2,262 seats, none of which is more than 65 feet (19.8 m) from the stage. The 1901-vintage Avon Theatre became a partner in the festival in 1967, and the Third Stage Theatre opened in 1971. The three theatres now draw 400,000 persons a year to "the Festival City."

STRATHROY

Pop. 9,186. In Caradoc T., Middlesex C., on the Sydenham River and Hwy. 81 and C. Rds. 9 & 39, 32 km W of London. A sawmill was built here as early as 1832, but the townsite was not laid out until 1850. The place was first known as Strath Valley, or Red Valley. In 1832 John Stewart Buchanan acquired the mill site and named the place after his hometown of Strathroy, a small Irish seaport. Edward Blake (1833-1912), born near Strathroy, was premier of Ontario from 1871 to 1872. He later held several posts in the federal government. Strathroy native Gen. Sir Arthur

William Currie (1875-1933) was one of Canada's most distinguished military figures. He saw action throughout the First World War and in 1917 was appointed commander-in-chief of the Canadian Corps in Europe.

STREETSVILLE

Pop. 9,690. In Toronto T., Peel C., on the Credit River and Hwys 10 & 401, 33 km W of Toronto. The place was settled around 1818 and first known as Credit Mills, taking its name from that of the river. When a post office was established in 1828, the community was named Streetsville after Timothy Street, an early settler who built the first saw- and grist mill.

STROUD

Pop. 1,000. In Innisfil T., Simcoe C., on Hwy. 11, 12 km SE of Barrie. The first home was built in 1840 by John Lawrence, and for a time the place was called Victoria, after the Queen of England. When a post office was to be established in 1873, it was found that a number of other communities also had the name Victoria. W. C., Little, member of Parliament for South Simcoe, suggested the community be named Stroud after his hometown in Gloucestershire, England. A wooden Methodist church was built in 1852 on Lawrence's farm, and a dozen years later the community built a brick church, using the original church as a Sunday school. In the winter of 1905, both buildings burned down.

STURGEON FALLS

Pop. 5,770. In Springer T., Nipissing Dist., on the Sturgeon River, 5 km upstream from Lake Nipissing, on Hwys. 17 & 64. A Hudson's Bay Company post had been established at the mouth of the Sturgeon River before 1880, but the present townsite was not settled until 1883, when the Canadian Pacific Railway line came through the region. The townsite then was called Barrier Falls. With the railway came many French-Canadians settlers; much of today's population has French as its mother tongue. For years Sturgeon Falls was known for its excellent caviar, taken from the sturgeon of Lake Nipissing. Overfishing has ended the commercial viability of this industry.

SUCKER CREEK I.R.

Pop. 200. In Manitoulin Dist. on Manitoulin Island and Hwy. 540, 8 km W of Little Current. The 1,573-acre (637-ha) reservation is the smallest on Manitoulin Island.

SUDBURY

Pop. 89,698. City in Reg. Mun. of Sudbury on Lake Ramsey and Hwys. 17, 69, & 144, 125 km W of North Bay. Sudbury, nicknamed "Nickel

Capital of the World," was created by the Canadian Pacific Railway, which established it as a siding in 1883. It was named by James Worthington, superintendent of the construction crews, after his wife's birthplace in Suffolk, England. In 1884, during construction of the rail bed, copper and nickel ores were discovered just west of the townsite, resulting in an influx of prospectors and mining interests. In the 1920s, a smelting method known as "heap roasting" was used. In this process, ore with a high sulphur content was piled on beds of timber, which were then burned. The piles burned for months, creating sulphurous fumes in which no vegetation could live, which left the Sudbury area resembling a moonscape—U.S. astronauts actually trained there for their moon landing. In the late 1970s a program called the Greening of Sudbury was launched. Hundreds of students spread tons of lime on soil in and around the city and planted a special variety of coarse grass and small deciduous trees.

Sudbury is on the edge of a massive indentation in the landscape called the Sudbury Basin. The elliptical depression, 59 km long and 27 km wide, is believed to have been caused by a meteorite two billion years ago, or a huge volcanic eruption, or a combination of the two. About 30 years ago, Sudbury erected The Big Nickel, the largest coin in the world. The replica, 30 feet (9.1 m) in diameter, is of the Canadian 1951 commemorative five-cent coin. In 1984 Northern Ontario's biggest tourism magnet opened at Sudbury. Science North is a hands-on science museum housed in two snowflake-shaped buildings that cling to a rocky ledge of the shore of Lake Ramsey.

SUMMER BEAVER
Pop. 280. In Kenora Dist. on the S shore of Nibinamik Lake, 470 km NE of Thunder Bay. The community takes its name from the lake, which is an Ojibway word for "summer beaver." The settlement was started in 1975, and in the same year the post office was established.

SUNDERLAND
Pop. 875. In the Reg. Mun. of Durham on the Beaverton River and Hwys. 7 & 12 and C. Rd. 10, 85 km NE of Toronto. In 1836 the post office was established as Brock, the name of the township in which the community was then located. In the 1860s the place was called Jones' Corner or Corners, but in 1868 the name was changed to Sunderland after a town in England.

SUNDRIDGE
Pop. 812. In Strong T., Parry Sound Dist., on the NW shore of Bernard Lake, part of the Magnetawan River system, and Hwy. 11 just N of its junction with Hwy. 124, 67 km S of North Bay. The community was

settled in the 1870s and enjoyed a period of growth in 1886, with the arrival of the Canadian National Railway. The first postmaster, John Paget, named the community Sun Ridge or Sunny Ridge, but the name became corrupted through use to Sundridge.

SUTTON

Pop. 2,470. In the Reg. Mun. of York on the Black River 3 km S of Jackson's Point on Lake Simcoe, 86 km N of Toronto. The town was founded in 1830. Nearby is York County Park, the location of Sibbald Memorial Museum, built before 1820 and home to a large collection of Scottish and English Georgian silver; as well, it houses early Canadian, English, and Scottish furniture and early 18th-century portraits and enamels by Henry Bone. Canadian historian and humourist Stephen Butler Leacock (1869-1944), head of McGill University's faculty of political science, spent his summers at nearby Old Brewery Bay at the north end of Lake Simcoe. His grave is beneath a rare umbrella-elm tree in the cemetery of St. George's Anglican Church on Sibbald Point Provincial Park Road, 5 km northeast of Sutton. Leacock's best-known humourous novel is *Sunshine Sketches of a Little Town*, in which he parodied many of Orillia's leading citizens. In 1957, Leacock's home and library were bought by the Town of Orillia and turned into a museum, the Stephen Leacock Memorial Home. Canadian novelist Mazo de la Roche is buried in the same cemetery.

SWASTIKA

Pop. 542. In Teck T., Timiskaming Dist., on the Blanche River and Hwy. 66, 8 km W of Kirkland Lake. The post office was established as Swastika in 1911. Bill Dusty, owner of Swastika Mining Company, named the community Swastika in 1906 after the good-luck charm worn by a young lady he met. The name comes from a cross supposed to denote good fortune. During the Second World War, when the Nazis were using a version of the swastika as their emblem, determined efforts were made to have the community's name changed to Winston, in honour of Britain's prime minister, Winston Churchill. The villagers refused to relinquish a name that had for them become a symbol of good faith, good luck, and goodwill. They argued that their name had been adopted before Germany took the symbol and, in any case, their swastika went "the other way."

SWEABURG

Pop. 574. In West Oxford T., Oxford C., on C. Rd. 12, 5 km S of Woodstock. First known as Floodtown, the post office was established as Sviaborg in 1857. The name is that of a fortress on the Gulf of Finland, heavily bombarded by the Allies during the Crimean War of 1854. An elderly resident of Floodtown had been reading about the place in a report of the Crimean War and suggested Floodtown be named Sviaborg. When the post office stamp arrived, the name had been misspelled as Sweaburg. The error was never corrected.

SYDENHAM

Pop. 720. In Loughborough T., Frontenac C., at the SW tip of Sydenham Lake on C. Rd. 5, 32 km N of Kingston. The first post office, opened in 1836, was named Loughborough after the township. In 1883 the name was changed to Sydenham to honour Lord Sydenham, governor-in-chief of Canada.

TAMWORTH

Pop. 274. In Sheffield T., Lennox and Addington C., on the Salmon River and C. Rds. 4 & 15, 62 km NW of Kingston. The community was first called Wheeler's Mills after early settler Calvin Wheeler, who moved from Vermont around 1840. In 1841 Wheeler built a sawmill and a grist mill, which encouraged settlement, mainly by immigrants fleeing the Irish potato famine. In 1848 the post office was established with Wheeler as postmaster, and he named the place Tamworth after Tamworth, England.

TARA

Pop. 758. In Arran T., Bruce C., on the Sauble River and C. Rds. 5, 10, & 17, 26 km SW of Owen Sound. One of the founders of the community, which was first known as Eblana, was Richard Berford, a member of the party that arrived to survey Arran Township in 1851. In the late 1850s, W. A. Gerolamy built a foundry and agricultural implement works. Gerolamy introduced perforated zinc for sieves in the fanning mills that the company made, and the innovation won prizes at three world fairs. The community changed its name to Tara to honour the place where Ireland's ancient kings were crowned, and was incorporated as a village in 1881. Sir William H. Hearst (1864-1941), born near Tara, was Ontario's seventh premier from 1914 to 1919. Frederick "Cyclone" Taylor (1885-1979) of Tara was one of hockey's first superstars. He attracted widespread attention with his exceptional skating and scoring ability and in 1960 was elected to the Hockey Hall of Fame.

TAVISTOCK

Pop. 1,885. In East Zorra-Tavistock T., Oxford C., on Hwy. 59 and C. Rds. 22, 23, 24, & 34, 15 km SE of Stratford. Capt. Henry Eckstein settled nearby in 1845, and in 1848, when he learned that a railway line was likely to come through the area, he moved to the present site of Tavistock, so his home would be near the railway station. Nine years after he moved, the Buffalo and Lake Huron Railway finally arrived. Eckstein called the community Freiburg after his hometown in Germany, and it was later called Inkerman. When the post office opened in 1857, the village was named Tavistock after a village in Devon, England.

TECUMSEH

Pop. 8,873. In Sandwich East T., Essex C., on the S shore of Lake St. Clair and Hwy. 2, 13 km E of Windsor. The town started in 1854 with the arrival of the Great Western Railway between London and Windsor. It was first called Ryegate and later named Tecumseh for the Shawnee Indian chief who fought on the British side during the War of 1812. It is believed that the chief and his braves stopped on the present site of the village during that campaign.

TEESWATER

Pop. 976. In Culross T., Bruce C., on the Teeswater River, Hwy. 4 and C. Rd. 6, 22 km SW of Walkerton. The village started in 1856 when farmers Matthew Hadwin, P. B. Brown, Alexander Gibson, and Ira Fulford had parts of their farms surveyed into lots. Development was slow until the arrival of the Toronto, Grey and Bruce Railway in 1874. When the post office was established in 1856, the village took its name from the river, which in turn had been named after the Tees River in England.

TEMAGAMI

Pop. 318. In Strathy T., Dist. of Temagami, on the NE arm of Lake Temagami and Hwy. 11, 92 km NW of North Bay. In 1834 the Hudson's Bay Company opened a small trading post on nearby Bear Island. The post was an outpost of a larger one on Lake Timiskaming, designed to protect the company's fur-trading territory from competition. The site of the post on Bear Island was first known as Sandy Inlet. A community grew on the lakeshore, and when a post office was established, it was named Temagami after the 86-square-mile (225 sq km) lake of the same name. Temagami is an Indian word meaning "deep water." Immediately south of Temagami in tiny Finlayson Point Provincial Park, a plaque honours Grey Owl, a conservationist, author, and lecturer who was also an unrepentant imposter. He claimed to have been born in Mexico of an Apache Indian mother, but it is believed that he was born in England in 1888, son of George Belaney, a Scot. He emigrated to the Temagami and Biscotasing area in 1906 and became a trapper, guide, and forest ranger. He adopted Indian ways and in 1925 married an Iroquois woman. He became well known through his writing and as a lecturer who used his woods lore for the cause of wildlife conservation in Canada.

TERRACE BAY

Pop. 2,639. On Lake Superior at the mouth of the Aguasabon River on Hwy. 17, 78 km NW of Marathon. The settlement was a flag stop on the Canadian Pacific Railway named Black until a large sulphite pulp mill was opened in 1948. Waterpower for the mill was produced by a drop of 300 feet (91 m) in the Aguasabon River near its mouth. Long Lake and the waters of the Kenogami River were diverted into the Aguasabon River to develop 55,000 horsepower, and the flow is carried by tunnel to a powerhouse at Terrace Bay. The post office opened as Terrace Bay in 1947. The community's name describes a succession of flat terraces separated by escarpments and cliffs. They were formed by glacial melt waters creating new drainage patterns in the Lake Superior basin 20,000 years ago, as the level of the lake gradually lowered.

THAMESFORD

Pop. 1,920. In East Nissouri and North Oxford ts., Oxford C., on the Middle Thames River and Hwys 2 & 19, 22 km NE of London. The place was first called St. Andrews and was named Thamesford when the post office was established in 1851.

THAMESVILLE

Pop. 955. In Camden T., Kent C., on the Thames River and Hwys. 2 & 21 and C. Rd. 23, 25 km NE of Chatham. The first settler was Lemuel Sherman, who built a log cabin beside the Thames River in 1805. The following year he erected a large pineboard barn which, during the War of 1812, served as a hospital for wounded soldiers. Sherman saw the retreat of Brigadier-General Proctor's British army up the Thames River in 1813. Shawnee Chief Tecumseh, recruiter of Indians to fight on the side of the British, died a few kilometres north of here during the Battle of the Thames in 1813. When a post office was established in 1834, it was named Thamesville.

THEDFORD

Pop. 610. In Bosanquet T., Lambton C., on Hwy. 79, 51 km NE of Sarnia. When the Grand Trunk Railway came through the area in 1859, a station was provided, at the site of what is now Thedford, to serve the people of the hamlet of Widder, about 2 km southwest of the rail line. Farmer Nelson Southworth gave the railroad the land on which the station was built, on the condition that he could name the place Thetford after his hometown in Vermont. When the name was changed from Widder Station in 1867, Thetford was misspelled Thedford.

THESSALON

Pop. 1,444. In Thessalon T., Algoma Dist., on the North Channel of Lake Huron at the mouth of the Thessalon River (which drains Ottertail, Desert, and Rock lakes) and Hwys. 17 & 129, 86 km SE of Sault Ste. Marie. The place was originally an Indian encampment called Neyashewun, meaning "a point of land." That name was corrupted through translation into French by the explorer René François de Bréhan Galinée who marked it on his map of 1670 as Tessalon. In 1755, cartographer Berlin charted it as Pointe aux Thessalons and Alexander Henry, recounting his travels, called the place O'Tossalon. In 1814 two armed American schooners, the *Tigress* and *Scorpion*, were captured by a British contingent from Fort Michilimackinac, in the waters between Drummond and St. Joseph Islands. When N. Dyment of Barrie built a sawmill there in 1877, he called the place Thessalon Mills. A large amount of square-cut timber from that mill was shipped by sailing vessels to Kincardine and Goderich. The lumber ships returned with supplies for the entire north shore of Lake Huron.

THORNBURY
Pop. 1,458. In Collingwood T., Grey C., on Nottawasaga Bay off Georgian Bay at the mouth of the Beaver River on Hwy. 26 and C. Rd. 13, 41 km E of Owen Sound. Upper Canada's deputy surveyor, Charles Rankin, surveyed the area in 1833 and left 900 acres (364.5) at the mouth of the Beaver River for a townsite, but did not survey it. His assistant, a Mr. Gifford, named the site Thornbury after his native town in Somersetshire, England. Rankin settled just west on a tract of 200 acres (81 ha) on Laura Bay. In the late 1840s, Solomon Olmstead from Carleton County came to the area looking for a mill site. He and his brother Rufus built a sawmill on the Beaver River, then a store and a grist mill. When the post office was established in 1853, it was named Thornbury.

THORNDALE
Pop. 581. In West Nissouri T., Middlesex C., on the River Wye, a tributary to the Thames and C. Rds. 27 & 28, 18 km NE of London. James Shanly bought a large property in West Nissouri Township in 1837 and named his estate Thorndale. In 1858 the Logan family laid out a village site. When the post office opened in 1859 it took the name Thorndale.

THORNE
Pop. 265. In Poitras T., Nipissing Dist., on the Ottawa River and Hwy. 63, 64 km NE of North Bay. The post office was established in 1948. The origin of the name is not known.

THORNHILL
Pop. 19,000. In Reg. Mun. of York, 8 km N of Toronto. In 1792, Lt.-Gov. John Graves Simcoe planned a road to link York (now Toronto) on Lake Ontario with Lake Simcoe, about 45 km north. The road was for military use and as a trade route for the North West Fur Company. Simcoe named it Yonge St. after his friend Sir George Yonge, minister of war in the Imperial Cabinet. Free lots of 200 acres (81 ha) each were offered on either side of Yonge Street as an incentive to settlement. Settlers were required to clear 10 acres (4 ha) plus 33 feet (10 m) for road allowance and to build a house, within two years. The first log house was built at the site of present-day Thornhill by Asa Johnson, and his stepson, Nathan Chapman, took up the next lot. Benjamin Thorne from Dorset, England, arrived in 1820 and became active in local affairs, among them petitioning for a post office. The settlement had been known as Atkinson's Mills, Lyon's Mills, Purdy's Mills, Dundurn, and Thorn's Mills. When the post office

was established in 1829, it took the name Thornhill, after Benjamin Thorne. In the late 1830s and early 1840s there were seven hotels in Thornhill, including Montgomery's Tavern, headquarters of the insurgents during the 1837 Rebellion. J. E. H. MacDonald (1873-1932), a founding member of the Group of Seven, lived and painted in Thornhill from 1913 until his death.

THORNTON

Pop. 663. In Essa and Innisfil ts., Simcoe C., on Hwy. 27 and C. Rd. 21, 17 km S of Barrie. Thornton developed during the 1820s and was first known as Henrysville or Henry's Corners after early settler John Henry, who was the first teacher and then the schoolmaster, and who also became the postmaster when an office opened in 1854. The name Henrysville caused confusion in the mails, so the post office requested a name change, and the community became Thornton after Henry Thornton who owned a grist mill, sawmill, and planing mill.

THOROLD

Pop. 16,589. City in the Reg. Mun. of Niagara on Lock Seven of the Welland Canal and Hwys. 58 & 406, 8 km S of St. Catharines. Thorold's first settlers arrived between 1784 and 1787. Most were officers and men of Butler's Rangers, a United Empire Loyalist company that had fought under Col. John Butler and wintered in the Niagara region during the American Revolutionary War. During the War of 1812 militia were raised from the township to defend the Niagara Peninsula, which was briefly in American hands in the summer of 1813. It was during this period that Laura Secord made her famous walk from Queenston to the headquarters of Lt. James Fitzgibbon at the DeCew house in Thorold Township. Her warning made possible the capture of the entire invading American force by a force of loyal Indians at Beaverdams, just outside present-day Thorold. The foundation of the DeCew house, which was destroyed by fire in 1943, has been preserved as an historic site.

Beaverdams is the oldest settlement completely within Thorold Township, and was an important settlement in the industrial and political life of the early years. It was never incorporated, and much of it was flooded during construction of the fourth Welland Canal. Egerton Ryerson, superintendent of education for Upper Canada from 1845 to 1875, was the first Methodist minister in the new church at Beaverdam in 1832. The township and the city were both named after Sir John Thorold, MP for Lincolnshire, England, who was greatly interested in colonial affairs. The first cotton factory in the province was a joint-stock company founded by local citizens in Thorold in 1847. Twenty water-powered looms produced sheeting, scrim, and batting in an operation that heralded the establishment of what was to become an important provincial industry.

THOROLD SOUTH

Pop. 1,734. Part of the City of Thorold in Reg. Mun. of Niagara on C. Rd. 53, 3 km S of Thorold. A post office was established as Thorold South in 1926.

THUNDER BAY

Pop. 109,269. On the shores of Thunder Bay, an inlet of the NW shore of Lake Superior, at the mouth of the Kaministikwia River and at Hwys. 11, 17, 61, 102, & 130, 335 km E of Fort Frances and 690 km NW of Sault Ste. Marie. The city was formed in 1970 by the amalgamation of the former cities of Fort William and Port Arthur, part of Neebing Towship, and that part of Shuniah Township known as McIntyre. Explorers, missionaries, and traders were in these parts as early as the mid-1600s, and the first settlement was a French fur-trading post established in 1678 by Daniel Greysolon Dulhut. The post was replaced with another French fort, which served as a trading post and operational base for the explorer Pierre Gaultier de La Verendrye.

Fort William: In the early 1800s the North West Company built a fort named Fort William after the company's principal director, William McGillivray. The fort became the company's most important post because it was the farthest west that supplies could be taken by canoe from Montreal in one season. The canoes then returned to Montreal laden with furs, just before winter set in.

Port Arthur: First known as The Hill City, Port Arthur began as a silver-mining settlement. The Gladman-Hind-Dawson expedition was organized in the mid-1850s to explore a route to the west and set up a base station. The route began to develop in 1858, when a Toronto group organized the Rescue Company to expedite trade with the prairies. A Crown lands agent, Robert McVicar, built the first residence in 1859. The Thunder Bay silver mine nearby went into operation in 1866, and three years later the federal government launched a road to the west under the direction of Simon J. Dawson. The military expedition under Col. Garnet Wolseley, sent to crush the first Riel Rebellion, used the road in 1870. Wolseley named the station Prince Arthur's Landing in honour of Prince Arthur, later duke of Connaught and governor general of Canada. After the railroad to the west was begun at Fort William in 1875, most of the supplies were landed at Prince Arthur's Landing. To ensure a link with the railhead at Fort William, Prince Arthur's Landing residents built their own short railroad in 1876. In 1882 the name Prince Arthur's Landing was changed to Port Arthur as requested by the Canadian Pacific Railway. The following year the CPR built a grain elevator in Port Arthur, and later that year the first Manitoba wheat was shipped. The grain and freight traffic grew until a dispute over taxes between the railroad and the town, which resulted in the CPR transferring all its business to Fort William in 1889.

Thunder Bay is the world's largest grain-handling centre and Canada's second-largest port. It has an extraordinary ethnic mix, with 42 nationalities clearly represented, 100 churches, and, at over 9,000, the largest Finnish population outside Finland. The Trans-Canada Highway between Thunder Bay and Nipigon is officially called the Terry Fox Courage Highway. In 1980, 21-year-old Terry Fox of British Columbia dipped his foot in the Atlantic Ocean at St. John's, Newfoundland, and started what he called the Marathon of Hope. He planned to run across Canada that summer—on one leg, because he had lost the other one to cancer—to raise money for cancer research. He managed 42 km a day and covered 5,372 km to Thunder Bay, but by then cancer had spread through his body and he had to stop. He returned home and died the following year. The province of Ontario has honoured him by erecting a statue to his memory at Thunder Bay Lookout, close to the end of his Marathon of Hope. Col. Elizabeth Smellie (1884-1968), a native of Port Arthur, became the first woman to attain the rank of colonel in the Canadian Armed Forces. In the First World War she served with the Royal Canadian Army Medical Corps in France and England, and in 1941 she organized the Canadian Women's Army Corps.

TILBURY

Pop. 4,186. In Tilbury East T., Kent C., on Hwys. 2 & 401 and C. Rd. 1, 29 km SW of Chatham. The town came into existence when the Canada Southern Railway opened its line between Fort Erie and Windsor in the early 1870s and established a station at the border of Kent and Essex counties. David Henderson opened a general store and operated a post office he called Henderson. By 1887 the community was incorporated into a village known as Tilbury Centre. The name described the community's being central to the townships of Tilbury North, Tilbury West, and Tilbury East. The township names came from Tilbury on the Thames in England. At one time there were five hotels selling liquor on the west side of Tilbury's main street. There were none on the east side of the street, which was in the dry county of Kent.

TILLSONBURG

Pop. 10,621. In Dereham T., Oxford C., on Otter Creek and Hwys. 3 & 19 and C. Rd. 37, 38 km S of Woodstock. In 1825, George Tillson, originally from Massachusetts, built a dam, sawmill, and forge on the site of the town named after him. The forge melted and manufactured bog iron ore, deposits of which were found nearby, and the community that sprang up around it was called Dereham Forge. When the town started its local government in 1836, Tillson was appointed commissioner of roads, and he insisted on the community having a main street 100 feet (30.4 m) wide, named Broadway. This was so a team of oxen could make a U-turn; all that space may have seemed a waste in the 1800s, but today Tillsonburg is one of very few Ontario communities still able to provide angled parallel parking on both sides of its main street. When Tillsonburg achieved town status in 1869, an "l" got dropped due to a clerical error. It stayed that way, officially, until 1902, when it took an act of the Ontario legislature to put the "l" back into Tillsonburg.

TIMMINS
Pop. 46,065. City in Cochrane Dist. on the Mattagami River and Hwy. 101, 140 km NW of Kirkland Lake. Although it was not founded until 1910, Timmins claims to be the largest city in Canada. That's because in 1973 it amalgamated with a number of nearby towns and villages and wound up being 3,000 square kilometres (1,158 square miles) in area. Nicknamed "the City With the Heart of Gold," Timmins was named after brothers Noah and Henry Timmins, who formed one of the early mining syndicates and developed a gold mine staked in 1911 by a man named Benny Hollinger. The Hollinger Mine yielded $10 million in gold annually—20 million ounces (625 tons, 567 tonnes) over its lifetime—and was for years second in production only to the Rand Mine in South Africa. Timmins also has Canada's deepest mine, the McIntyre Mine, which is 7,400 feet (2255.5 m) deep. In 1934, Roy Herbert Thomson bought the weekly *Timmins Press* and turned it into a daily newspaper. By the mid-1960s he owned 124 newspapers in eight countries and was made Baron Thomson of Fleet.

TIVERTON
Pop. 707. In Bruce and Kincardine ts., Bruce C., on Hwy. 21 and C. Rd. 15, 67 km NE of Goderich. The first settler was Timothy Allan, who arrived in 1850. When a post office was established in 1860, the residents, who were of predominantly Scottish stock, chose the name St. Andrews. A place of that name already existed in Ontario, so the post office was renamed Tiverton after a place in England. In 1897 the village was swept by a disastrous fire, which destroyed most of its businesses.

TOBERMORY
Pop. 600. In St. Edmunds T., Bruce C., at the N tip of the Bruce Peninsula, the mouth to Georgian Bay from Lake Huron, the N terminus of Hwy. 6, the N terminus of the Bruce Trail, and the S terminus of a summer-only ferry service to Manitoulin Island, 112 km NW of Owen Sound. Two

snug harbours, known as Big Tub and Little Tub, serve as marine centres for the northern part of the Bruce Peninsula and occasionally accommodate Great Lakes ships sitting out a storm. Capt. John Charles Earl, the township's first pioneer, settled at Big Tub in 1871. A decade later, when the post office was established, it was named after a look-alike fishing port on Scotland's Isle of Mull. Fathom Five National Marine Park, Canada's first national marine park, includes 19 of the Cape Hurd Islands (including two "flowerpot" islands, just off Tobermory) and the waters in between, which attract divers to the 21 sail and steam vessel wrecks within the park.

TORONTO

Pop. 598,939. City, metropolitan municipality, and capital of the Province of Ontario since 1867, on the N shore of Lake Ontario at the mouths of the Don and Humber Rivers, and Hwys. 2, 5, 7, 11, 27, 400, 401, 404, 409, 427, and Queen Elizabeth Way, 60 km NE of Hamilton. The name Toronto is of Indian origin and thought to mean "place of meeting" or "trees rising out of the water." The name first appears as Tarantou on Sanson's map of 1656 and in varying forms has been applied at different times to most of the region between Lake Ontario and Lake Simcoe. In the 17th century a Seneca village called Teiaigon stood near the mouth of the Humber River, where the trail from Lake Ontario to Georgian Bay started. Etienne Brûlé was the first white man to visit the site when he descended the Humber River in 1615. In 1787 the British government bought about one-third of what is now York County from three Mississauga chiefs for £1,700. In 1793 John Graves Simcoe, lieutenant-governor of Upper Canada, was directed to establish his capital at what is now Toronto. Simcoe named it York in honour of the duke of York, son of King George III, a name it retained—despite local objections—until its incorporation as a city in 1834. Simcoe held a meeting of his executive council at York that year, but later meetings were held at what is now Niagara-on-the-Lake, until permanent buildings were completed at York in 1797. "Muddy York," as it was nicknamed, grew up close to the malarial Don marshes, and its major defences were built farther west, at the entrance to the harbour. Under the threat of war with the United States, Fort York and a shipyard were begun in 1812. When an American invading force landed near the present Sunnyside Beach in 1813, the York garrison withdrew after brief skirmishing. Before leaving, however, the British mined the fort's magazine, which blew up as the Americans arrived, killing Gen. Zebulon M. Pike. The Americans burned the parliament and garrison buildings and looted deserted houses; in retaliation, the British burned part of Washington, D.C., in 1814. Fort York has been restored and is now one of Toronto's many tourist attractions.

York remained a small and undistinguished capital until the late 1820s, when the rich farmlands nearby were settled, and the settlement became a grain market and distribution centre. Between 1827 and 1834, the year in which Toronto was incorporated as a city, the population jumped to 9,000 from 1,800. When Upper and Lower Canada were united in 1841, the capital of the United Province of Canada was established, first at Kingston and then, from 1845 to 1849, in Montreal. After the Rebellion Losses Riots in Montreal, the capital alternated every two years between Toronto and Quebec. At Confederation in 1867, Toronto became the capital of the province of Ontario.

Torontonian "Ned" Hanlan (1855-1908) took up rowing as a child and turned professional in 1876. For four years he held the world singles sculls championship. The Royal Canadian Yacht Club, started as the Toronto Boat Club in 1852 and with quarters on the Toronto Islands, was the first sailing association in the province. An historic plaque at 60 Richmond St. E. recalls Sir Sandford Fleming, inventor of Standard Time. At a meeting of the Canadian Institute in 1879, Fleming first presented his idea for a standardized worldwide system for reckoning time. His proposal led to the International Prime Meridian Conference in Washington five years later, at which the present system of Standard Time was adopted. Woodbine is the oldest permanent racing establishment in Ontario and was the site of the running of the Queen's Plate from 1883 to 1955. The track became "Old Woodbine" in 1956, when a New Woodbine was opened in Etobicoke; in 1963 it was renamed Greenwood. Mary Pickford (1893-1979) began her acting career on stage at the age of five and was later nicknamed "America's Sweetheart." She played children's roles well into her adult life. Canada's first air-mail flight in 1918 ended at the Leaside flying field. A JN-4 Curtiss aircraft from the Royal Air Force detachment at Leaside was chosen for the first air-mail delivery in Canada. The plane took off from Montreal at 10:30 a.m., refuelled at Kingston, and landed in Toronto with its cargo of 120 letters at 4:55 p.m.

Today, Metropolitan Toronto consists of five cities and one borough: Toronto, North York, York, Etobicoke, Scarborough, and the Borough of East York. Together they cover a total of 400 square kilometres (144 square miles). Approximately two-thirds of Metro Toronto's three million residents were born and raised somewhere else. Half a million Italians make Metro the largest Italian community outside Italy. Metro is also home to the largest Chinese community in Canada and the biggest Portuguese community in North America. Toronto has a wealth of architecture—from Casa Loma, a magnificent 98-room castle built between 1911 and 1914, to the world's tallest freestanding structure, the CN Tower. There's a one-of-a-kind City Hall building, which still looks futuristic, even though it was built in 1965, and the Romanesque Revival-style 1899 Old City Hall, with its Georgia pine floors and gargoyles, is still in use and may be visited. As real-estate prices have climbed, so have Toronto skyscrapers, and the city's skyline seems to change monthly as new glass-sheathed temples to business and commerce rear into the sky.

TOTTENHAM

Pop. 2,856. In Tecumseth T., Simcoe C., on C. Rd. 10, 48 km SW of Barrie. John Tegart, who arrived in 1823, was the first settler. Two years later Alexander Totten arrived and built a store. Successive settlers built around the store. The post office was established in 1858 as Tottenham, and Alexander Totten was the first postmaster.

TOWNSEND

Pop. 268. Part of the Town of Simcoe, Reg. Mun. of Haldimand-Norfolk, on Nanticoke Creek and C. Rds. 69 & 70, 17 km NE of Simcoe. The community was created in 1980 and gets its postal service from nearby Jarvis. The origin of the name is not known.

TRENTON

Pop. 14,765. In Sidney T., Hastings C., on the Bay of Quinte off Lake Ontario at the mouth of the Trent River and Trent Canal, which links the Bay of Quinte with Georgian Bay and Hwys. 2 & 33, 4 km S of Hwy. 401, 18 km SW of Belleville. Settlement began in 1790 as United Empire Loyalists took up their land grants. John Strachan, the first Anglican Bishop of York (now Toronto) owned a tract of land in the area and in 1829 laid out lots on a site he called Annwood. Annwood eventually merged with Trenton, which was first known as River Trent, Port Trent, Trent Port, and finally, in 1853, Trenton. In 1910 fire destroyed the Gilmour Sash and Door Factory, and in 1918 the British Chemical Company ammunition plant was destroyed by fire and the resultant explosions. No lives were lost, and eight Trentonians who remained at vital posts in the danger zone throughout the night of explosions were later awarded Order of the British Empire medals.

In 1919 Trenton briefly became the Hollywood of Canada when the government set up a film plant in town and produced a number of films. The experiment was short-lived, and the only reminder today of that era is a street called Film Street. When the Depression hit Trenton in the 1930s, the influential Sen. William Alexander Fraser managed to have the town chosen as the home of the Royal Canadian Air Force. An enormous building program followed, and during the Second World War the station served as the Commonwealth Air Training Base. The base is still in operation as Canadian Forces Base Trenton. Three major fires devastated Trenton's downtown business section during 1978.

TROUT CREEK

Pop. 640. In South Himsworth T., Parry Sound Dist., on Hwys. 11 & 522, 40 km S of North Bay. The hamlet was settled in 1868 mostly by pioneers of British, Polish, and German descent. It was known as Melbourne until the post office opened in 1887 as Barkerton. In 1890 the name was changed to Trout Creek.

TURKEY POINT

Pop. 418. In the Reg. Mun. of Haldimand-Norfolk on C. Rds. 10 & 42, 24 km SW of Simcoe. There is archaeological evidence that Indians frequented this area thousands of years before the arrival of Europeans. The French were here as early as 1670. In 1793 hundreds of United Empire Loyalists moved to the north shore of Lake Erie. In order to protect their settlements from attack, Lt.-Gov. John Graves Simcoe decided to build a fortress (Fort Norfolk) on Turkey Point. The nearby town of Charlotteville (after Queen Charlotte, wife of George III) was designated the capital of the Western District of Upper Canada. During the War of 1812, when the Americans controlled Lake Erie, the seat of government was moved inland. In 1815 the Charlotteville courthouse burned down, and the capital was then moved to Vittoria and later to London. Fort Norfolk fell into disrepair and was abandoned. In 1925 a summer post office was established as Turkey Point.

TWEED

Pop. 1,549. In Hungerford T., Hastings C., on Stoco Lake, (an enlargement of the Moira River) and Hwy. 37 and C. Rd. 38, 40 km NW of Belleville. Richard Woodcock was the first settler. He arrived in 1828 and the following year built a dam across the river. By 1830 Allan Munroe had built another dam and erected the first saw- and grist mill at the site. The place was first known as Hungerford Mills after the township. (Part of it had been surveyed in 1797 and named after Sir Francis Rawdon-Hastings, a leader in the American Revolution and a descendant of the Barons of Hungerford.) The Munroe mills changed hands a number of times, until they were acquired by James Jamison, a Scot who had traded his foundry business in Belleville for the mills and surrounding land. He divided the land into village lots and named the place Tweed after his hometown in Scotland. In 1967 Tweed residents elected what is believed to have been the first all-female council in Canada.

TYENDINAGA

Pop. 882. In Tyendinaga T., Hastings C., 2 km W of Hwy. 49, 23 km E of Belleville. The community was named after Mohawk Chief Tyendinaga, whose English name was Joseph R. Brant.

TYRONE

Pop. 219. Part of the Town of Newcastle, Reg. Mun. of Durham, on C. Rd. 14, 13 km NW of Bowmanville. The post office was established in 1852. The first name suggested for the post office was Mount Hope. Since another settlement was already using that name, another had to be chosen. Most settlers in the west end of the village were originally from County Tyrone in Ireland and favoured that name; those settlers at the east end were mainly from Devon in Cornwall, England, and preferred the name Devon. It was decided to resolve the matter with a cricket match, which the west-enders won. Robert McLaughlin (1836-1921) was born on a farm near Tyrone. He was a self-taught craftsman of exceptional skill. He established the McLaughlin Carriage Works, which became the largest carriage works in the British Empire.

UNION

Pop. 357. In Yarmouth T., Elgin C., on Hwy. 4, 14 km SE of St. Thomas. In 1851 survey roads created by surveyors Col. M. Burwell and D. Hanney of St. Thomas converged. At the point where they met a settlement began, and when the post office was established, the place was named Union.

UNIONVILLE

Pop. 14,000. Part of the Town of Markham, Reg. Mun. of York, on the River Rouge and Hwy. 7 and C. Rd. 3, 29 km NE of Toronto. German settlers who were brought to this area in 1794 by William von Moll Berczy, were the first township residents and they formed one of the earliest Lutheran congregations in Ontario. Berczy, a German painter, went to London in 1790 as agent for a land company and under its auspices brought a large group of German settlers to New York State. Two years later, following a dispute with the company, he transferred his colony to Upper Canada and settled north of York (now Toronto). The origin of the name is not known.

UPSALA

Pop. 349. In Upsala T., Thunder Bay Dist., on Hwy. 17, 141 km NW of Thunder Bay. The place was settled in 1923 by veterans of the First World War who were offered lots at one dollar apiece. The post office was established in 1925. The community took its name from the township, which was named after Upsala in Sweden. Some of the residents grow award-winning yields per acre of potato crops.

UXBRIDGE

Pop. 4,209. In the Reg. Mun. of Durham on Beaver Creek and Hwy. 47 and C. Rds. 1 & 8, 66 km NE of Toronto. Uxbridge Township was part of a parcel of land granted in 1798 to a group of French Royalists, under the Comte de Puisaye, who had fled to England during the French Revolution. Few of the emigrés went to Upper Canada and, of those who arrived, only a few settled. In 1803 the government of Canada regained control of the unsettled lands and had them surveyed so they could be opened for regular settlement. The area that was to become the town of Uxbridge was immediately settled by 12 Quaker families from Pennsylvania. Joseph Gould was the first settler in 1806. The place was known as Gouldville until the post office opened in 1832 and was called Uxbridge after the township in which the community was then located. The township was named after Uxbridge in Middlesex, England. Just west of present-day Uxbridge is the second meeting house, built in 1820 by Quaker families to replace a log structure they had erected in 1806. Uxbridge was the first town in Ontario to receive an official coat of arms—in 1956. About 13 km north of Uxbridge, surrounded by farm fields, is the architecturally unusual Thomas Foster Memorial Temple, dedicated in 1936 as the final resting place of Thomas Foster (thrice mayor of Toronto) and members of his family. The memorial, intended to be executed as a smaller replica of the Taj Mahal at Agra, India, was built instead in the form of a Christian church, in the purest Byzantine tradition. The interior is finished with vari-coloured marble and rich mosaics.

VVV

VAL CARON
Pop. 4,036. Part of the Town of Valley East, Reg. Mun. of Sudbury, on C. Rds. 15 & 80, 12 km N of Sudbury. The post office was established in 1944, and Clarence Bissillon was appointed the first postmaster. Postmasters have traditionally had the right to name their offices after themselves, but Bissillon's request for that name was turned down as being too difficult a name to spell. The post office then named the place Val Caron after the first missionary in the district, Rev. Father Hormisdas Caron.

VAL GAGNE
Pop. 277. In Taylor T., Nipissing Dist., .5 km E of Hwy. 11, 18 km SE of Iroquois Falls. The post office was established as Nushka Station in 1911. In 1916 the community was destroyed by the forest fire that also wiped out Porquis Junction, Iroquois Falls, Kelso, Matheson, and Ramore. Residents rebuilt their town, and when the post office was re-established in 1920, they renamed the community Val Gagne. In 1921 the local station of the Timiskaming and Northern Ontario Railway, which had been called Nushka Station, was renamed Val Gagne Station. The origin of the name is not known.

VALLEY EAST
Pop. 19,119. Town in the Reg. Mun. of Sudbury created in 1973 by regional government by annexing the Townships of Neelon and Garson and geographic Township of Lumsden to the Township of Valley East.

VAL RITA
Pop. 275. In Owens T., Cochrane Dist., on Hwy. 11, 14 km NW of Kapuskasing. The post office was established as Secord in 1923. In 1925 the name was changed to Val Rita for St. Rita, patron saint of St. Rita parish.

VAL THERESE
Pop. 903. Part of the Town of Valley East, Reg. Mun. of Sudbury, on C. Rds. 80 & 96, 21 km N of Sudbury. The post office was established as Val Therese in 1964. The origin of the name is not known.

VANIER
Pop. 18,190. A city within the Reg. Mun. of Ottawa-Carleton on the Rideau River immediately east of central Ottawa. Vanier's 2.5 square kilometres (1 sq mi) are surrounded by the expanded capital city. The first settlers of this detached portion of Gloucester Township arrived in

the 1820s, and the site became known as Cummings Island after Charles Cummings, who established a general store and carriage shop. In the 1870s the name was changed to Janeville, presumably after Jane, wife of John McArthur, who owned the land now traversed by the McArthur Road. In 1909 Janeville and the hamlets of Clarkstown and Clandeboye joined under the name Eastview, which was incorporated as a town in 1909 and a city in 1963. In 1963 the city was renamed Vanier after the late Gov. Gen. Georges Vanier. Many of Eastview's men served in the Second World War and, to honour the town's contribution, one of the navy's frigates was named HMCS *Eastview*.

VANKLEEK HILL
Pop. 1,745. In West Hawkesbury T., Prescott and Russell C., on Hwy. 34 and C. Rd. 10, 83 km E of Ottawa. The first settler was United Empire Loyalist Simeon Van Kleek from Poughkeepsie, New York, whose 500-acre (202.5-ha) grant in 1798 included the entire site of the present town. The first building erected was a tavern, operated by Van Kleek's son, Simon. More than half the town now is of French descent.

VARS
Pop. 370. In the Reg. Mun. of Ottawa-Carleton on C. Rds. 8 & 17, 24 km SE of Ottawa. The post office was established in 1886 and named Vars after the birthplace in France of Father Guillaume, an early parish priest.

VAUGHAN
Pop. 88,475. A town in the Reg. Mun. of York on the Humber River, formed in 1971 by regional government. Part of Vaughan Township was annexed to Richmond Hill, and the Town of Woodbridge and parts of King Township amalgamated with the Township of Vaughan to form the Town of Vaughan.

VERNER
Pop. 1,076. In Caldwell T., Nipissing Dist., on the Veuve River and Hwys. 17, 64, & 575, 54 km W of North Bay. The community came into being with the completion of the Canadian Pacific Railway line between North Bay and Sudbury. After helping to build the line, some of the workmen returned with their families, cleared the land, and farmed. The place was first called Burnside because the settlers discovered fire had swept both sides of the railway track at that point. The post office was established as Burnside in 1886, although the railway station was named Verner Station. The origin of the name is not known.

VERNON
Pop. 370. In the Reg. Mun. of Ottawa-Carleton on Hwy. 31, 36 km SE of Ottawa. The post office was established as Vernon in 1862. The origin of

the name is not known. Alexander Cameron Rutherford (1857-1941) a native of Osgoode Township in which Vernon used to be located, was premier, provincial treasurer, and minister of education in the first Alberta government following that province's formation in 1905.

VERONA
Pop. 769. In Portland T., Frontenac C., on the Napanee River and Hwy. 38, 40 km NW of Kingston. The community was first known as Buzztown. The post office was established as Verona in 1858. The origin of both names is unknown.

VICTORIA HARBOUR
Pop. 1,080. In Tay T., Simcoe C., on Hogg's Bay off Severn Sound off Georgian Bay at the mouth of the Hogg River, 45 km NW of Orillia. In 1869, John Kean and Albert Fowlie of Orillia opened a large sawmill on the site of the present village, which was first known as Hogg's Bay. At one time the place was nicknamed "Canary Town" because most of the houses were painted yellow by the major employer, Victoria Harbour Lumber Company. In 1871 the Midland Railway arrived and the settlement was given its present name to honour Queen Victoria. A cairn a short distance south of the community on the Hogg River marks the site of the palisaded Huron village and Jesuit mission, St. Louis, where missionaries Jean de Brébeuf and Gabriel Lalemant were captured. The Iroquois destroyed the fortification.

VIENNA
Pop. 391. In Bayham T., Elgin C., on Big Otter Creek and Hwy. 19, 21 km SW of Tillsonburg. One of the earliest settlers was Capt. Samuel Edison, a Loyalist from New Jersey and grandfather of the well-known inventor, Thomas Alva Edison. Captain Edison, who had first moved to Nova Scotia, arrived in 1811. During the War of 1812, he served in the Middlesex Militia. Village lots were laid out by deputy surveyor Mahlon Burwell in 1830. Colonel Burwell had planned to name the place Shrewsbury, but Edison's suggestion of Vienna, where his wife had been born, was more widely accepted. The post office was established as Vienna in 1838. By 1855 the community had a population of 1,200; in that year, fire destroyed a large part of the commercial section of town. In 1867 another major fire, coinciding with a decline in the lumber industry, ended the community's growth. During the 1840s and 1850s, Thomas Edison was a regular summer visitor at the home of his grandfather. In 1933 the Edison home was moved to the Ford Museum in Dearborn, Michigan.

VINELAND
Pop. 2,500. Part of the Town of Lincoln in the Reg. Mun. of Lincoln on

C. Rds. 24 & 81, 11 km W of St. Catharines. Settlement began in 1790 with the arrival of United Empire Loyalist settlers, many of whom were Mennonites and who built Canada's first Mennonite church in 1801. The post office was established in 1894 as Vineland, the place having been named by Mrs. Franklin W. Moyer, wife of a local shopkeeper, to describe an area of the Niagara Peninsula where grapes grew in abundance.

VINELAND STATION

Pop. 392. Part of the Town of Lincoln in the Reg. Mun. of Niagara on C. Rds. 24 & 81, 16 km W of St. Catharines. The post office was established in 1912. The name was taken from nearby Vineland.

VIRGIL

Pop. 1,100. Part of the Town of Niagara-on-the-Lake, Reg. Mun. of Niagara, on Hwy. 55 and C. Rd. 11, 13 km NE of St. Catharines. The community was settled around 1783 and first known as Four Mile Creek and then Cross Roads. Later the place was called Lawrenceville after Rev. George Lawrence. In 1895 the post office was established as Virgil. The origin of the name is not known.

VIRGINIA

Pop. 1,738. In the Reg. Mun. of York on Hwy. 48, 8 km E of Sutton, 72 km NE of Toronto. The post office was established as Virginia in 1874. The origin of the name is not known.

VIRGINIATOWN

Pop. 1,010. In McGarry T, Timiskaming Dist., on the NE tip of Larder Lake on Hwy. 66, 38 km E of Kirkland Lake. The community was born of a gold rush in 1906 and named after Virginia, wife of George B. Webster, president of the Kerr-Addison Gold Mine. For a time the mine was first-ranked in production in Canada.

VITTORIA

Pop. 378. In Delhi T., Reg. Mun. of Haldimand-Norfolk, on Young's Creek, 8 km S of Simcoe. The first settler was a Mr. McCall, who arrived in 1794. The place was first called Tisdale's Mills and for a time was the judicial seat of the London District. After the courthouse and jail were completed in 1817, the community was renamed Vittoria in honour of an important British victory over Napoleon during the Peninsular campaign. In 1826 the jail and courthouse burned down, and the judicial capital was moved to London. The Rev. Adolphus Egerton Ryerson (1803-1882) was born near Vittoria. He was head of Ontario's department of education for 30 years and established Ontario's present system of public education, making free elementary and secondary schooling available to all children in the province.

WABIGOON
Pop. 266. In Kenora Dist. on the E shore of Wabigoon Lake and Hwy. 17, 15 km SE of Dryden. The post office was established as Wabigoon in 1897. Wabigoon is an Indian name that means "white feather" and may have referred to white lilacs around the lake.

WAHNAPITAE
Pop. 1,529. Part of the Town of Nickel Centre in the Reg. Mun. of Sudbury on Hwys. 17 & 537, 19 km E of Sudbury. The post office was established as Wahnapitae in 1887. The origin of the name is unknown.

WALDEN
Pop. 9,411. A town in the Reg. Mun. of Sudbury, established in 1973 by the amalgamation of the towns of Lively and Waters, united townships of Drury, Denison, and Graham, Township of Waters and Geographic Townships of Dieppe, Lorne, and Louise.

WALKERTON
Pop. 4,687. In Brant T., Bruce C., on the Saugeen River and Hwy. 4 and C. Rd. 2, 77 km SW of Owen Sound. In 1849, William Jasper and Edward Boulton built the first house. A year later, Joseph Walker, an Irishman and by trade a miller, built the first sawmill in the settlement that was then called Elgin. The community developed on Walker's farm lots and its name was changed to Walkerton. For nine years Walker tried to have it declared the county town. Eventually he was successful, and when Walkerton was incorporated as a town in 1871, Walker became the first mayor.

WALLACEBURG
Pop. 11,462. In Chatham T., Kent C., at the confluence of the North and East branches of the Sydenham River, on Hwys 40 & 78, 27 km NW of Chatham. The community was originally known as The Forks because of its location at the confluence of the river branches. Most of its first settlers came from Lord Selkirk's nearby Baldoon Settlement, which they were forced to abandon after frequent floodings of the low-lying lands, bouts of malaria, and, finally, an invasion during the War of 1812 by American militia who carried off their livestock. James Johnson had squatted at the site around 1809 and established a trading post, which became known as Johnson's Point. When the post office was established in 1837, the first postmaster, Hugh McCallum, named the community Wallaceburg in honour of Sir William Wallace, the champion of Scottish independence. In 1840, James Baby surveyed a nearby area, erected a

large frame building, taught school, and operated a store. He had hoped to name his village Babyville, but it was absorbed by Wallaceburg. A major contribution to firearms design was made here in 1878, when inventor James Paris Lee (1831-1904) developed the box magazine, a significant improvement on the standard tube magazine.

WALLACETOWN

Pop. 284. In Dunwich T., Elgin C., on Hwy. 3 and C. Rd. 8, 28 km SW of St. Thomas. The first settler, in 1819, was John Currie. The post office was established as Wallacetown in 1852. One of the sights in the Wallacetown area is St. Peter's Church, at nearby Tyrconnell. The Gothic Revival-style church was built in the middle of the original Talbot Settlement in 1827. The adjacent cemetery contains the graves of many early settlers, including Col. Thomas Talbot (1771-1853). Talbot first came to Canada in 1790 as a subaltern in the 24th Regiment of the British Army and two years later was appointed private secretary to Lt.-Col. John Graves Simcoe with whom he visited the western part of what is now Ontario. He returned to England in 1794, sold his army commission in 1802 and returned to Upper Canada. From the British government he obtained a grant of many thousand of acres, established himself at Port Talbot on Lake Erie and founded the Talbot Settlement, of which the capital, St. Thomas still bears his name. Many communities in the counties of Essex, Kent, Lambton, Norfolk, Oxford, Elgin, and Middlesex owe their origin to his colonizing efforts. He ruled his vast territory in almost patriarchal state for nearly 50 years.

WALLENSTEIN

Pop. 267. In Wellesley T., Waterloo C., on the Conestogo River and Hwy. 86 and C. Rd. 10, 27 km NW of Kitchener. The community's first settler was Jacob Wallenstein who arrived in 1860 and built a hotel. When the post office was established in 1867, Wallenstein was the first postmaster and named the place after himself.

WALPOLE ISLAND

Pop. 1,374. In Lambton C., in the NE portion of Lake St. Clair at the mouth of the St. Clair River, 52 km S of Sarnia. The island is about 16 km long and 5-6 km wide, and is linked by toll ferry to Algonac, Michigan. On a chart prepared for Commodore Sir Edward Owen in 1815, the island is called St. Mary's, but the channels and a bay are called Walpole after Lt. Arthur Walpole, who died in 1842. Walpole served in Canada and prepared the Fort Erie plan in 1818-19.

WALSINGHAM

Pop. 244, In Walsingham T., Norfolk C., on Big Creek and Hwy. 59, 30 km SE of Tillsonburg. The community's first name was Spring Arbor.

The first settlers in the early 1800s were the Cope family, after which the place was known for a time as Cope's Landing. The post office was established in 1831 as Walsingham, after the township.

WANUP
Pop. 396. In Cleland T., Sudbury Dist., on Hwy. 537, 16 km SE of Sudbury. The place was settled around 1904 by employees of the Canadian National Railway. The post office was established in 1935 as Wanup. The origin of the name is not known.

WARMINSTER
Pop. 391. In Medonte T., Simcoe C., on Hwy. 12, 10 km NW of Orillia. The place was first known as Barrs Corners. When the post office was established in 1868, postmaster William G. Deacon named the community Warminster after his hometown in England.

WARREN
Pop. 455. In Ratter and Dunnet T., Reg. Mun. of Sudbury on Hwy. 17, 29 km E of Sturgeon Falls. The post office was established in 1879 as Warren, named after George M. Warren, the first postmaster.

WARSAW
Pop. 272. In Otonabee T., Peterborough C., on the Katchewanook River and C. Rds. 4 & 38, 20 km NE of Peterborough. The place was first settled in 1834 by Thomas Hartwell and was known for a time as Dummer's Mills. The mills were owned by Zacceus Burnham of Cobourg and managed by his cousin, Thomas George Choate, after whom the place was briefly called Choate's Mills. In 1839 Thomas Choate applied for the first post office and named the community Warsaw. The origin of the name is not known.

WARWICK
Pop. 204. In Warwick T., Lambton C., on Bear Creek and Hwy. 7, 31 km E of Sarnia. When the post office opened in 1837, the community was called Warwick West after the township, which had been named for Warwick County in England. In 1839 the "west" was dropped.

WASAGA BEACH
Pop. 4,807. In Sunnidale T., Simcoe C., on Nottawasaga Bay off Georgian Bay and the mouth of the Nottawasaga River, and at Hwy. 92, 40 km NW of Barrie. The name is from Nottawasaga, derived from the Indian for "outlet of Iroquois river." At the mouth of the river is Nancy Island, formed by the wreck of the schooner *Nancy*. Originally a trading ship of the North West Company, it was commandeered by the British Navy during the War of 1812 and outfitted for war. In 1913, during a naval battle with three American ships, the *Nancy* sought refuge in the

Nottawasaga River, but ran aground and burned. Silt and sand built up around the charred hulk and formed a small island. In 1925 what remained of the hull was dug up and put on display in an environmentally controlled chamber. A museum on the island depicts local events of the War of 1812 and displays artifacts recovered from the *Nancy*. The population of Wasaga Beach multiplies many times over in summer, when holidayers flock to its 14-km-long sandy beach.

WASHAGO

Pop. 224. In Rama T., Simcoe C., at the N end of Lake Couchiching at the mouth of the Severn River and on Hwy. 169 immediately E of Hwy. 11, 19 km NE of Orillia. The area was opened up by the lumber trade, and in 1853 the St. George family was granted lands in the region, including the townsite. The terms of the grant called for St. George to build grist and sawmills. He built the sawmill to help his timber business, but the grist mill wasn't erected for 20 years, which slowed development of the area. The place was first known as Severn Landing. When the post office opened in 1868, St. George asked Chief Bigwin, a local Indian, to choose a name. Bigwin named the place Washago, meaning "sparkling waters." The Wasdell Falls Hydro-Electric Generating Station was opened in 1914, about 5 km northwest of Washago. Sir Adam Beck officially opened the plant, which was the first station built by the Hydro-Electric Power Commission of Ontario. It served the region until 1955.

WATERDOWN

Pop. 2,737. In the Reg. Mun. of Hamilton-Wentworth on Grindstone Creek and the Queen Elizabeth Way, 8 km N of Hamilton. Alexander McDonnell was the first to own land at the site, having been given a land grant in 1796. When he failed to develop his holding, the land was granted in 1805 to Alexander Brown, a former officer of the North West Company. Brown built the first mill at Great Falls on Grindstone Creek, and his sons later constructed Brown's Wharf on nearby Lake Ontario. The post office was established in 1840. Mill builder Henry Van Wagner is said to have named the community Waterdown because of the water in Grindstone Creek rushing down out of the forest.

WATERFORD

Pop. 2,849. Part of the City of Nanticoke, Reg. Mun. of Haldimand-Norfolk on Nanticoke Creek and C. Rd. 24, 10 km N of Simcoe. Jacob Slaght settled in 1812, followed by a number of United Empire Loyalists. The place was first called Avery's Mills. When the post office was established in 1826, the settlement was named Waterford after an American town from which some of the settlers had come.

WATERLOO

Pop. 67,435. A city in the Reg. Mun. of Waterloo on the Grand River and Hwys. 7 & 86, immediately NW of Kitchener. In 1798, Joseph Brant, acting for the Six Nations Indians, sold 94,000 acres (38,070 ha) of land to Richard Beasley, James Wilson, and Jean Baptiste Rosseaux. In 1800 Beasley began to sell land to immigrants of German descent from Pennsylvania. Joseph Sherk and Samuel Betzner were the first permanent settlers. In 1802, new settler Samuel Bricker discovered that the deeds the settlers held were worthless; Beasley had not been sole owner of the land he sold and the tract was heavily mortgaged. In 1804 two of the settlers were sent to Pennsylvania to persuade relatives and old friends to buy the land in Waterloo for $20,000. Under the leadership of John Eby, a joint-stock company known as the German Company was eventually formed. Bricker was appointed agent, and Daniel Erb became his assistant. The $20,000 was wrapped in rags and brought to Waterloo County by wagon. The wagon that carried the money is now in the Waterloo County Museum.

Abraham Erb, who moved from Franklin County, Pennsylvania, in 1806, is credited with founding Waterloo, which is named after Waterloo in Belgium. Erb built a sawmill and then in 1816, a grist mill, which saved area farmers having to haul their wheat to Dundas for milling. The mill drew many colonists to the district, but settlement was stymied for many years by Erb's refusal to sell any of his land in small lots. In 1844 the Kuntz family established a brewery, which eventually became Carling's Brewery. In 1807 Joseph Seagram bought a partnership in the local distillery and eventually took over the entire operation. In 1874 Waterloo County's first Saengerfest, a major choir and band festival, was held. It was so successful that a special arena was built for the annual event. In 1882 the Waterloo Musical Society was organized and the Waterloo Band Festival was started in 1932. Waterloo is a partner with Kitchener in the annual Oktoberfest celebrations, started in 1969.

WATFORD

Pop. 1,447. In Warwick T, Lambton C., on Hwy. 79, 53 km W of London. Named Brown's Corners in 1850 for the first settler, George Brown. When the post office was established in 1854, with Brown as postmaster, the name was changed to Watford after an English village in Hertfordshire. One of the first automobiles in Canada was built in Watford in 1900 by a local blacksmith, D. A. Maxwell, who spent two years perfecting the vehicle.

WAUBAUSHENE

Pop. 868. In Tay T., Simcoe C., on Matchedash Bay off Georgian Bay and Hwy. 69, 32 km NW of Orillia. The Indian name means "meeting of the rocks" or "place of narrows." The first clearing was made in 1833 by Michael Labatte, and a post office was opened in 1840. The community adjoins the site of a trading post established by a man named Cowan, who traded to Fort Mackinaw before the Indian treaties of 1778-1804.

WAWA

Pop. 4,206. In McMurray T., Algoma Dist., on the Magpie River and Hwy. 101, 1 km E of Hwy. 17 and 10 km inland from Lake Superior, 222 km N of Sault Ste. Marie. The name is Ojibway for "wild goose." In 1898, William Teddy and his Indian wife discovered gold on the shore of Wawa Lake, starting one of the biggest gold rushes in Ontario history. The post office was established in 1899 as Wawa. In 1951 the name was changed to Jamestown to honour Sir James Dunn, a New Brunswick native who became one of North America's greatest industrialists and, in 1935, chair and president of Algoma Steel Corp. of Sault Ste. Marie. Dunn died in 1956, and in 1960 the community name was changed back to Wawa.

WEAGAMOW LAKE

Pop. 452. In Kenora Dist. on the N shore of Weagamow Lake, 520 km NW of Thunder Bay. In 1961 the post office was established as Round Lake. In 1968 the name was changed to Weagamow Lake, a contraction of Wauwiyaeyaun meaning "round or oval lake."

WEBBWOOD

Pop. 524. In Hallam T., Sudbury Dist., on the Spanish River and Hwy. 17, 77 km SW of Sudbury. The post office was established in 1889, the name honouring Andrew Webb, the first settler.

WEBEQUIE

Pop. 486. In Kenora Dist. on Eastwood Island in Winis Lake, 520 km NE of Thunder Bay. The Fort Hope Indian Band lives in this settlement. In 1966 the post office was established as Webequie, a Cree word describing "the side-to-side motion of the fish duckling as it is chased on the lake surface."

WELCOME

Pop. 243. In Hope T., Northumberland C., on Hwy. 2 and C. Rd. 10, 4 km NW of Port Hope. The post office was established as Welcome in 1864. The word Welcome is believed to have been atop signboards at this site which pointed the way to other communities. When a settlement developed here, it took the name Welcome.

WELLAND

Pop. 44,569. A city in the Reg. Mun. of Niagara on the Welland Ship Canal and the Welland River (Chippewa Creek) and Hwy. 58 and C. Rds.

27 & 29, 24 km SW of Niagara Falls. Welland was created by the first Welland Canal, completed in 1829. A feeder canal, supplying water from the Grand River, 32 km SW, crossed the Chippewa Creek by means of a large wooden aqueduct. Settlement grew up around this structure, and the hamlet was called Aqueduct until 1842. The community was then named Merrittsville to honour William Hamilton Merritt, financial agent for the Welland Canal Company and a leading promoter of the canal. When the settlement was incorporated in 1858, the name was changed to Welland after the river, which had been named by Lt.-Gov. Simcoe after the Welland River in Lincolnshire, England. In 1988 Welland started Festival of Arts Murals as a way to draw tourists to the city, and there are now 27 large murals.

WELLESLEY

Pop. 1,107. In Wellesley T., Reg. Mun. of Waterloo, on the Nith River and C. Rds. 5 & 12, 29 km W of Kitchener. The community was first called Smithville after John Smith, a squatter who settled in the area some time before the township was surveyed in 1842 and built the first sawmill. When the post office was established in 1851, the community was named Wellesley after the township.

WELLINGTON

Pop. 1,217. In Hillier T., Prince Edward County, on Wellington Bay of Lake Ontario and Hwy. 33, 16 km SW of Picton. The first settler at Wellington's original site was Daniel Reynolds, a United Empire Loyalist and trapper and trader, from Albany, New York. Reynolds lived among the Indians, who nicknamed him "Old Smoke" and helped him build his stone house in 1786. Today it is the oldest dwelling in the Township. It is recorded that in 1792, the lieutenant-governor and Lady Simcoe, en route from Kingston to Newark, were forced to take shelter from a storm in Reynolds' home. Lady Simcoe became ill and stayed there for several weeks while her husband and the official party continued on. The settlement was first called Smokeville, but when the post office was established in 1830, it was named Wellington after the "Iron Duke," Arthur Wellesley, duke of Wellington.

WENDOVER

Pop. 464. In North Plantagenet T., Prescott and Russell C., on the Ottawa River and Hwy. 17 and C. Rd. 19, 44 km NE of Ottawa. The post office was established as Wendover in 1867 after a Wendover in England.

WESTBROOK

Pop. 553. In Kingston T., Frontenac C., on Hwy. 2, 11 km NW of Kingston. The community was first known as Slab City because the local mill produced fine slabs of wood for building early houses. Slabs are the first cuts from logs. William Marshall, a brewer and farmer, was acquainted with Lord William Westbrooke, and when the post office was established in 1860, Marshall suggested the community be named Westbrooke after him. The first post office was called West Brook. In 1950 the name contracted to Westbrook.

WEST FLAMBOROUGH

Pop. 352. In Flamborough T., Reg. Mun. of Hamilton-Wentworth, on Hwy. 8, 7 km NW of Hamilton. The post office was established in 1840; J. Brackenbridge Strathy was the first postmaster. The community took its name from the township, which was named after the famed Flamborough Head, in the heights of Yorkshire, England.

WEST LAKE

Pop. 246. In Hallowell T., Prince Edward C., on West Lake and C. Rd. 12, 14 km SW of Picton. The settlement was first called West Point. The post office was established in 1865, and the community took its name from West Lake, on which it is situated. West Lake is an almost landlocked, triangular-shaped lake off Wellington Bay. The first seminary in Canada of the Society of Friends was opened in 1841 a few kilometres northeast of West Lake. The West Lake Boarding School was opened the same year to girls, and the following year a second building was opened to house male students. The school was remotely situated and inadequately supported, and was forced to close in 1865. It is now a private dwelling.

WEST LORNE

Pop. 1,314. In Aldborough T., Elgin C., on Hwy. 76, 40 km SW of St. Thomas. Scots were the first settlers in the early 1800s, followed by a wave of Germans after 1846. When the Canada Southern Railway was building its line through the area in 1872, German settlers provided land and requested that the station be called Bismarck after the German chancellor. When the post office opened the following year, it was known as West Lorne after the marquess of Lorne, but in the same year the name was changed to West Clayton, Dutton, Lorne, and finally back to West Lorne. Until 1903, when West Lorne was officially adopted as the name, the community was known as Bismarck, or Lorne, or Bismarck-Lorne.

WESTMEATH

Pop. 272. In Westmeath T., Renfrew C., on the E shore of Allumette Lake, a widening in the Ottawa River, and C. Rds. 12 & 31, 25 km E of Pembroke. When the post office was established in 1832, the settlement was named Bellowston after the first settler, Caleb Strong Bellows, who was also the first postmaster. The name was later changed to Westmeath after the township, which is itself named after a county in Ireland.

WESTMINSTER

Pop. 6,062. Part of the City of London, on the Thames River and Hwys 4 & 401. The first settler was Archibald McMillan in 1812, when the North Talbot Road was a blazed trail. A survey was carried out by Col. Mahlon Burwell and completed in 1820 by Colonel Bostwick. Westminster, first called Byron, is named after the township in which it was formerly located.

WESTPORT

Pop. 647. In North Crosby T., Leeds and Grenville C., at the head of Upper Rideau Lake and Hwy. 42 and C. Rds. 10, 12, & 36, 69 km W of Brockville. The township was surveyed in 1803, and the first settler in the vicinity of the townsite was George Hastings, who arrived in 1819 from Rhode Island. A decade later William Manhard and his brothers Peter and David built sawmills in the area, which then became known as Manhard's Mills. In 1841 the post office was established as Westport, likely because of the community being the most westerly port on the Rideau Lakes. In summer many vacationers visit the 33 lakes within 24 km of Westport.

WHEATLEY

Pop. 1,539. In Mersea T., Essex C., and Romney T., Kent C., on Muddy Creek, 2 km from Lake Erie and Hwy. 3 and C. Rd. 1, 13 km NE of Leamington. The community was settled in the early 1800s as newcomers located along the Talbot Road. The place was first known as Pegtown—either because there were seven cobblers in the community or because the homes, built without foundations, were propped up on posts, or pegs. When the post office was established in 1864, the community was called Wheatley after early settler Richard Wheatley. Gas wells were discovered near Wheatley in 1905, and by 1907 the village was lighted at night by gas lamps. Wheatley has the largest freshwater fish-processing plant in the world, and Wheatley Provincial Park is nearby.

WHITBY

Pop. 49,948. A town in the Reg. Mun. of Durham on Lake Ontario and Hwys 2, 12, & 401, 46 km NE of Toronto. Peter Perry is considered the founder of Whitby, although Jabez Lynde settled on Lynde's Creek in 1804. Perry arrived in 1836 and opened the "Red Store" at what became known as Perry's Corners. Before Perry arrived the place had been called Big Bay, Port Whitby, Windsor Bay, Crawford's Corners, and Hamer's Corners. By 1848 the harbour had become so busy that a plank road was constructed to Port Perry to facilitate the movement of grain from farms in the northern part of the region to the shipping facilities at Windsor

Bay. The community was incorporated in 1855, and because there was another Windsor in Ontario, the place was named Whitby after a seaside town in Yorkshire, England. In 1871 a rail line was completed from Whitby to Port Perry, and by 1877 it extended to Lindsay. The line's official name was the Whitby, Port Perry and Lindsay Railway, but its nickname, "The Nip and Tuck," was popular. The railway was intended to move goods to and from Whitby's harbour but it eventually spelled the doom of the harbour and its related businesses, because rail travel proved a cheaper and more efficient means of transporting goods.

WHITCHURCH-STOUFFVILLE

Pop. 16,705. A town in the Reg. Mun. of York created in 1971 by regional government by the incorporation of parts of Whitchurch Township and Markham Township and the Village of Stouffville.

WHITEDOG

Pop. 831. In Kenora-Rainy River Dist. on Tetu Lake and Hwy. 525, 50 km NW of Kenora. The post office was established in 1957 as Whitedog Falls but closed the following year. In 1961 it was reopened as Whitedog. The origin of the name is not known.

WHITEFISH

Pop. 902. In Sudbury Dist on C. Rd. 55, 29 km SW of Sudbury. In 1824 the Hudson's Bay Company built a trading post at Whitefish Lake to discourage independent traders from working the area north of the French River. In 1887 the post was moved to Naughton to facilitate rail shipments. The post office was established in 1888 as Whitefish. The origin of the name is not known.

WHITE LAKE

Pop. 300. In McNab T., Renfrew C., on Waba Creek and C. Rd. 2, 13 km SW of Arnprior. The post office was established as White Lake in 1848. The origin of the name is not known.

WHITE RIVER

Pop. 1,132. In Hunt T., Algoma Dist., on White River and Hwys. 17 & 631, 93 km NW of Wawa. In 1887 the post office was established, taking its name from the river that flows through the townsite. A huge thermometer beside the Trans-Canada Highway advertises "White River—coldest place in Canada," and shows a reading of -72 degrees Fahrenheit (-57 Celsius). (On Jan. 3, 1935, a reading of -73 degrees Fahrenheit [-57.5 Celsius] was recorded at Iroquois, Ontario.) The town is raising money for a statue to honour Winnie the Pooh, the lovable character from A. A. Milne's children's books. Winnie's name was a contraction of Winnipeg, hometown of Lt. Harry Colebourn, who bought the bear cub for $20 at White River railway station while he was passing through on a troop train bound for Valcartier, Quebec. Colebourne, a veterinarian with the Second Canadian Rifles, took Winnie to England. When his regiment headed for the battlefields of France, Winnie was left in the care of the Zoological Society of London. Winnie went to the zoo in 1914, and shortly after that Milne took his young son Christopher Robin to the zoo. Christopher liked the bear cub—and the rest is literary history.

WHITEVALE

Pop. 273. Part of the Town of Pickering, Reg. Mun. of Durham, 1 km S of Hwy. 7 on C. Rd. 27, 11 km NW of Pickering. The post office was established in 1861 and named after early settler Trueman White, who built the first mill.

WHITNEY

Pop. 766. In Airy T., Nipissing Dist., on the Madawaska River and Hwy. 60, 47 km W of Barry's Bay. The post office was established as Whitney in 1895. The community was named after E. C., Whitney, managing director of the St. Anthony Lumber Company.

WIARTON

Pop. 2,080. In Amabel T., Bruce C., on Colpoy's Bay off Georgian Bay and Hwy. 6 and C. Rds. 21 & 26, 33 km NW of Wiarton. The first settler was James Lennox, who arrived in 1866. Three years later when lots were offered for sale, B. B. Miller, a Scot who had been teaching school in Arran and Elderslie, and who had stores in Paisley and Oxenden, arrived. Miller may not have been the first settler, but he rapidly became involved in the community's affairs. He opened a hotel, took charge of the post office; and held the offices of clerk of the First Division Court, the first Indian lands agent, the first police magistrate, and the town's first reeve and mayor. When the post office was established in 1868, the community was called Wiarton after the English birthplace of Sir Edmund Walker Head, governor general of Canada at the time the Bruce Peninsula was surveyed. Wiarton's nickname is "Gateway to the Bruce Peninsula."

WIKWEMIKONG

Pop. 767. On Smith Bay off Georgian Bay on the extreme E end of Manitoulin Island. The Ojibway Indian reserve is believed to be North America's only unceded Indian reserve and is therefore—in theory at least—not part of Canada. After the War of 1812, the government of Upper Canada wanted to make the land on the southern shore of Georgian Bay available to settlers. The government also realized that tribes living near whites had been ravaged by disease and alcohol. It was proposed that the Natives be segregated on Manitoulin Island, and this was accomplished by a treaty in 1836. There were 268 Native residents. The government sponsored the founding of an "establishment," and by 1842 there were 700 settlers, including a commissioner, surgeon, minister, teacher, several mechanics, carpenters, and blacksmiths.

The government supported the "establishment" for 20 years before concluding that the attempt to segregate the Natives was a failure. The government then tried to void the 1836 treaty and to persuade the Natives to cede their land so it could be sold to settlers. The money was to be held in trust for the Natives, who were to be paid the interest annually. Treaty signatures were obtained from the groups living west of Heywood Sound and Manitoulin Gulf, but the treaty was rejected by the Wikwemikong Indians. Missionaries protested the new treaty, claiming signatures had been obtained by unethical methods. The government finally agreed to set aside a special reserve for the Wikwemikong residents, a 300-square-mile (777-sq-km) area, which is technically not a part of Canada. One of Manitoulin Island's most colourful events is the Wikwemikong Pow Wow held on Civic Holiday weekend each year. Wikwemikong is Ojibway for "bay of the beaver."

WILBERFORCE
Pop. 309. In Monmouth T., Haliburton C., on Poverty Lake at the head of the Irondale River and Hwy. 648 and C. Rd. 4, 26 km E of Haliburton. Isaac Ritchie and his sons were early settlers. The post office was established as Wilberforce in 1880. The name honours William Wilberforce (1759-1833), a philanthropist and statesman born in Hull, England. Wilberforce was a prominent anti-slavery crusader and an advocate of emigration.

WILCOX LAKE
Pop. 1,377. In the Reg. Mun. of York on C. Rds. 11 & 34, 10 km N of Richmond Hill. The community is believed to have been named in honour of Col. William Willcocks, a judge in the area in 1802.

WILDFIELD
Pop. 300. In Albion and Toronto Gore ts., Peel C., on C. Rds. 8 & 14, 10 km NW of Woodbridge. The place was first called Grantville or Grantsville but by 1859 the settlement was known locally as Gooseville. The post office was established as Gribben in 1873 and changed to Wildfield in 1891. In 1950 a pastor L. J. Austin proposed the name Maryfield, but it did not come into use. The origin of the name Wildfield is not known.

WILLIAMSBURG
Pop. 449. In Williamsburg T., Stormont, Dundas, and Glengarry C., on Hwy. 31 and C. Rd. 18, 8 km NW of Morrisburg. The place was named after Prince William Henry, son of George III. Dr. Mahlon W. Locke

(1880-1942) operated an internationally known clinic in Williamsville during the 1920s and 1930s. His technique of "manipulative surgery" for the relief of rheumatism and arthritis drew patients from as far away as Europe.

WILLIAMSFORD

Pop. 255. In Holland T., Grey C., on the North Saugeen River and Hwy. 6 and C. Rd. 24, 21 km SE of Owen Sound. The post office was established in 1874, and the settlement was named after the first postmaster, Alfred Williams.

WILLIAMSTOWN

Pop. 251. In Charlottenburgh T., Stormont, Dundas, and Glengarry C., on the Raisin River and C. Rds. 17 & 19, 29 km NE of Cornwall. The community was founded in 1778 by United Empire Loyalists led by Sir John Johnson. It was first called Ballaviellen, a Gaelic word meaning "mill town." When the post office was established in 1833 the name was changed to Williamstown to honour William Johnson, father of Sir John Johnson. In 1802 more than 400 Scottish Highlanders, many named MacMillan, emigrated to Canada from Invernesshire under the leadership of cousins Archibald and Alan MacMillan. They settled in Argenteuil County, Lower Canada; and Glengarry and Stormont counties, Upper Canada. St. Andrew's Church was built in 1812 to house the province's first Presbyterian congregation, which formed in Williamstown in 1787. Sir Alexander Mackenzie, the explorer of the Canadian West, donated a bell for the church and persuaded friends in Scotland to provide a communion service. Although its eastern headquarters were in Montreal and its inland depots were at Grand Portage and later Fort William, the North West Company's roots were in Glengarry County. Many employees were recruited from the county's Scottish settlements, and several senior partners made their homes in Williamstown. Duncan Cameron (1764-1848), who commanded the Red River area for the North West Company during the company's fierce rivalry with the Hudson's Bay Company, returned to live in Williamstown in 1820. The Williamstown Fair has been held since 1808 on a 12-acre (4.8 ha) site donated by Sir John Johnson.

WILNO

Pop. 287. In Sherwood and Hagerty T., Renfrew C., on Hwy. 60/62, 10 km NE of Barry's Bay. The community is in a valley, surrounded by high hills. In 1864, 300 Poles left the adverse social and political conditions of their partitioned homeland and came to Renfrew County. They soon established a thriving agricultural community, and in the early 1900s their numbers were augmented by another wave of immigrants from

Poland. In 1885 the post office was established, and the place was named Wilno after a town in Poland from which many of the settlers had come.

WINCHESTER

Pop. 2,167. In Winchester T., Stormont, Dundas, and Glengarry C., on C. Rd. 3 just E of Hwy. 31 and N of Hwy. 43, 51 km SE of Ottawa. Ben Bates, who arrived in 1836, was the first recorded settler. The place was named Bates Corners until the post office opened in 1855 as West Winchester after the township. The township had been named after the Colonial Secretary, the earl of Winchester; some sources claim the place was named after the City of Winchester in Hampshire, England. In 1890 the name was shortened to Winchester.

WINDSOR

Pop. 190,198. A city in Essex C., on the Detroit River and on Hwys 2, 3, 18, & 401, across the river from Detroit and linked to it by a vehicular suspension bridge, auto tunnel, and rail tunnel, 190 km SW of London. Jesuit missionaries operated a post in 1640, and the French had a fortified post on the site in 1734 called Fort Pontchartrain. Urban development within the present city of Windsor occurred following the American acquisition of the Michigan side of the river in 1796. This resulted in the founding of Sandwich to replace Detroit as capital of the Western District. Sandwich was subsequently annexed by Windsor. The place was known by a string of names—La Traverse, South Side, The Ferry, Richmond, and South Detroit—before Windsor was chosen in 1836, after Windsor in England. As it grew, Windsor annexed Sandwich, Walkerville, East Windsor, Riverside, Ojibway, and parts of Sandwich West, East, and South Townships. Windsor, nicknamed "the Rose City," is home of the University of Windsor, the St. Clair College of Applied Arts and Technology, the Hiram Walker Historical Museum (located in the 1811 Francois Baby House), and the Art Gallery of Windsor.

WINGHAM

Pop. 2,970. In Turnberry T., Huron C., at the confluence of the North and South branches of the Maitland River and Hwys 4 & 86, 112 km N of London. Wingham's first settler came from Owen Sound to try his luck in the northern part of Huron County, which had just been opened in the late 1850s. Wingham is only 80 km south of Owen Sound, but to get there in 1858, Edward Farley and his family had to take a roundabout route with all their possessions. From Owen Sound they went by boat to Collingwood, and from there by the Northern Railway to Toronto. From there they travelled by the recently completed Grand Trunk Railway to Stratford—then the end of steel. In Stratford, Farley hired teams and wagons, but the roads were so bad the teams left the family at the settlement of Blyth and turned back. Farley managed to round up two teams of oxen and got as far as Bodwin in Morris Township, where the road ended. There he built a huge raft on which the family piled its possessions and floated downstream to the site of present-day Wingham, which Farley named Lower Wingham. When the post office was established in 1862, the name was shortened to Wingham.

WINONA

Pop. 1,217. In the City of Stoney Creek, Reg. Mun. of Hamilton-Wentworth, on Hwy. 8, 19 km SE of Hamilton. When the post office opened in 1851, the place was called Ontario. With Confederation in 1867, Upper Canada took the name Ontario. The name of the community was changed to Winona despite strong local feelings that there was nothing wrong with calling it Ontario, Ontario. Winona is named for Winonah, the eldest daughter of Shawnee Chief Tecumseh, said to have jumped to her death from the Niagara Escarpment. We-non-ah is a Dacotah Indian word for "first-born daughter."

WOODBRIDGE

Pop. 19,800. Part of the Town of Vaughan, Reg. Mun. of York, on the Humber River and Hwy. 7, 26 km NW of Toronto. The first settler was Rowland Burr, who built a flour mill in 1837 and laid out town lots. The community was known as Burwick or Burwick's Mills until the post office was established in 1855. A post office by that name already existed. At the suggestion of the then reeve of Vaughan Township, the community was called Woodbridge after a town in England.

WOODLAND BEACH

Pop. 325. In Tiny T., Simcoe C., on the E shore of Nottawasaga Bay off Georgian Bay, 30 km NE of Collingwood. A summer post office was established in 1929.

WOODSTOCK

Pop. 26,295. In Blandford and East Oxford ts., Oxford C., on the Thames River at Cedar Creek and Hwys. 2 & 59, 43 km NE of London. Rear Admiral Henry Vansittart is considered to be the founder of Woodstock, although most of the work was done by his agent, Capt. Andrew Drew. During the 1837 Rebellion, Drew commanded the Canadian force that destroyed the American steamer *Caroline*. Drew went to the area in 1832 and on Vansittart's behalf bought a tract of land in what is now the east side of the city, surveyed it into lots, and built houses for himself and for Vansittart. The west side of what is now the City of Woodstock had already been laid out as a town plot by Lt.-Gov. John Graves Simcoe. The community was first known as Town Plot; later, one half was called Oxford and the other, Brighton. Vansittart arrived in 1834, built a store and a tavern, and financed the construction of St. Paul's Church, which was consecrated in 1838 and is still in use. The post office was established in 1835, and the place was called Woodstock after a village in Oxfordshire, England. Woodstock town hall was built in 1852 and is now home of the Oxford County Museum. A plaque at his former home on Vansittart Avenue recalls Thomas "Carbide" Willson who in 1892 discovered a commercial process for producing calcium carbide, a chemical compound used in the manufacture of acetylene gas.

WOODVILLE
Pop. 616. In Mariposa and Eldon ts., Victoria C., on a branch of the Beaverton River and Hwy. 46 and C. Rds. 2 & 9, 27 km W of Lindsay. In 1828 a number of Scots were brought to the area by a Squire Cameron, who sold them land at a dollar an acre. The community was first called Irish's Corners and given the name Woodville when the post office was established in 1853. In 1877 a plebiscite was held to rename the community Otago. Although the plebiscite carried by one vote, the name was not changed. The origin of the name Woodville is not known.

WOOLER
Pop. 322. In Murray T., Northumberland C., on Cold Creek and C. Rd. 5, 12 km NW of Trenton. The area was settled by United Empire Loyalists and immigrants from the British Isles. When the post office was established in 1854, the place was called Smith's Corners after Thomas Smith, who operated a store and tavern in the community. Several years later, residents petitioned the post office for an official designation for their post office. Since they were in Northumberland County, they chose Wooler, the name of a community in Northumberland County, England. At one time in the community's history, a toll gate collected a toll of two cents per stagecoach to defray road maintenance costs.

WROXETER
Pop. 317. In Howick T., Huron C., on the Maitland River and Hwy. 87 and C. Rd. 12, 7 km SE of Wingham. The townsite was part of a large tract of land bought by the Hon. James Patton and two men named Boys and Torre. In 1856 Thomas and Robert Gibson acquired some of that land and the water rights and, with their brother John, built saw- and flour mills on the Maitland River. James Patton's brother, Andrew, built the first frame house in 1858, surveyed the community, and laid out a townsite, naming it after Wroxeter in Wales. In the same year a post office was established, and Andrew Patton was appointed postmaster. In 1874 a branch of the Toronto, Grey and Bruce Railway reached the community. Railway construction workers considerably swelled the population, and civic leaders took advantage of the situation to conduct a census.

Including the railway workers, and with a canny disregard for village boundaries, the head count reached 750, enabling Wroxeter to incorporate as a village.

WUNNUMMIN LAKE

Pop. 289. In Kenora Dist. on Wunnummin Lake, 492 km N of Thunder Bay. The post office was established in 1964. Wunnummin is an Indian name meaning "the lake of beaver meal fragments," (wood chips).

WYOMING

Pop. 1,824. In Plympton T., Lambton C., on Hwy. 21 and C. Rd. 25, 22 km E of Sarnia. The townsite was laid out in 1856 by W. McMullen, and in the same year a public auction was held to sell lots. The place was named Wyoming after a place in Pennsylvania, by officials of the Great Western Railway whose line reached the community in 1858. When oil was discovered at nearby Oil Springs in 1858, Wyoming experienced an unprecedented boom as the nearest shipping depot for oil products, and at one time there were four oil refineries. Barrels were hauled to Wyoming on "jumpers" or "stone boats" through a swampy road nicknamed "the Canal." By 1863 the oil wells had diminished, the refineries had closed, and both Oil Springs and Wyoming went into decline.

YYY

YARKER

Pop. 302. In Camden T., Lennox and Addington C., on the Napanee River and C. Rds. 1, 4, & 6, 26 km NW of Kingston. A 1,000-acre (405-ha) parcel including the village site was acquired in 1796 by Lt.-Gov. John Graves Simcoe. The land was inherited by Henry A. Simcoe, who sold the land and water privileges to Sidney Warner in 1840. Warner sold the portion north of the river to George Miller and the south portion to David Vader. Vader built a mill and the place was known as Vader's Mills. Later the name changed to Simcoe Falls. In 1859 the community received a post office, with instructions that the name be changed since there was another place in Ontario called Simcoe. From a list of possible names submitted, postal authorities chose Yarker, suggested by mill owner Alexander McVean and honouring George W. Yarker, a prosperous Kingston mill owner. The Benjamin Manufacturing Company, originally manufacturers of light buggy wheels and, latterly, baskets and crates, was the community's major employer. In 1928 the factory was destroyed by fire.

YORK

Pop. 131,537. City on the N shore of Lake Ontario 60 km NE of Hamilton. The city was created in 1983 from the former Township of York and the Town of Weston, which joined in 1967. York is bounded on the west by the Humber River, Bathurst St. to the east, and St. Clair Ave. to the south and the northern boundary is south of Hwy. 401. (See entry under Toronto.)

YOUNG'S POINT

Pop. 312. In Smith T., Peterborough C., on the Otonabee River at the foot of Stony Lake and Hwy. 28, 24 km NE of Peterborough. The place was founded by Patrick Young in 1818. In 1865 a post office was established with John Young as postmaster, and the place was called Young's Point.

ZZZ

ZEPHYR

Pop. 360. In Reg. Mun. of Durham on C. Rd. 39, 49 km NW of Whitby. The post office was established as Zephyr in 1865. The origin of the name is not known.

ZURICH

Pop. 800. In Hay T., Huron C., on Hwy. 84 and C. Rd. 2, 34 km S of Goderich. Most of the early settlers were Germans, but the founder of the village was Swiss. Frederick K. Knell laid out a townsite on his land in 1854 and named the place Zurich after the city in Switzerland. Sir Stephen Willison, a political journalist and one-time editor of the Toronto *Globe* and the Toronto *News*, was born near Zurich in 1856. He was knighted in 1913 for his contributions to journalism.

Sources

A Guide to Provincial Plaques in Ontario, Mary Ellen Perkins, Ontario Ministry of Culture and Communications, 1989.

A Taste of Ontario Country Inns, David E. Scott, Whitecap Publishing Ltd., 1991.

Colombo's Canadian References, John Robert Colombo, Oxford University Press, 1976.

Encyclopedia Canadiana, Grolier of Canada, 1977.

Ghost and Post Offices of Ontario, Floreen Ellen Carter, Personal Impressions Publishing, 1986.

Larousse Spanish/French dictionaries, 1975/1976.

Municipal Directory 1992 (of Ontario), 1992.

Ontario For Free, David E. Scott. Whitecap Publishing Ltd., 1992.

On The Road, David E. Scott, London Free Press, 1986.

Place Names of Ontario, Floreen Ellen Carter, Phelps Publishing Company, 1984.

Places in Ontario, Nick and Helma Mika, Mika Publishing Company, Vol. I, 1977; Vol. II, 1981; Vol. III, 1983.

The Ontario Getaway Guidebook, David E. Scott. Whitecap Publishing Ltd., 1991.

Abbreviations

C.	County
Cs.	Counties
Dist.	District
E	East
Hwy.	Highway
Hwys.	Highways
km	kilometre(s) (0.6 mile)
Mun.	Municipality
N	North
NE	Northeast
NW	Northwest
Reg.	Regional
Rd.	Road
Rds.	Roads
S	South
SE	Southeast
SW	Southwest
T.	Township
ts.	townships
W	West

About the Author

Photo:
Wendy Scott

David E. Scott has been a writer, photographer, and editor for the past three decades, with a brief reprieve in the early seventies as the owner of a bar-restaurant in Andorra. A great lover of travel, he has lived in many countries and toured almost a hundred. He is an international award-winning journalist whose travel books and articles have brought him much acclaim; in 1989 he won an outstanding achievement award from the southwestern Ontario Travel Association. His other books for Whitecap include *A Taste of Ontario Country Inns, The Ontario Getaway Guidebook* and *Ontario for Free (and Almost Free)*. He presently resides in Ailsa Craig, Ontario.